SUSE Linux Enterprise Server 12 - Deployment Guide

A catalogue record for this book is available from the Hong Kong Public Libraries.

Published in Hong Kong by Samurai Media Limited.

Email: info@samuraimedia.org

ISBN 978-988-8406-49-4

Contents

About This Guide

Installations of SUSE Linux Enterprise Server are possible in many different ways. It is impossible to cover all combinations of boot, or installation server, automated installations or deploying images. This manual should help with selecting the appropriate method of deployment for your installation.

Part I, "Architecture-Specific Installation Considerations"

> The standard deployment instructions differ depending on the architecture used. For differences and requirements regarding the architecture, see this part.

Part II, "Manual Deployment"

> Most tasks that are needed during installations are described here. This includes the manual setup of your computer and additional software and remote installations.

Part IV, "Imaging and Creating Products"

> Mass installations often require the preparation of images or products furnished with the features that are needed in this special case. Several options are described that allow the administrator to prepare these deployment methods.

Part V, "Automated Installations"

> To do unattended installations, either use the installation with AutoYaST or prepare an image with kiwi or firstboot. This part describes methods to deploy these installations with a minimum of user interaction.

Many chapters in this manual contain links to additional documentation resources, including additional documentation that is available on the system and documentation available on the Internet.

For an overview of the documentation available for your product and the latest documentation updates, refer to http://www.suse.com/doc or to the following section.

1 Available Documentation

We provide HTML and PDF versions of our books in different languages. The following manuals for users and administrators are available for this product:

Article "Installation Quick Start"

> Lists the system requirements and guides you step-by-step through the installation of SUSE Linux Enterprise Server from DVD, or from an ISO image.

Deployment Guide

> Shows how to install single or multiple systems and how to exploit the product inherent capabilities for a deployment infrastructure. Choose from various approaches, ranging from a local installation or a network installation server to a mass deployment using a remote-controlled, highly-customized, and automated installation technique.

Book "Administration Guide"

> Covers system administration tasks like maintaining, monitoring and customizing an initially installed system.

Book "Virtualization Guide"

> Describes virtualization technology in general, and introduces libvirt—the unified interface to virtualization—and detailed information on specific hypervisors.

Book "Storage Administration Guide"

> Provides information about how to manage storage devices on a SUSE Linux Enterprise Server.

Book "AutoYaST"

> AutoYaST is a system for installing one or more SUSE Linux Enterprise systems automatically and without user intervention, using an AutoYaST profile that contains installation and configuration data. The manual guides you through the basic steps of auto-installation: preparation, installation, and configuration.

Book "Security Guide"

> Introduces basic concepts of system security, covering both local and network security aspects. Shows how to use the product inherent security software like AppArmor or the auditing system that reliably collects information about any security-relevant events.

Book "Security and Hardening Guide"

Deals with the particulars of installing and setting up a secure SUSE Linux Enterprise Server, and additional post-installation processes required to further secure and harden that installation. Supports the administrator with security-related choices and decisions.

Book "System Analysis and Tuning Guide"

An administrator's guide for problem detection, resolution and optimization. Find how to inspect and optimize your system by means of monitoring tools and how to efficiently manage resources. Also contains an overview of common problems and solutions and of additional help and documentation resources.

Book "GNOME User Guide"

Introduces the GNOME desktop of SUSE Linux Enterprise Server. It guides you through using and configuring the desktop and helps you perform key tasks. It is intended mainly for end users who want to make efficient use of GNOME as their default desktop.

Find HTML versions of most product manuals in your installed system under `/usr/share/doc/manual` or in the help centers of your desktop. Find the latest documentation updates at http://www.suse.com/doc where you can download PDF or HTML versions of the manuals for your product.

2 Feedback

Several feedback channels are available:

Bugs and Enhancement Requests

For services and support options available for your product, refer to http://www.suse.com/support/.

To report bugs for a product component, go to https://scc.suse.com/support/requests, log in, and click *Create New*.

User Comments

We want to hear your comments about and suggestions for this manual and the other documentation included with this product. Use the User Comments feature at the bottom of each page in the online documentation or go to http://www.suse.com/doc/feedback.html and enter your comments there.

Mail

For feedback on the documentation of this product, you can also send a mail to doc-team@suse.de. Make sure to include the document title, the product version and the publication date of the documentation. To report errors or suggest enhancements, provide a concise description of the problem and refer to the respective section number and page (or URL).

3   Documentation Conventions

The following typographical conventions are used in this manual:

- /etc/passwd: directory names and file names

- *placeholder*: replace *placeholder* with the actual value

- PATH: the environment variable PATH

- **ls**, --help: commands, options, and parameters

- user: users or groups

- Alt , Alt - F1 : a key to press or a key combination; keys are shown in uppercase as on a keyboard

- *File*, *File* › *Save As*: menu items, buttons

- x86_64 ⟩ This paragraph is only relevant for the x86_64 architecture. The arrows mark the beginning and the end of the text block. ◁
  System z, POWER ⟩ This paragraph is only relevant for the architectures z Systems and POWER. The arrows mark the beginning and the end of the text block. ◁

- *Dancing Penguins* (Chapter *Penguins*, ↑Another Manual): This is a reference to a chapter in another manual.

1 Planning for SUSE Linux Enterprise Server

The implementation of an operating system either in an existing IT environment or as a completely new rollout must be carefully prepared. SUSE Linux Enterprise Server 12 SP1 provides a variety of new features. It is impossible to describe all the new features here. The following is a list of major enhancements that might be of interest.

Xen 4.0 Virtualization

Runs many virtual machines on a single server, each with its own instance of an operating system. For more information, see *Book* "Virtualization Guide".

YaST

Several new configuration options have been developed for YaST. These are normally described in the chapters about the technology involved.

SPident

The management utility SPident gives an overview of the installed software base and clarifies the current service pack level of the system.

Directory Services

Several LDAP-compliant directory services are available:

- Microsoft Active Directory

- OpenLDAP

AppArmor

Harden your System with the AppArmor technology. This service is described in depth in *Book* "Security Guide".

AIDE

This is an intrusion detection system that can be set up to detect unauthorized changes to the system.

iSCSI

iSCSI provides an easy and reasonably inexpensive solution for connecting Linux computers to central storage systems. Find more information about iSCSI in *Book* "Storage Administration Guide".

Network File System v4

Starting with version 10, SUSE Linux Enterprise Server supports NFS also in version 4. This gives you performance improvements, strong security, and a "stateful" protocol.

Oracle Cluster File System 2

OCFS2 is a general-purpose journaling file system that is fully integrated in the Linux 2.6 kernel and later. Find an overview of OCFS2 in the *Administration Guide*.

Linux Kernel Crash Dump

Debugging kernel-related problems is now much easier when using Kexec and Kdump. This technology is available on AMD64, Intel 64, and POWER platforms.

1.1 Considerations for Deployment of a SUSE Linux Enterprise Server

At the beginning of the planning process, you should try to define the project goals and needed features. This must always be done individually for each project, but the questions to answer should include the following:

- How many installations should be done? Depending on this, the best deployment methods differ. See also *Chapter 5, Deployment Strategies*.

- Will the system run as physical host or as a virtual machine?

- Will the system be in a hostile environment? Have a look at *Book "Security Guide", Chapter 1 "Security and Confidentiality"* to get an overview of consequences.

- How will you get regular updates? All patches are provided online for registered users. Find the registration and patch support database at http://download.suse.com/.

- Do you need help for your local installation? SUSE provides training, support, and consulting for all topics pertaining to SUSE Linux Enterprise Server. Find more information about this at http://www.suse.com/products/server/.

- Do you need third-party products? Make sure that the required product is also supported on the desired platform. SUSE can provide help to support software on different platforms when needed.

1.2 Deployment of SUSE Linux Enterprise Server

To make sure that your system will run flawlessly, always try to use certified hardware. The hardware certification process is an ongoing process and the database of certified hardware is updated regularly. Find the search form for certified hardware at http://www.suse.com/yessearch/Search.jsp.

Depending on the number of desired installations, it is beneficial to use installation servers or even completely automatic installations. Have a look at *Chapter 5, Deployment Strategies* for more information. When using Xen virtualization technologies, network root file systems or network storage solutions like iSCSI should be considered.

SUSE Linux Enterprise Server provides you with a broad variety of services. Find an overview of the documentation in this book in *Book "Administration Guide", Preface "About This Guide"*. Most of the needed configurations can be made with YaST, the SUSE configuration utility. In addition, many manual configurations are described in the corresponding chapters.

In addition to the plain software installation, you should consider training the end users of the systems and help desk staff.

1.3 Running SUSE Linux Enterprise Server

The SUSE Linux Enterprise Server operating system is a well-tested and stable system. Unfortunately, this does not prevent hardware failures or other causes for downtime or data loss. For any serious computing task where data loss could occur, a regular backup should be done.

For optimal security and data safety, you should make regular updates of all the operated machines. If you have a mission critical server, you should run a second identical (pre-production) machine where you can apply all changes for testing purposes before doing so in production. This also gives you the possibility of switching machines in the case of hardware failure.

I Architecture-Specific Installation Considerations

2 Installation on AMD64 and Intel 64

This chapter describes the steps necessary to prepare for the installation of SUSE Linux Enterprise Server on AMD64 and Intel 64 computers. It introduces the steps required to prepare for various installation methods. The list of hardware requirements provides an overview of supported systems supported by SUSE Linux Enterprise Server. Find information about available installation methods and several common known problems. Also learn how to control the installation, provide installation media, and boot with regular methods.

2.1 Required Background

To keep the scope of these guidelines manageable, certain technical assumptions have been made:

- You have some computer experience and are familiar with common technical terms.

- You are familiar with the documentation for your system and the network on which it runs.

- You have a basic understanding of Linux systems.

For an overview of the documentation available for your product and the latest documentation updates, refer to http://www.suse.com/doc.

2.2 System Requirements for Operating Linux

The SUSE® Linux Enterprise Server operating system can be deployed on a wide range of hardware. It is impossible to list all the different combinations of hardware SUSE Linux Enterprise Server supports. However, to provide you with a guide to help you during the planning phase, the minimum requirements are presented here.

If you want to be sure that a given computer configuration will work, find out which platforms have been certified by SUSE. Find a list at http://www.suse.com/yessearch/Search.jsp.

2.2.1 Hardware for Intel 64 and AMD64

The Intel 64 and AMD64 architectures support the simple migration of x86 software to 64 bits. Like the x86 architecture, they constitute a value-for-money alternative.

CPU

All CPUs available on the market to date are supported. This includes dual-core CPUs.

Maximum Number of CPUs

The maximum number of CPUs supported by software design is 8192 for Intel 64 and AMD64. If you plan to use such a large system, verify with our hardware system certification Web page for supported devices, see http://www.suse.com/yessearch/.

Memory Requirements

A minimum of 512 MB of memory is required for a minimal installation. However, the minimum recommended is 1024 MB or, alternatively, 512 MB per CPU on multiprocessor computers. Add 150 MB for a remote installation via HTTP or FTP. Note that these values are only valid for the installation of the operating system—the actual memory requirement in production depends on the system's workload.

Hard Disk Requirements

The disk requirements depend largely on the installation selected and how you use your machine. Minimum requirements for different selections are:

System	Hard Disk Requirements
Minimal System	800 MB - 1GB
Minimal X Window System	1.4 GB
GNOME Desktop	3.5 GB
All patterns	8.5 GB
Using snapshots for virtualization	min. 8 GB

Boot Methods

The computer can be booted from a CD or a network. A special boot server is required to boot over the network. This can be set up with SUSE Linux Enterprise Server.

2.2.2 Supported Virtualization Hosts

SUSE Linux Enterprise Server can also be installed as VM Guests on various virtualization hosts. The following host operating systems and virtualization platforms are supported:

- KVM on SUSE Linux Enterprise Server 11 SP3+

- Xen on SUSE Linux Enterprise Server 11 SP3+

- Citrix XenServer 6.0 / 6.1

- Microsoft Windows 2008 SP2+ / 2008 R2+ / 2012+

- Oracle VM 3.0 / 3.1 / 3.2

- VMware ESX 5.1 / ESXi 5.1 / ESX 5.2 / ESXi 5.2

2.3 Installation Considerations

This section encompasses many factors that need to be considered before installing SUSE Linux Enterprise Server on AMD64 and Intel 64 hardware.

2.3.1 Installation Type

SUSE Linux Enterprise Server is normally installed as an independent operating system. With the introduction of Virtualization, it is also possible to run multiple instances of SUSE Linux Enterprise Server on the same hardware. However, the installation of the VM Host Server is performed like a typical installation with some additional packages. The installation of virtual guests is described in *Book "Virtualization Guide", Chapter 9 "Guest Installation"*.

2.3.2 Boot Methods

Depending on the hardware used, the following boot methods are available for the first boot procedure (prior to the installation of SUSE Linux Enterprise Server).

Boot Option	Use
CD or DVD drive	The simplest booting method. The system requires a locally-available CD-ROM or DVD-ROM drive for this.
Flash disks	Find the images required for creating boot disks on the first CD or DVD in the `/boot` directory. See also the `README` in the same directory. Booting from a USB memory stick is only possible if the BIOS of the machine supports this method.
PXE or bootp	Must be supported by the BIOS or by the firmware of the system used. This option requires a boot server in the network. This task can be handled by a separate SUSE Linux Enterprise Server.
Hard disk	SUSE Linux Enterprise Server can also be booted from hard disk. For this, copy the kernel (`linux`) and the installation system (`initrd`) from the `/boot/loader` directory of the first CD or DVD onto the hard disk and add an appropriate entry to the boot loader.

2.3.3 Installation Source

When installing SUSE Linux Enterprise Server, the actual installation data must be available in the network, on a hard disk partition, or on a local DVD. To install from the network, you need an installation server. To make the installation data available, set up any computer in a Unix or Linux environment as an NFS, HTTP, SMB, or FTP server. To make the installation data available from a Windows computer, release the data with SMB.

The installation source is particularly easy to select if you configure an *SLP server* in the local net-work. For more information, see *Section 13.2, "Setting Up the Server Holding the Installation Sources"*.

2.3.4   Installation Target

Most installations are to a local hard disk. Therefore, it is necessary for the hard disk controllers to be available to the installation system. If a special controller (like a RAID controller) needs an extra kernel module, provide a kernel module update disk to the installation system.

Other installation targets may be various types of block devices that provide sufficient disk space and speed to run an operating system. This includes network block devices like `iSCSI` or `SAN`. It is also possible to install on network file systems that offer the standard Unix permissions. How-ever, it may be problematic to boot these, because they must be supported by the `initramfs` before the actual system can start. Such installations are useful if there is a need to start the same system in different locations or if you intend to use Xen features like domain migration.

2.3.5   Different Installation Methods

SUSE Linux Enterprise Server offers several different methods for controlling installation:

- Installation on the console

- Installation via serial console

- Installation with AutoYaST

- Installation with KIWI images

- Installation via SSH

- Installation with VNC

By default, the graphical console is used. If you have a many similar computers to install, it is advisable to create an AutoYaST configuration file or a KIWI preload image and make this available to the installation process. See also the documentation for `autoyast2` in *Chapter 25, Automated Installation* and **KIWI** at http://doc.opensuse.org/projects/kiwi/doc/.

2.4 Boot and Installation Media

When installing the system, the media for booting and for installing the system may be different. All combinations of supported media for booting and installing may be used.

2.4.1 Boot Media

Booting a computer depends on the capabilities of the hardware used and the availability of media for the respective boot option.

Booting from DVD

This is the most common possibility of booting a system. It is straightforward for most computer users, but requires a lot of interaction for every installation process.

Booting from a USB Hard Disk

Depending on the hardware used, it is possible to boot from a USB hard disk. The respective media must be created as described in *Section 6.2.2, "PC (x86_64): System Start-up"*.

Booting from the Network

You can only boot a computer directly from the network if this is supported by the computer's firmware or BIOS. This booting method requires a boot server that provides the needed boot images over the network. The exact protocol depends on your hardware. Commonly you need several services, such as TFTP and DHCP or PXE boot. If you need a boot server, also read *Section 13.1.3, "Remote Installation via VNC—PXE Boot and Wake on LAN"*.

2.4.2 Installation Media

The installation media contain all the necessary packages and meta information that is necessary to install a SUSE Linux Enterprise Server. These must be available to the installation system after booting for installation. Several possibilities for providing the installation media to the system are available with SUSE Linux Enterprise Server.

Installation from DVD

All necessary data is delivered on the boot media. Depending on the selected installation, a network connection or add-on media may be necessary.

Networked Installation

If you plan to install several systems, providing the installation media over the network makes things a lot easier. It is possible to install from many common protocols, such as NFS, HTTP, FTP, or SMB. For more information on how to run such an installation, refer to *Chapter 13, Remote Installation*.

2.5   Installation Procedure

This section offers an overview of the steps required for the complete installation of SUSE® Linux Enterprise Server in the required mode. *Part II, "Manual Deployment"* contains a full description of how to install and configure the system with YaST.

2.5.1   Booting from a Local Interchangeable Drive

DVD-ROM and USB storage devices can be used for installation purposes. Adjust your computer to your needs:

1. Make sure that the drive is entered as a bootable drive in the BIOS.

2. Insert the boot medium in the drive and start the boot procedure.

3. The installation boot menu of SUSE Linux Enterprise Server allows transferring different parameters to the installation system. See also *Section 13.4.2, "Using Custom Boot Options"*. If the installation should be performed over the network, specify the installation source here.

4. If unexpected problems arise during installation, use safe settings to boot.

2.5.2   Installing over the Network

An installation server is required to perform the installation by using a network source. The procedure for installing this server is outlined in *Section 13.2, "Setting Up the Server Holding the Installation Sources"*.

If you have an SLP server, select SLP as the installation source in the first boot screen. During the boot procedure, select which of the available installation sources to use.

If the DVD is available on the network, use it as an installation source. In this case, specify the parameter `install=<URL>` with suitable values at the boot prompt. Find a more detailed description of this parameter in *Section 13.4.2, "Using Custom Boot Options"*.

2.6   Controlling the Installation

Control the installation in one of several ways. The method most frequently used is to install SUSE® Linux Enterprise Server from the computer console. Other options are available for different situations. Find more information about the available installation methods in *Chapter 5, Deployment Strategies*.

2.6.1   Installation on the Computer Console

The simplest way to install SUSE Linux Enterprise Server is using the computer console. With this method, a graphical installation program guides you through the installation. This installation method is discussed in detail in *Chapter 6, Installation with YaST*.

You can still perform the installation on the console without a working graphics mode. The text-based installation program offers the same functionality as the graphical version. Find some hints about navigation in this mode in *Book "Administration Guide", Chapter 2 "YaST in Text Mode", Section 2.1 "Navigation in Modules"*.

2.6.2   Installation Using a Serial Console

For this installation method, you need a second computer that is connected by a *null modem* cable to the computer on which to install SUSE Linux Enterprise Server. Depending on the hardware, even the firmware or BIOS of the computer may already be accessible to the serial console. If this is possible, you can carry out the entire installation using this method. To activate the serial console installation, additionally specify the parameter `console=ttyS0` at the boot prompt after the boot process has completed and before the installation system starts.

On most computers, there are two serial interfaces, *ttyS0* and *ttyS1*. For the installation, you need a terminal program like minicom or screen. To initiate the serial connection, launch the screen program in a local console by entering the following command:

```
screen /dev/ttyS0 9600
```

This means that screen listens to the first serial port with a baud rate of 9600. From this point on, the installation proceeds similarly to the text-based installation over this terminal.

2.6.3   Installation with SSH

If you do not have direct access to the computer hardware and, for example, the installation should be launched from a management console, control the entire installation process over the network. To do this, enter the parameters `ssh=1` and `ssh.password=SECRET` at the boot prompt. An SSH daemon is then launched in the system and you can log in as user `root` with the password `SECRET`.

To connect, use **ssh -X**. X-Forwarding over SSH is supported, if you have a local X server available. Otherwise, YaST provides a text interface over ncurses. YaST then guides you through the installation. This procedure is described in detail in *Section 13.1.5, "Simple Remote Installation via SSH—Dynamic Network Configuration"*.

If you do not have a DHCP server available in your local network, manually assign an IP address to the installation system. Do this by entering the option `HostIP=IPADDR` at the boot prompt.

2.6.4   Installation over VNC

If you do not have direct access to the system, but want a graphical installation, install SUSE Linux Enterprise Server over VNC. This method is described in detail in *Section 13.5.1, "VNC Installation"*.

As suitable VNC clients are also available for other operating systems, such as Microsoft Windows and MacOS, the installation can also be controlled from computers running those operating systems.

2.6.5   Installation with AutoYaST

If you need to install SUSE Linux Enterprise Server on several computers with similar hardware, it is recommended you perform the installations with the aid of AutoYaST. In this case, start by installing one SUSE Linux Enterprise Server and use this to create the necessary AutoYaST configuration files.

AutoYaST is extensively documented in *Chapter 25, Automated Installation*.

2.7 Dealing with Boot and Installation Problems

Prior to delivery, SUSE® Linux Enterprise Server is subjected to an extensive test program. Despite this, problems occasionally occur during boot or installation.

2.7.1 Problems Booting

Boot problems may prevent the YaST installer from starting on your system. Another symptom is when your system does not boot after the installation has been completed.

Installed System Boots, Not Media

Change your computer's firmware or BIOS so that the boot sequence is correct. To do this, consult the manual for your hardware.

The Computer Hangs

Change the console on your computer so that the kernel outputs are visible. Be sure to check the last outputs. This is normally done by pressing Ctrl – Alt – F10 . If you cannot resolve the problem, consult the SUSE Linux Enterprise Server support staff. To log all system messages at boot time, use a serial connection as described in *Section 2.6, "Controlling the Installation"*.

Boot Disk

The boot disk is a useful interim solution if you have difficulties setting the other configurations or if you want to postpone the decision regarding the final boot mechanism. A boot disk may also be a suitable solution in connection with OS/2 or Windows NT. For more details on creating boot disks, see *Book "Administration Guide", Chapter 11 "The Boot Loader GRUB 2" grub2-mkrescue* .

Virus Warning after Installation

There are BIOS variants that check the structure of the boot sector (MBR) and erroneously display a virus warning after the installation of GRUB 2. Solve this problem by entering the BIOS and looking for corresponding adjustable settings. For example, switch off *virus protection*. You can switch this option back on again later. It is unnecessary, however, if Linux is the only operating system you use.

2.7.2   Problems Installing

If an unexpected problem occurs during installation, information is needed to determine the cause of the problem. Use the following directions to help with troubleshooting:

- Check the outputs on the various consoles. You can switch consoles with the key combination `Ctrl`-`Alt`-`Fn`. For example, obtain a shell in which to execute various commands by pressing `Ctrl`-`Alt`-`F2`.

- Try launching the installation with "Safe Settings" (press `F5` on the installation screen and choose *Safe Settings*). If the installation works without problems in this case, there is an incompatibility that causes either `ACPI` or `APIC` to fail. In some cases, a BIOS or firmware update fixes this problem.

- Check the system messages on a console in the installation system by entering the command `dmesg -T`.

2.7.3   Redirecting the Boot Source to the Boot DVD

To simplify the installation process and avoid accidental installations, the default setting on the installation DVD for SUSE Linux Enterprise Server is that your system is booted from the first hard disk. At this point, an installed boot loader normally takes over control of the system. This means that the boot DVD can stay in the drive during an installation. To start the installation, choose one of the installation possibilities in the boot menu of the media.

3 Installation on IBM POWER

This chapter describes the procedure for preparing the installation of SUSE® Linux Enterprise Server on IBM POWER systems.

3.1 Requirements

A standard installation requires at least 512 MB of RAM. The installation of a standard system with the GNOME desktop requires at least 3.5 GB of free hard disk space; for more information about hard disk space requirements, see *Hard Disk Requirements*.

3.1.1 Hardware Requirements

The SUSE® Linux Enterprise Server operating system can be operated on a wide range of hardware. To provide you with a guide to help you during the planning phase, the minimum requirements are presented here.

If you want to be sure that a given computer configuration will work, check the database of hardware certified by SUSE. Find a list of certified hardware at http://www.suse.com/yessearch/ Search.jsp.

SUSE Linux Enterprise Server may support additional IBM POWER systems not listed below. For the latest information, see the IBM Information Center for Linux at http://publib.boulder.ibm.com/infocenter/lnxinfo/v3r0m0/index.jsp?topic=%2Fliaam%2Fliaamdistros.htm.

Find up-to-date firmware at IBM FixCentral (http://www.ibm.com/support/fixcentral/). Select your system from the Product Group list.

3.1.1.1 IBM POWER8 Processor-Based Servers

All POWER8 servers are supported that are PowerKVM-capable.

POWER8 SERVERS

- 8247-21L (IBM Power® System S120L)

- 8247-22L (IBM Power System S220L)

- 8284-22A (IBM Power System S2200)

- 8286-41A (IBM Power System S1400)

- 8286-42A (IBM Power System S2400)

3.1.2 Software Requirements

A Web browser able to connect to PowerKVM running on the PowerLinux server is required. With this Web browser you will perform pre-installation steps using the Kimchi Web interface.

3.2 Preparation

This section describes the preparatory steps that must be taken before the actual installation of SUSE Linux Enterprise Server. The installation procedure depends on the system used. See the following documentation:

- For IBM PowerLinux servers with IBM PowerKVM using Kimchi, see *Section 3.2.1, "Installation on IBM PowerLinux Servers with IBM PowerKVM using Kimchi"*.

If SUSE® Linux Enterprise Server needs to be installed on several systems or partitions, it is recommended you create a network installation source. The same source can also be used for the concurrent installation on several partitions or several systems. The configuration of a network installation source is described in *Section 13.2.1, "Setting Up an Installation Server Using YaST"*.

The installation can be controlled with a VNC client. For more information about VNC, see *Section 13.1.1, "Simple Remote Installation via VNC—Static Network Configuration"*.

To participate in the `linuxppc-dev` mailing list, register using the forms at http://lists.ozlabs.org/listinfo/linuxppc-dev/. The following links are pertinent to the maintenance of an installation:

- http://www.suse.com/support/kb/ is an effective help tool for assisting customers in solving problems. A corresponding article is published whenever SUSE discover that a special case could lead to serious problems. Search the portal using keywords like POWER or PowerKVM.

- Find security alerts at http://www.suse.com/support/security/. SUSE also maintains two security-related mailing lists to which anyone may subscribe.

- `suse-security` — General discussion of security regarding Linux and SUSE. All security alerts for SUSE Linux Enterprise Server are sent to this list.

- `suse-security-announce` — The SUSE mailing list exclusively for security alerts.

3.2.1   Installation on IBM PowerLinux Servers with IBM PowerKVM using Kimchi

This section covers the preparatory steps for installing SUSE® Linux Enterprise Server on IBM PowerLinux systems with PowerKVM. It explains the installation from an ISO image with the Kimchi Web interface. Kimchi is a tool for administrating IBM PowerKVM.

This section assumes you have PowerKVM running on your IBM PowerLinux server. If PowerKVM is not preinstalled see "Configuring IBM PowerKVM on Power Systems" on http://www-01.ibm.com/support/knowledgecenter/linuxonibm/liabp/liabpkickoff.htm for installing and setting up PowerKVM.

3.2.1.1   Creating a SUSE Linux Enterprise Server Template with Kimchi

Templates are the installation source for PowerKVM guests.

PROCEDURE 3.1: CREATING A TEMPLATE WITH KIMCHI

1. In the Web browser, enter the URL of the PowerLinux server where PowerKVM is running, for example `https://powerlinux_ip:8001` (replace `powerlinux_ip` with the IP address of your system).

2. Click the *Templates* tab to activate the *Templates* page.

3. Click the green plus sign (+) to create the SUSE Linux Enterprise Server template. Provide either a local or a remote ISO image of SUSE Linux Enterprise Server. Check *I want to use a specific ISO file*, and specify the path to the file of the ISO image.

4. To configure the newly created template, click *Actions* › *Edit*, and change the default values as required by your workload.

For more information, see "Setting up a template using Kimchi" on http://www-01.ibm.com/ support/knowledgecenter/linuxonibm/liabp/liabpkimchitemplate.htm.

3.2.1.2   Installing SUSE Linux Enterprise Server as a Guest with Kimchi

1. In the Web browser, enter the URL of the PowerLinux server where PowerKVM is running, for example `https://powerlinux_ip:8001` (replace `powerlinux_ip` with the IP address of your system).

2. Click the *Guests* tab to activate the *Guests* page.

3. Click the green plus sign (+) to create the SUSE Linux Enterprise Server guest.

4. Enter a *Virtual Machine Name* for the SUSE Linux Enterprise Server guest.
   Choose the SUSE Linux Enterprise Server template created in *Section 3.2.1.1, "Creating a SUSE Linux Enterprise Server Template with Kimchi"* and click *Create*.

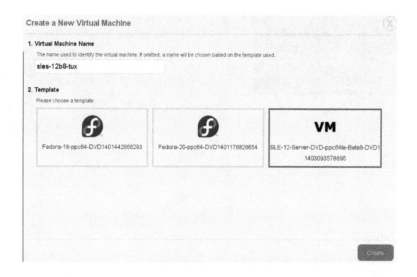

The SUSE Linux Enterprise Server guest is created and ready to be started.

5. Click the red power button to start the SUSE Linux Enterprise Server guest. Alternatively, select *Start* from the *Actions* pull-down button.

6. Click *Actions › Connect,* and connect your VNC viewer to the installation process as outlined in *Section 13.5.1.2, "Connecting to the Installation Program".*

Now you can continue with the default installation via VNC.

3.2.2   Installation on IBM PowerLinux Servers with IBM PowerKVM using `virt-install`

Alternatively, use the `virt-install` command line tool, if you need to install multiple virtual machines on IBM PowerLinux Server systems. `virt-install` allows many installation scenarios; in the following a remote installation scenario via VNC and PXE boot is outlined. For more information about `virt-install`, see *Book "Virtualization Guide", Chapter 9 "Guest Installation", Section 9.2 "Installing from the Command Line with* `virt-install`*".*

Prepare a repository with the installation sources and PXE boot enabled target system as described in *Section 13.1.3, "Remote Installation via VNC—PXE Boot and Wake on LAN".*

On the command line, enter something similar as follows (adjust the options according to your needs and matching your hardware):

```
virt-install --name server_sle12 --memory 4096 --vcpus=2 --pxe \
```

```
--graphics vnc --os-variant sles11 \
--disk pool=default,size=3000,format=qcow2,allocation=1G,bus=virtio \
-w mac=mac_address,model=spapr-vlan
```

It will use VNC graphics, and it will automatically launch the graphical client.

4 Installation on IBM z Systems

This chapter describes the procedure for preparing the installation of SUSE® Linux Enterprise Server on IBM z Systems systems. It provides all information needed to prepare the installation on the LPAR and z/VM side.

4.1 General Information and Requirements

This section gives basic information about the system requirements (like supported hardware), level of MicroCode, and software. It also covers the different installation types and how to do an IPL for the first installation. For detailed technical information about IBM z Systems on SUSE Linux Enterprise Server refer to http://www.ibm.com/developerworks/linux/linux390/documentation_suse.html.

4.1.1 System Requirements

This section provides a list of hardware for IBM z Systems supported by SUSE Linux Enterprise Server. Next, the level of the MicroCode (MCL) used in your IBM z Systems system, which is very important for the installation, is covered. Additional software to install and use for installation is mentioned at the end of this section.

4.1.1.1 Hardware

SUSE Linux Enterprise Server has run successfully on the following platforms:

- IBM zEnterprise System z196 2817

- IBM zEnterprise System z114 2818

- IBM zEnterprise EC12 (zEC12) 2827

- IBM zEnterprise BC12 (zBC12) 2828

- IBM z Systems z13 (2964)

4.1.1.1.1 Memory Requirements

Different installation methods have different memory requirements during installation. After installation is completed, the system administrator may reduce memory to the desired size. SUSE recommends using:

1 GB	For installation under z/VM.
1 GB	For installation under LPAR.
1 GB	For installation under KVM.

 Note: Memory Requirements with Remote Installation Sources

For installation from NFS, FTP, or SMB installation sources or whenever VNC is used, 512MB of memory is required as a minimum. Otherwise, the installation attempt is likely to fail. Further note that the number of devices visible to the z/VM guest or LPAR image affects memory requirements. Installation with literally hundreds of accessible devices (even if unused for the installation) may require more memory.

4.1.1.1.2 Disk Space Requirements

The disk requirements depend largely on the installation. Commonly, you need more space than the installation software itself needs to have a system that works properly. Minimal requirements for different selections are:

800 MB	Minimal Installation
1.4 GB	Minimal Installation + Base System
2.6 GB	Default Installation
3.6 GB+	Recommended (this is with graphical desktop, development packages and Java).

4.1.1.1.3   Network Connection

A network connection is needed to communicate with your SUSE Linux Enterprise Server system. This can be one or more of the following connections or network cards:

- OSA Express Ethernet (including Fast and Gigabit Ethernet)

- HiperSockets or Guest LAN

- 10 GBE, VSWITCH

- RoCE (RDMA over Converged Ethernet)

The following interfaces are still included, but no longer supported:

- CTC (or virtual CTC)

- ESCON

- IP network interface for IUCV

For installations under KVM make sure the following requirements are met to enable the VM Guest to access the network transparently:

- The virtual network interface is connected to a host network interface.

- The host network interface is connected to a network in which the virtual server will participate.

- if the host is set up to have a redundant network connection by grouping two independent OSA network ports into a bonded network interface, The identifier for the bonded network interface is bond0 (or, if more than one bonded interface exists, bond1, bond2,...). See http://www.ibm.com/support/knowledgecenter/SSNW54_1.1.0/com.ibm.kvm.v110.admin/toc.htm for further information about how to configure network bonding.

- If the host network connection had *not* been set up redundantly, the identifier of the single network interface has to be used. It has the form enccw0.0.*nnnn*, where *nnnn* is the device number of the desired network interface.

4.1.1.2   MicroCode Level, APARs, and Fixes

Documentation about restrictions and requirements for this release of SUSE Linux Enterprise Server can be found on IBM developerWorks at http://www.ibm.com/developerworks/linux/linux390/documentation_suse.html. It is recommended always to use the highest service level available. Contact your IBM support for minimum requirements.

4.1.1.2.1   z/VM

- z/VM 5.4

- z/VM 6.2

- z/VM 6.3, we strongly suggest installing the APAR VM65419 (or higher) to improve the output of qclib.

Negotiate the order of installation with your IBM support, because it might be necessary to activate the VM APARs before installing the new MicroCode levels.

4.1.1.3   Software

To install SUSE Linux Enterprise Server via non-Linux–based NFS or FTP, you might experience problems with NFS or FTP server software. The Windows standard FTP server can cause errors, so installing via SMB on these machines is generally recommended.

To connect to the SUSE Linux Enterprise Server installation system, one of the following methods is required (SSH or VNC are recommended):

SSH with Terminal Emulation (xterm compatible)

SSH is a standard Unix tool that should be present on any Unix or Linux system. For Windows, there is an SSH client called Putty. It is free to use and is available from http://www.chiark.greenend.org.uk/~sgtatham/putty/.

VNC Client

For Linux, a VNC client called vncviewer is included in SUSE Linux Enterprise Server as part of the `tightvnc` package. For Windows, TightVNC is also available. Download it from http://www.tightvnc.com/. Alternatively, use the VNC Java client and a Java-enabled Web browser.

X Server

Find a suitable X server implementation on any Linux or Unix workstation. There are many commercial X Window System environments for Windows and Macintosh. Some can be downloaded as free trial versions. A trial version of the Mocha X Server from MochaSoft can be obtained at http://www.mochasoft.dk/freeware/x11.htm.

 Tip: Additional Information

Consult the README located in the root directory of DVD 1 of your SUSE Linux Enterprise Server before installing SUSE Linux Enterprise Server on IBM z Systems. This file completes the documentation presented in this book.

4.1.2   Installation Types

This section gives an overview of the different types of installation possible with SUSE Linux Enterprise Server for IBM z Systems:

LPAR

Installation of SUSE Linux Enterprise Server using a logical partition (LPAR).

z/VM

Installation of SUSE Linux Enterprise Server as a guest operating system within z/VM.

KVM

Installation of SUSE Linux Enterprise Server as a guest operating system within KVM.

Depending on the mode of installation (LPAR or z/VM), there are different possibilities for starting the installation process and IPLing the installed system.

4.1.2.1   LPAR

If you install SUSE Linux Enterprise Server for IBM z Systems into a logical partition (LPAR), assign memory and processors to the instance. Installing into LPAR is recommended for highly loaded production machines. Running in LPAR also makes higher security standards available. Networking between LPARs is possible over external interfaces or Hipersockets. In case you plan to use your installation for virtualization with KVM, installing into LPAR is highly recommended.

4.1.2.2 z/VM

Running SUSE Linux Enterprise Server for IBM z Systems in z/VM means that SUSE Linux Enterprise Server is a guest system within z/VM. An advantage of this mode is that you have full control over SUSE Linux Enterprise Server from z/VM. This is very helpful for kernel development or kernel-based debugging. It is also very easy to add or remove hardware to and from Linux guests. Creating additional SUSE Linux Enterprise Server guests is simple and you can run hundreds of Linux instances simultaneously.

4.1.2.3 KVM Guest

Being able to install SUSE Linux Enterprise Server for IBM z Systems as a KVM guest requires a KVM server instance installed into LPAR (refer to www.ibm.com/support/knowledge-center/SSNW54_1.1.0/com.ibm.kvm.v110.install/abstract.htm for more information). For the guest installation, the same rules and features as for KVM on the x86_64 architecture apply—see *Book "Virtualization Guide"* for details. Further details on installing KVM gueats are prodided by IBM; refer to http://www.ibm.com/support/knowledgecenter/SSNW54_1.1.0/com.ibm.kvm.v110.kvmlp/KVM.htm-

4.1.3 IPL Options

This section provides the information needed to do an IPL for the first installation. Depending on the type of installation, different options need to be used. The VM reader, load from CD-ROM or server and load from an SCSI-attached DVD-ROM options are discussed. Installing the software packages, which is done over the network, does not require the IPL medium.

4.1.3.1 VM Reader

To IPL from a VM reader, transfer the necessary files into the reader first. For convenience of administration, it is recommended to create a user linuxmnt that owns a minidisk with the files and scripts needed for IPL. This minidisk is then accessed read-only by the Linux guests.

4.1.3.2 Load from Removable Media or Server

For IPLing into an LPAR, it is possible to either load the kernel image directly from the SE's or the HMC's CD/DVD-ROM device or from any remote system accessible through FTP. This function can be performed from the HMC. The installation process requires a file with a mapping of the location of the installation data in the file system and the memory locations where the data is to be copied. For SUSE Linux Enterprise Server this file is called `suse.ins` and located in the root directory of the file system on the DVD 1.

In the left navigation pane of the HMC expand *Systems Management* > *Systems* and select the mainframe system you want to work with. Choose the LPAR where you want to boot SUSE Linux Enterprise Server from the table of LPARs and select *Load from Removable Media or Server*.

Now either choose *Hardware Management Console CD-ROM/DVD* or *FTP Source*. If having chosen the latter option, provide the servers address or name and your credentials. In case the `suse.ins` file is not located in the root directory of the server, provide the path to this file. Continue to the *Select the software to load* menu and select the `suse.ins` entry. Start the installation with *OK*.

4.1.3.3 Load from SCSI-Attached DVD

To IPL from an SCSI DVD, you need access to an FCP adapter connected to a DVD drive. You need the values for WWPN and LUN from the SCSI drive. For details, see *Section 4.2.4.1.2, "IPL from FCP-Attached SCSI DVD"*.

4.1.3.4 Load from the Network with zPXE

IPLing from the Network with zPXE requires a Cobbler server providing the kernel, RAM disk and a parmfile. It is initiated by running the ZPXE EXEC script. See *Section 4.2.1.3, "Using a Cobbler Server for zPXE"* for details. zPXE is only available on z/VM.

4.2 Preparing for Installation

In this section, learn how to make the data accessible for installation, install SUSE Linux Enterprise Server using different methods, and prepare and use the IPL of the SUSE Linux Enterprise Server installation system. Also find out about network configuration and network installation.

4.2.1 Making the Installation Data Available

This section provides detailed information about making the SUSE Linux Enterprise Server IBM z Systems installation data accessible for installation. Depending on your computer and system environment, choose between NFS or FTP installation. If you are running Microsoft Windows workstations in your environment, you can also use the Windows network (including the SMB protocol) to install SUSE Linux Enterprise Server on your IBM z Systems system.

 Tip: IPL from DVD

Since Service Pack 1 of SUSE Linux Enterprise Server Version 10, it is possible to IPL from DVD and use the DVD as the installation medium. This is very convenient if you have restrictions setting up an installation server providing installation media over your network. The prerequisite is an FCP-attached SCSI DVD Drive.

 Note: No Installation "From Hard Disk"

It is not possible to install from hard disk by putting the content of the DVD to a partition on a DASD.

4.2.1.1 Using a Linux Workstation or SUSE Linux Enterprise Server DVD

If you have a Linux workstation running in your computer environment, use the workstation to provide the installation data to the IBM z Systems installation process by NFS or FTP. If the Linux workstation runs under SUSE Linux Enterprise Server, you can set up an installation server (NFS or FTP) using the YaST *Installation Server* module as described in *Section 13.2.1, "Setting Up an Installation Server Using YaST"*.

4.2.1.1.1 Over NFS

Use NFS (network file system) to make the installation media available.

Important: Exporting Mounted Devices with NFS

Exporting the file system root (/) does not imply the export of mounted devices, such as DVD. Explicitly name the mount point in `/etc/exports`:

```
/media/dvd  *(ro)
```

After changing this file, restart the NFS server with the command **sudo systemctl restart nfsserver**.

4.2.1.1.2 Over FTP

Setting up an FTP server on a Linux system involves the installation of the server software itself, such as wuftpd or proftpd, and other possible configuration tasks. Using YaST, the installation step is straightforward: select the package to install and start the installation. Skip the configuration of the FTP server if no anonymous FTP should be used for the installation. Instead, use an FTP login with a valid user name and password. You should create a user account for this task only. The FTP daemon does not need to be started by hand. It can be started by inetd if an FTP connection is requested. To activate the new settings, enter **rcxinetd** restart.

4.2.1.1.3 SUSE Linux Enterprise Server on DVD

DVD1 of the SUSE Linux Enterprise Server for IBM z Systems contains a bootable Linux image for Intel-based workstations and an image for z Systems.

For Intel-based workstations, boot from this DVD, answer the questions regarding your language and keyboard layout, and select *Start rescue system*. You need at least 64 MB RAM for this. No disk space is needed because the entire rescue system resides in the workstation's RAM. This approach takes some Linux and networking experience, because you need to set up the networking of the workstation manually.

For System z, IPL your LPAR/VM guest from this DVD as described in *Section 4.2.4.1.2, "IPL from FCP-Attached SCSI DVD"*. After entering your network parameters, the installation system treats the DVD as the source of installation data. Because z Systems cannot have an X11-capable terminal attached directly, choose between VNC or SSH installation. SSH also provides a graphical installation by tunneling the X connection through SSH with **ssh -X**.

4.2.1.2 Using a Microsoft Windows Workstation

If there is a Microsoft Windows workstation available in your network, use this computer to make the installation media available. The easiest way to do this is to use the SMB protocol, already included in the Windows operating system. Be sure to activate *SMB over TCP/IP* as this enables the encapsulation of SMB packages into TCP/IP packages. Find details in the Windows online help or other Windows-related documentation that covers networking. Another option is to use FTP. This also requires some third-party software for Windows.

4.2.1.2.1 With SMB

To make the installation media available with SMB, insert the SUSE Linux Enterprise Server DVD 1 into the DVD drive of the Windows workstation. Then create a new share using the DVD-ROM drive's letter and make it available for everyone in the network.

The installation path in YaST can be:

```
smb://DOMAIN;USER:PW@SERVERNAME/SHAREPATH
```

Where the placeholders mean:

DOMAIN

Optional workgroup or active directory domain.

USER,

PW

Optional user name and password of a user who can access this server and its share.

SERVERNAME

The name of the server that hosts the share(s).

SHAREPATH

The path to the share(s).

4.2.1.2.2 With NFS

Refer to the documentation provided with the third party product that enables NFS server services for your Windows workstation. The DVD-ROM drive containing the SUSE Linux Enterprise Server DVDs must be in the available NFS path.

4.2.1.2.3 With FTP

Refer to the documentation provided with the third party product that is enabling FTP server services on your Windows workstation. The DVD-ROM drive containing the SUSE Linux Enterprise Server DVDs must be in the available FTP path.

The FTP server that is bundled with some Microsoft Windows releases implements only a subset of the FTP command set and is not suitable for providing the installation data. However, other products (such as the FTP server that is part of Hummingbird Exceed or WAR-FTPD) have been reported as functional.

4.2.1.2.4 Using an FCP-Attached SCSI DVD Drive

After you IPLed from the SCSI DVD as described in *Section 4.1.3.3, "Load from SCSI-Attached DVD"*, the installation system uses the DVD as the installation medium. In that case, you do not need the installation media on an FTP, NFS, or SMB server. However, you need the network configuration data for your SUSE Linux Enterprise Server, because you must set up the network during the installation to perform a graphical installation by VNC or by X.

4.2.1.3 Using a Cobbler Server for zPXE

IPLing from the network requires a Cobbler server, to provide the kernel, initrd, and the installation data. Preparing the Cobbler server requires four steps:

- Importing the Installation Data
- Adding a Distribution
- Adding Profiles
- Adding Systems

4.2.1.3.1 Importing the Installation Data

Importing the media requires the installation source to be available on the Cobbler server—either from DVD or from a network source. Run the following command to import the data:

```
cobbler import --path=PATH❶ --name=IDENTIFIER❷ --arch=s390x
```

❶ Mount point of the installation data.

② A string identifying the imported product, for example "sles12_s390x". This string is used as the name for the subdirectory where the installation data is copied to. On a Cobbler server running on SUSE Linux Enterprise this is `/srv/www/cobbler/ks_mirror/IDENTIFIER`. This path may be different if Cobbler runs on another operating system.

4.2.1.3.2   Adding a Distribution

By adding a distribution, you tell Cobbler to provide the kernel and the initrd required to IPL via zPXE. Run the following command on the Cobbler server to add SUSE Linux Enterprise Server for IBM z Systems:

```
cobbler distro add --arch=s390 --breed=suse --name="IDENTIFIER" ① \
  --os-version=sles10② \
  --initrd=/srv/www/cobbler/ks_mirror/IDENTIFIER/boot/s390x/initrd③ \
  --kernel=/srv/www/cobbler/ks_mirror/IDENTIFIER/boot/s390x/linux④ \
  --kopts="install=http://cobbler.example.com/cobbler/ks_mirror/IDENTIFIER"⑤
```

① Custom identifier for the distribution, for example "SLES 12 SP1 z Systems". Must be unique.

② Operating system identifier. Use `sles10`.

③ Path to the initrd. The first part of the path (`/srv/www/cobbler/ks_mirror/IDEN-TIFIER/`) depends on the location where Cobbler imported the data and the subdirectory name you chose when importing the installation data.

④ Path to the kernel. The first part of the path (`/srv/www/cobbler/ks_mirror/IDEN-TIFIER/`) depends on the location where Cobbler imported the data and the subdirectory name you chose when importing the installation data.

⑤ URl to the installation directory on the Cobbler server.

4.2.1.3.3   Adjusting the Profile

When adding a distribution (see *Section 4.2.1.3.2, "Adding a Distribution"*) a profile with the corresponding *IDENTIFIER* is automatically generated. Use the following command to make a few required adjustments:

```
cobbler distro edit \
```

Making the Installation Data Available

```
--name=IDENTIFIER ❶  --os-version=sles10 ❷  --ksmeta="" ❸
--kopts="install=http://cobbler.example.com/cobbler/ks_mirror/IDENTIFIER" ❹
```

❶ Identifier for the profile. Use the same string as specified when having added the distribution.

❷ Operating system version. Distribution to which the profile should apply. You must use the string specified with `--name=IDENTIFIER` in the importing step here.

❸ Option needed for templating kickstart files. Not used for SUSE, so set to an empty value as specified in the example.

❹ Space-separated list of Kernel parameters. Should include at least the `install` parameter as shown in the example.

4.2.1.3.4 Adding Systems

The last step that is required is to add systems to the Cobbler server. A system addition needs to be done for every z Systems guest that should boot via zPXE. Guests are identified via their z/VM user ID (in the following example, an ID called "linux01" is assumed). Note that this ID needs to be a lowercase string. To add a system, run the following command:

```
cobbler system add --name=linux01 --hostname=linux01.example.com \
--profile=IDENTIFIER --interface=qdio \
--ip-address=192.168.2.103 --subnet=192.168.2.255 --netmask=255.255.255.0 \
--name-servers=192.168.1.116 --name-servers-search=example.com \
--gateway=192.168.2.1 --kopts="KERNEL_OPTIONS"
```

With the `--kopts` option you can specify the kernel and installation parameters you would normally specify in the parmfile. The parameters are entered as a space-separated list in the form of *PARAMETER1=VALUE1 PARAMETER2=VALUE2*. The installer will prompt you for missing parameters. For a completely automated installation you need to specify all parameters for networking, DASDs and provide an AutoYaST file. The following shows an example for a guest equipped with an OSA interface using the same network parameters as above.

```
--kopts=" \
AutoYaST=http://192.168.0.5/autoinst.xml \
Hostname=linux01.example.com \
Domain=example.com \
```

```
HostIP=192.168.2.103 \
Gateway=192.168.2.1 \
Nameserver=192.168.1.116 \
Searchdns=example.com \
InstNetDev=osa; \
Netmask=255.255.255.0 \
Broadcast=192.168.2.255 \
OsaInterface=qdio \
Layer2=0 \
PortNo=0 \
ReadChannel=0.0.0700 \
WriteChannel=0.0.0701 \
DataChannel=0.0.0702 \
Portname=DT70 \
DASD=600"
```

4.2.2 Installation Types

This section provides information about which steps must be performed to install SUSE Linux Enterprise Server for each of the installation modes and where to find the appropriate information. After the preparations mentioned in the previous chapters have been accomplished, follow the installation overview of the desired installation mode to install SUSE Linux Enterprise Server on your system.

As described in *Section 4.2.1, "Making the Installation Data Available"*, there are three different installation modes for Linux on IBM z Systems:

- LPAR installation

- z/VM installation

- KVM guest installation

PROCEDURE 4.1: OVERVIEW OF AN LPAR INSTALLATION

1. Prepare the devices needed for installation. See *Section 4.2.3.1, "LPAR Installation"*.

2. IPL the installation system. See *Section 4.2.4.1, "LPAR Installation"*.

Installation Types

3. Configure the network. See *Section 4.2.5, "Network Configuration"*.

4. Connect to the SUSE Linux Enterprise Server installation system. See *Section 4.2.6, "Connecting to the SUSE Linux Enterprise Server Installation System"*.

5. Start the installation using YaST and IPL the installed system. See *Chapter 6, Installation with YaST*.

PROCEDURE 4.2: INSTALLATION OVERVIEW OF Z/VM INSTALLATION

1. Prepare the devices needed for installation. See *Section 4.2.3.2, "z/VM Installation"*.

2. IPL the installation system. See *Section 4.2.4.2, "z/VM Installation"*.

3. Configure the network. See *Section 4.2.5, "Network Configuration"*.

4. Connect to the SUSE Linux Enterprise Server installation system. See *Section 4.2.6, "Connecting to the SUSE Linux Enterprise Server Installation System"*.

5. Start the installation using YaST and IPL the installed system. See *Chapter 6, Installation with YaST*.

PROCEDURE 4.3: OVERVIEW OF A KVM GUEST INSTALLATION

1. Create a virtual disk image and write a domain XML file. See *Section 4.2.3.3, "KVM Guest Installation"*.

2. Prepare the installation target and IPL the VM Guest. See *Section 4.2.4.3, "KVM Guest Installation"*.

3. *Section 4.2.5.3, "Set up the Network and Select the Installation Source"*.

4. Connect to the SUSE Linux Enterprise Server installation system. See *Section 4.2.6, "Connecting to the SUSE Linux Enterprise Server Installation System"*.

5. Start the installation using YaST and IPL the installed system. See *Chapter 6, Installation with YaST*.

4.2.3 Preparing the IPL of the SUSE Linux Enterprise Server Installation System

4.2.3.1 LPAR Installation

Configure your IBM z Systems system to start in ESA/S390 or Linux-only mode with an appropriate activation profile and IOCDS. Consult IBM documentation for more on how to achieve this. Proceed with *Section 4.2.4.1, "LPAR Installation"*.

4.2.3.2 z/VM Installation

4.2.3.2.1 Adding a Linux Guest

The first step is to attach and format one or multiple DASDs in the system to be used by the Linux guest in z/VM. Next, create a new user in z/VM. The example shows the directory for a user LINUX1 with the password LINPWD, 1 GB of memory (extendable up to 2 GB), 32 MB of expanded RAM (XSTORE), some minidisks (MDISK), two CPUs and an OSA QDIO device.

 Tip: Assigning Memory to z/VM guests

> When assigning memory to a z/VM guest, make sure that the memory size suits the needs of your preferred installation type. See *Section 4.1.1.1.1, "Memory Requirements"*. To set the memory size to 1 GB, use the command **CP DEFINE STORAGE 1G**. After the installation has finished, reset the memory size to the desired value.

EXAMPLE 4.1: CONFIGURATION OF A Z/VM DIRECTORY

```
USER LINUX1 LINPWD 1024M 2048M G
*  _____
* LINUX1
*  _____
* This VM Linux guest has two CPUs defined.

CPU 01 CPUID 111111
CPU 02 CPUID 111222
IPL CMS PARM AUTOCR
IUCV ANY
IUCV ALLOW
```

```
MACH ESA 10
OPTION MAINTCCW RMCHINFO
SHARE RELATIVE 2000
XSTORE 32M
CONSOLE 01C0 3270 A
SPOOL 000C 2540 READER *
SPOOL 000D 2540 PUNCH A
SPOOL 000E 3203 A
* OSA QDIO DEVICE DEFINITIONS
DEDICATE 9A0 9A0
DEDICATE 9A1 9A1
DEDICATE 9A2 9A2
*
LINK MAINT 0190 0190 RR
LINK MAINT 019E 019E RR
LINK MAINT 019D 019D RR
* MINIDISK DEFINITIONS
MDISK 201 3390 0001 0050 DASD40 MR ONE4ME TWO4ME THR4ME
MDISK 150 3390 0052 0200 DASD40 MR ONE4ME TWO4ME THR4ME
MDISK 151 3390 0253 2800 DASD40 MR ONE4ME TWO4ME THR4ME
```

This example uses minidisk 201 as the guest's home disk. Minidisk 150 with 200 cylinders is the Linux swap device. Disk 151 with 2800 cylinders holds the Linux installation.

Now add (as the user MAINT) the guest to the user directory with **DIRM FOR LINUX1 ADD**. Enter the name of the guest (LINUX1) and press F5 . Set up the environment of the user with:

```
DIRM DIRECT
DIRM USER WITHPASS
```

The last command returns a reader file number. This number is needed for the next command:

```
RECEIVE <number> USER DIRECT A (REPL)
```

You can now log in on the guest as user LINUX1.

If you do not have the dirmaint option available, refer to the IBM documentation to set up this user.

Proceed with *Section 4.2.4.2, "z/VM Installation"*.

4.2.3.3 KVM Guest Installation

Prerequisite for a KVM guest installation are a domain XML file defining the virtual machine and at least on virtual disk image to be used for the installation.

4.2.3.3.1 Create a Virtual Disk Image

By default libvirt searches for disk images in /var/lib/libvirt/images/ on the VM Host Server. Images can also be stored anywhere else on the file system, however, it is recommended to store all images in a single location for easier maintainability. The following example creates a qcow2 image with a size of 10 GB in /var/lib/libvirt/images/. For more information refer to *Book "Virtualization Guide", Chapter 27 "Guest Installation", Section 27.2 "Managing Disk Images with* **qemu-img**".

1. Log in to the KVM host server.

2. Run the following commend to create the image:

   ```
   qemu-img create -f qcow2 /var/lib/libvirt/images/s12lin_qcow2.img 10G
   ```

4.2.3.3.2 Write a Domain XML File

A domain XML file is used to define the VM Guest. To create the domain XML file open an empty file s12-1.xml with an editor and create a file like in the following example.

EXAMPLE 4.2: EXAMPLE DOMAIN XML FILE

The following example creates a VM Guest with a single CPU, 1 GB RAM and the virtual disk image created in the previous section (*Section 4.2.3.3.1, "Create a Virtual Disk Image"*. It assumes that the host network interface to which the virtual server is attached is bond0. Please change the source devices element to match your network setup.

```
<domain type="kvm">
```

```
  <name>s12-1</name>
  <description>Guest-System SUSE Sles12</description>
  <memory>1048576</memory>
  <vcpu>1</vcpu>
  <os>
   <type arch="s390x" machine="s390-ccw-virtio">hvm</type>
   <!-- Boot kernel - remove 3 lines after successfull installation -->
   <kernel>/var/lib/libvirt/images/s12-kernel.boot</kernel>
   <initrd>/var/lib/libvirt/images/s12-initrd.boot</initrd>
   <cmdline>linuxrcstderr=/dev/console</cmdline>
  </os>
  <iothreads>1</iothreads>
  <on_poweroff>destroy</on_poweroff>
  <on_reboot>restart</on_reboot>
  <on_crash>preserve</on_crash>
  <devices>
   <emulator>/usr/bin/qemu-system-s390x</emulator>
   <disk type="file" device="disk">
    <driver name="qemu" type="qcow2" cache="none" iothread="1" io="native"/>
    <source file="/var/lib/libvirt/images/s12lin_qcow2.img"/>
    <target dev="vda" bus="virtio"/>
   </disk>
   <interface type="direct">
    <source dev="bond0" mode="bridge"/>
    <model type="virtio"/>
   </interface>
   <console type="pty">
    <target type="sclp"/>
   </console>
  </devices>
</domain>
```

4.2.4   IPLing the SUSE Linux Enterprise Server Installation System

4.2.4.1 LPAR Installation

There are different ways to IPL SUSE Linux Enterprise Server into an LPAR. The preferred way is to use the *Load from CD-ROM or server* feature of the SE or HMC.

4.2.4.1.1 IPL from DVD-ROM

Mark the LPAR to install and select *Load from CD-ROM or server*. Leave the field for the file location blank or enter the path to the root directory of the first DVD-ROM and select continue. In the list of options that appears, select the default selection. *Operating system messages* should now show the kernel boot messages.

4.2.4.1.2 IPL from FCP-Attached SCSI DVD

You can use the *Load* procedure by selecting *SCSI* as *Load type* to IPL from SCSI. Enter the WWPN (Worldwide port name) and LUN Logical unit number) provided by your SCSI bridge or storage (16 digits—do not omit the trailing 0s). The boot program selector must be 2. Use your FCP adapter as *Load address* and perform an IPL.

4.2.4.2 z/VM Installation

This section is about IPLing the installation system to install SUSE Linux Enterprise Server for IBM z Systems on a z/VM system.

4.2.4.2.1 IPL from the z/VM Reader

You need a working TCP/IP connection and an FTP client program within your newly defined z/VM guest to transfer the installation system via FTP. Setting up TCP/IP for z/VM is beyond the scope of this manual. Refer to the appropriate IBM documentation.

Log in as the z/VM Linux guest to IPL. Make the content of the directory `/boot/s390x` on DVD 1 of the SUSE Linux Enterprise Server for IBM z Systems available by FTP within your network. From this directory, get the files `linux`, `initrd`, `parmfile`, and `sles12.exec`. Transfer the files with a fixed block size of 80 characters. Specify it with the FTP command **locsite fix 80**. It is important to copy `linux` (the Linux kernel) and `initrd` (the installation image) as binary files, so use the `binary` transfer mode. `parmfile` and `sles12.exec` need to be transferred in ASCII mode.

The example shows the steps necessary. In this example, the required files are accessible from an FTP server at the IP address 192.168.0.3 and the login is lininst. It may differ for your network.

EXAMPLE 4.3: TRANSFERRING THE BINARIES VIA FTP

```
FTP 192.168.0.3
VM TCP/IP FTP Level 530
Connecting to 192.168.0.3, port 21
220 ftpserver FTP server (Version wu-2.4.2-academ[BETA-18](1)
Thu Feb 11 16:09:02 GMT 2010) ready.
USER
lininst
331 Password required for lininst
PASS
******
230 User lininst logged in.
Command:
binary
200 Type set to I
Command:
locsite fix 80
Command:
get /media/dvd1/boot/s390x/linux sles12.linux
200 PORT Command successful
150 Opening BINARY mode data connection for /media/dvd1/boot/s390x/linux
(10664192 bytes)
226 Transfer complete.
10664192 bytes transferred in 13.91 seconds.
Transfer rate 766.70 Kbytes/sec.
Command:
get /media/dvd1/boot/s390x/initrd sles12.initrd
200 PORT Command successful
150 Opening BINARY mode data connection for /media/dvd1/boot/s390x/initrd
(21403276 bytes)
226 Transfer complete.
21403276 bytes transferred in 27.916 seconds.
```

```
Transfer rate 766.70 Kbytes/sec.
Command:
ascii
200 Type set to A
Command:
get /media/dvd1/boot/s390x/parmfile sles12.parmfile
150 Opening ASCII mode data connection for /media/dvd1/boot/s390x/parmfile
(5 bytes)
226 Transfer complete.
5 bytes transferred in 0.092 seconds.
Transfer rate 0.05 Kbytes/sec.
Command:
get /media/dvd1/boot/s390x/sles12.exec sles12.exec
150 Opening ASCII mode data connection for /media/dvd1/boot/s390x/sles12.exec
(891 bytes)
226 Transfer complete.
891 bytes transferred in 0.097 seconds.
Transfer rate 0.89 Kbytes/sec.
Command:
quit
```

Use the REXX script sles12.exec you downloaded to IPL the Linux installation system. This script loads the kernel, parmfile, and the initial RAM disk into the reader for IPL.

EXAMPLE 4.4: SLES12 EXEC

```
/* REXX LOAD EXEC FOR SUSE LINUX S/390 VM GUESTS      */
/* LOADS SUSE LINUX S/390 FILES INTO READER           */
SAY ''
SAY 'LOADING SLES12 FILES INTO READER...'
'CP CLOSE RDR'
'PURGE RDR ALL'
'SPOOL PUNCH * RDR'
'PUNCH SLES12 LINUX A (NOH'
'PUNCH SLES12 PARMFILE A (NOH'
'PUNCH SLES12 INITRD A (NOH'
'IPL 00C'
```

With this script you can IPL the SUSE Linux Enterprise Server installation system with the command **sles12**. The Linux kernel then starts and prints its boot messages.

To continue the installation, proceed to *Section 4.2.5, "Network Configuration"*.

4.2.4.2.2   IPL from FCP-Attached SCSI DVD

To IPL in z/VM, prepare the SCSI IPL process by using the SET LOADDEV parameter:

```
SET LOADDEV PORTNAME 200400E8 00D74E00 LUN 00020000 00000000 BOOT 2
```

After setting the LOADDEV parameter with the appropriate values, IPL your FCP adapter, for example:

```
IPL FC00
```

To continue the installation, proceed with *Section 4.2.5, "Network Configuration"*.

4.2.4.2.3   IPL from a Cobbler Server with zPXE

To IPL from a Cobbler server with zPXE you need to transfer the zpxe.rexx script via FTP from the Cobbler server to your z/VM guest. The z/VM guest needs a working TCP/IP connection and an FTP client program.

Log in as the z/VM Linux guest to IPL and transfer the script with a fixed size of 80 characters in ASCII mode (see *Example 4.3, "Transferring the Binaries via FTP"* for an example). The zpxe.rexx script is available on the Cobbler server at /usr/share/doc/packages/s390-tools/.

zpxe.rexx is supposed to replace the PROFILE EXEC of your guest. Make a backup copy of the existing PROFILE EXEC and rename ZPXE REXX to PROFILE EXEC. Alternatively call ZPXE REXX from the existing PROFILE EXEC by using a new line with the following content: 'ZPXE REXX'.

The last step is to create a configuration file, ZPXE CONF, telling ZPXE REXX which Cobbler server to contact and which disk to IPL. Run **xedit zpxe conf a** and create ZPXE CONF with the following content (replace the example data accordingly):

```
HOST cobbler.example.com
IPLDISK 600
```

On the next log in to your z/VM guest, the Cobbler server will be connected. If an installation is scheduled on the Cobbler server, it will be executed. To schedule the installation, run the following command on the Cobbler server:

```
cobbler system edit --name ID❶ --netboot-enabled 1❷ --profile PROFILENAME❸
```

❶ z/VM user ID.

❷ Enable IPLing from the network.

❸ Name of an existing profile, see *Section 4.2.1.3.3, "Adjusting the Profile"*.

4.2.4.3   KVM Guest Installation

To start the guest installation, you first need to start the VM Guest defined in *Section 4.2.3.3.1, "Create a Virtual Disk Image"*. Prerequisite for this is to first make the Kernel and initrd required for IPLing available.

4.2.4.3.1   Preparing the installation source

Kernel and initrd of the installation system need to be copied to the VM Host Server to be able to IPL the VM Guest into the installation system.

1. Log in to the KVM host and make sure you can connect to the remote host or device serving the installation source.

2. Copy the following two files from the installation source to `/var/lib/libvirt/images/`. If the data is served from a remote host, use **ftp**, **sftp** or **scp** to transfer the files:

   ```
   /boot/s390x/initrd
   /boot/s390x/cd.ikr
   ```

3. Rename the files on the KVM host:

   ```
   cd /var/lib/libvirt/images/
   mv initrd s12-initrd.boot
    mv cd.ikr s12-kernel.boot
   ```

4.2.4.3.2 IPL the VM Guest

To IPL the VM Guest, log in to the KVM host and run the following command:

```
virsh  create s12-1.xml --console
```

After the start of the VM Guest has completed, the installation system starts and you will see the following message:

```
Domain s12-1 started
Connected to domain s12-1
Escape character is ^]
Initializing cgroup subsys cpuset
Initializing cgroup subsys cpu
Initializing
cgroup subsys cpuacct
.

.

Please make sure your installation medium is available.
Retry?
0) <-- Back <--
1) Yes
2) No
```

Answer *2) No* and choose *Installation* on the next step. Proceed as described in *Section 4.2.5.3, "Set up the Network and Select the Installation Source"*.

4.2.5   Network Configuration

Wait until the kernel has completed its start-up routines. If you are installing in basic mode or in an LPAR, open the *Operating System Messages* on the HMC or SE.

First, choose *Start Installation* in the linuxrc main menu then *Start Installation or Update* to start the installation process. Select *Network* as your installation medium then select the type of network protocol you will be using for the installation. *Section 4.2.1, "Making the Installation Data Available"* describes how to make the installation data available for the various types of network connections. Currently, *FTP, HTTP, NFS,* and *SMB/CIFS* (Windows file sharing) are supported.

Now choose an OSA or HiperSockets network device over which to receive the installation data from the list of available devices. The list may also contain CTC, ESCON, or IUCV devices, but they are no longer supported on SUSE Linux Enterprise Server.

4.2.5.1   Configure a HiperSockets Interface

Select a Hipersocket device from the list of network devices. Then enter the numbers for the read, write and data channels:

EXAMPLE 4.5: SUPPORTED NETWORK CONNECTION TYPES AND DRIVER PARAMETERS

```
Choose the network device.


 1) IBM parallel CTC Adapter (0.0.0600)

 2) IBM parallel CTC Adapter (0.0.0601)

 3) IBM parallel CTC Adapter (0.0.0602)

 4) IBM Hipersocket (0.0.0800)

 5) IBM Hipersocket (0.0.0801)

 6) IBM Hipersocket (0.0.0802)

 7) IBM OSA Express Network card (0.0.0700)

 8) IBM OSA Express Network card (0.0.0701)

 9) IBM OSA Express Network card (0.0.0702)

10) IBM OSA Express Network card (0.0.f400)

11) IBM OSA Express Network card (0.0.f401)

12) IBM OSA Express Network card (0.0.f402)

13) IBM IUCV


> 4


Device address for read channel. (Enter '+++' to abort).
[0.0.800]> 0.0.800


Device address for write channel. (Enter '+++' to abort).
[0.0.801]> 0.0.801


Device address for data channel. (Enter '+++' to abort).
```

```
[0.0.802]> 0.0.802
```

4.2.5.2   Configure an OSA Express Device

Select an OSA Express device from the list of network devices and provide a port number. Then enter the numbers for the read, write and data channels and the port name, if applicable. Choose whether to enable OSI Layer 2 support.

The port number was added to support the new 2 port OSA Express 3 Network devices. If you are not using an OSA Express 3 device, enter 0. OSA Express cards also have the option of running in an "OSI layer 2 support" mode or using the older more common "layer 3" mode. The card mode affects all systems that share the device including systems on other LPARs. If in doubt, specify 2 for compatibility with the default mode used by other operating systems such as z/VM and z/OS. Consult with your hardware administrator for further information on these options.

EXAMPLE 4.6: NETWORK DEVICE DRIVER PARAMETERS

```
Choose the network device.


 1)  IBM parallel CTC Adapter (0.0.0600)

 2)  IBM parallel CTC Adapter (0.0.0601)

 3)  IBM parallel CTC Adapter (0.0.0602)

 4)  IBM Hipersocket (0.0.0800)

 5)  IBM Hipersocket (0.0.0801)

 6)  IBM Hipersocket (0.0.0802)

 7)  IBM OSA Express Network card (0.0.0700)

 8)  IBM OSA Express Network card (0.0.0701)

 9)  IBM OSA Express Network card (0.0.0702)

10)  IBM OSA Express Network card (0.0.f400)

11)  IBM OSA Express Network card (0.0.f401)

12)  IBM OSA Express Network card (0.0.f402)

13)  IBM IUCV


> 7


Enter the relative port number. (Enter '+++' to abort).
> 0
```

```
Device address for read channel. (Enter '+++' to abort).
[0.0.0700]> 0.0.0700


Device address for write channel. (Enter '+++' to abort).
[0.0.0701]> 0.0.0701


Device address for data channel. (Enter '+++' to abort).
[0.0.0702]> 0.0.0702


Enable OSI Layer 2 support?

0) <-- Back <--
1) Yes
2) No

> 1


MAC address. (Enter '+++' to abort).
> +++
```

4.2.5.3   Set up the Network and Select the Installation Source

When all network device parameters have been entered, the respective driver is installed and you see the corresponding kernel messages.

Next, decide whether to use DHCP autoconfiguration for setting up the network interface parameters. Because DHCP only works on a few devices and requires special hardware configuration settings, you probably want to say *NO* here. When you do so, you are prompted for the following networking parameters:

- The IP address of the system to install

- The corresponding netmask (if not having been specified with the IP address)

- The IP address of a gateway to reach the server

- A list of search domains covered by the domain name server (DNS)

- The IP address of your domain name server

EXAMPLE 4.7: NETWORKING PARAMETERS

```
Automatic configuration via DHCP?


0) <-- Back <--
1) Yes
2) No


> 2


Enter your IPv4 address.
 Example: 192.168.5.77/24. (Enter '+++' to abort).
> 192.168.0.20/24


Enter the IP address of the gateway. Leave empty if you do not need one. (Enter '
+++' to abort).
> 192.168.0.1


Enter your search domains, separated by a space:. (Enter '+++' to abort).
> example.com


Enter the IP address of your name server. Leave empty if you do not need one. (En
ter '+++' to abort).
> 192.168.0.1
```

Finally, you are prompted for details on the installation server, such as the IP address, the directory containing the installation data, and login credentials. Once all required data is entered, the installation system loads.

4.2.6 Connecting to the SUSE Linux Enterprise Server Installation System

After having loaded the installation system, linuxrc wants to know what type of display you want to use to control the installation procedure. Possible choices are X11 (X Window System), VNC (Virtual Network Computing protocol), SSH (text mode or X11 installation via Secure Shell), or ASCII Console. Selecting VNC or SSH is recommended.

When choosing the latter (ASCII Console), YaST will be started in text mode and you can perform the installation directly within your terminal. See *Book "Administration Guide", Chapter 2 "YaST in Text Mode"* for instructions on how to use YaST in text mode. Using the ASCII Console is only useful when installing into LPAR.

 Note: Terminal Emulation for ASCII Console

To be able to work with YaST in text mode, it needs to run in a terminal with VT220/Linux emulation (also called ASCII console). You cannot use YaST in a 3270 terminal, for example.

4.2.6.1 Initiating the Installation for VNC

1. After the installation option VNC has been chosen, the VNC server starts. A short note displayed in the console provides information about which IP address and display number is needed for a connection with vncviewer. Alternatively, a URL is given here for entry into your Java-enabled browser to connect to the installation system.

2. Start a VNC client application on your client system. Either use vncviewer or the VNC Java client and a Java-enabled Web browser.

3. Enter the IP address and the display number of the SUSE Linux Enterprise Server installation system when prompted to do so.
   If you connect via a Java-enabled browser, enter a URL containing the IP address of the installation system and the appropriate port number in the format:

   ```
   http://<IP address of installation system>:5801/
   ```

4. After the connection has been established, start installing SUSE Linux Enterprise Server with YaST.

4.2.6.2 Initiating the Installation for the X Window System

🛈 **Important: X Authentication Mechanism**

The direct installation with the X Window System relies on a primitive authentication mechanism based on host names. This mechanism is disabled on current SUSE Linux Enterprise Server versions. Installation with SSH or VNC is preferred.

1. Make sure that the X server allows the client (the system that is installed) to connect. Set the variable **DISPLAYMANAGER_XSERVER_TCP_PORT_6000_OPEN="yes"** in the file /etc/sysconfig/displaymanager. Then restart the X server and allow client binding to the server using **xhost <client IP address>**.

2. When prompted at the installation system, enter the IP address of the machine running the X server.

3. Wait until YaST opens then start the installation.

4.2.6.3 Initiating the Installation for SSH

To connect to an installation system with the name earth using SSH, execute **ssh -X earth**. If your workstation runs on Microsoft Windows, use the SSH and telnet client and terminal emulator Putty which is available from http://www.chiark.greenend.org.uk/~sgtatham/putty/. Set *Enable X11 forwarding* in Putty under *Connection › SSH › X11*. If you use another operating system, execute **ssh -X earth** to connect to an installation system with the name earth. X-Forwarding over SSH is supported if you have a local X server available. Otherwise, YaST provides a text interface over ncurses.

A login prompt appears. Enter root and log in with your password. Enter **yast.ssh** to start YaST. YaST then guides you through the installation.

Proceed with the detailed description of the installation procedure that can be found in *Chapter 6, Installation with YaST*.

4.2.7 The SUSE Linux Enterprise Server Boot Procedure on IBM z Systems

The boot process for SLES 10 and 11 followed the scheme provided below. For in-depth information refer to the documentation provided at http://www.ibm.com/developerworks/linux/linux390/documentation_suse.html.

1. Provide the Kernel.

2. Provide or create an initrd for the given Kernel.

3. Provide the correct paths for the initrd and the Kernel in `/etc/zipl.conf`.

4. Install the configuration provided by `/etc/zipl.conf` to the system.

With SLES 12 the way SUSE Linux Enterprise Server is booted on IBM z Systems has changed. Several reasons led to this change:

- Alignment with other architectures: From an administrative point of view SLES systems should behave the same on all architectures.

- Btrfs: The zipl boot loader is technically incompatible with Btrfs, the new default root file system for SLES (see *Book "Storage Administration Guide", Chapter 1 "Overview of File Systems in Linux", Section 1.2.1 "Btrfs"* for details).

- Support for system rollbacks with Snapper: Snapper, in combination with Btrfs, provides bootable system snapshots which can be used for system rollbacks (see *Book "Administration Guide", Chapter 3 "System Recovery and Snapshot Management with Snapper"* for details).

For those reasons, starting with SLES 12, GRUB 2 replaces zipl on IBM SUSE Linux Enterprise Server for z Systems. GRUB 2 on the x86_64 architecture includes device drivers on the firmware level to access the file system. On the mainframe there is no firmware and adding `ccw` to GRUB 2 would not only be a huge task, but also would be a reimplementation of zipl in GRUB 2. Therefore SUSE Linux Enterprise Server uses a two-stage approach:

Stage One:

A separate partition containing the Kernel and an initrd is mounted to `/boot/zipl` (somewhat similar to `/boot/efi` on UEFI platforms). This Kernel and the initrd are loaded via zipl using the configuration from `/boot/zipl/config`.

This configuration adds the keyword `initgrub` to the Kernel command line. Once the Kernel and initrd are loaded, the initrd activates the devices required to mount the root file system (see `/boot/zipl/active_devices.txt`). Afterwards a GRUB 2 userland program is started, which reads `/boot/grub2/grub.cfg`.

Stage Two:

The Kernel and the initrd specified in `/boot/grub2/grub.cfg` are started via **kexec**. All devices listed in `/boot/zipl/active_devices.txt` are activated, the root file system is mounted and the boot procedure continues like on the other architectures.

4.3 The parmfile—Automating the System Configuration

The installation process can be partly automated by specifying the crucial parameters in the `parmfile`. The `parmfile` contains all the data required for network setup and DASD configuration. In addition to that, it can be used to set up the connection method to the SUSE Linux Enterprise Server installation system and the YaST instance running there. User interaction is thus limited to the actual YaST installation controlled by YaST dialogs.

The following parameters can be passed to the installation routine, which takes them as default values for installation. All IP addresses, server names, and numerical values are examples. Replace these values with the ones needed in your installation scenario.

The number of lines in the parmfile is limited to 10. Specify more than one parameter on a line. Parameter names are not case-sensitive. Separate the parameters by spaces. You may specify the parameters in any order. Always keep the `PARAMETER=value` string together in one line. For example:

```
Hostname=s390zvm01.suse.de HostIP=10.11.134.65
```

 Tip: Using IPv6 during the Installation

By default you can only assign IPv4 network addresses to your machine. To enable IPv6 during installation, enter one of the following parameters at the boot prompt: `ipv6=1` (accept IPv4 and IPv6) or `ipv6only=1` (accept IPv6 only).

Some of the following parameters are required. If they are missing, the automatic process pauses and asks you to enter the value manually.

4.3.1   General Parameters

`AutoYaST=` *<URL>* `Manual=0`

The `AutoYaST` parameter specifies the location of the `autoinst.xml` control file for automatic installation. The `Manual` parameter controls if the other parameters are only default values that still must be acknowledged by the user. Set this parameter to `0` if all values should be accepted and no questions asked. Setting `AutoYaST` implies setting `Manual` to `0`.

`Info=` *<URL>*

Specifies a location for a file from which to read additional options. This helps to overcome the limitations of 10 lines (and 80 characters per line under z/VM) for the parmfile. More documentation on the Info file can be found in *Section 25.1.5, "Creating the* `info` *File"*. Since the Info file can typically only be accessed through the network on z Systems, you cannot use it to specify options required to set up the network, that is options described in *Section 4.3.2, "Configuring the Network Interface"*. Also other linuxrc specific options such as for debugging need to be specified in the parmfile to be effective.

> **Tip: Creating a File with Autoinstallation Information**
>
> At the very end of the installation of a system you can check *Clone This System for Autoyast*. This creates a ready-to-use profile as `/root/autoinst.xml` that can be used to create clones of this particular installation. To create an autoinstallation file from scratch or to edit an existing one, use the YaST module *Autoinstallation*. For more information about AutoYaST, refer to *Chapter 25, Automated Installation*.

4.3.2 Configuring the Network Interface

 Important: Configuring the Network Interface

The settings discussed in this section apply only to the network interface used during installation. Configure additional network interfaces in the installed system by following the instructions given in *Book "Administration Guide", Chapter 19 "Basic Networking", Section 19.5 "Configuring a Network Connection Manually"*.

Hostname=zseries.example.com

Enter the fully qualified host name.

Domain=example.com

Domain search path for DNS. Allows you to use short host names instead of fully qualified ones.

HostIP=192.168.1.2

Enter the IP address of the interface to configure.

Gateway=192.168.1.3

Specify the gateway to use.

Nameserver=192.168.1.4

Specify the DNS server in charge.

InstNetDev=osa

Enter the type of interface to configure. Possible values are `osa`, `hsi`, `ctc`, `escon`, and `iucv` (CTC, ESCON, and IUCV are no longer officially supported).

For the interfaces of type `hsi` and `osa`, specify an appropriate netmask and an optional broadcast address:

```
Netmask=255.255.255.0
Broadcast=192.168.255.255
```

For the interfaces of type `ctc`, `escon`, and `iucv` (CTC, ESCON, and IUCV are no longer officially supported), enter the IP address of the peer:

```
Pointopoint=192.168.55.20
```

OsaInterface=<lcs|qdio>

> For osa network devices, specify the host interface (qdio or lcs).

Layer2=<0|1>

> For osa QDIO Ethernet and hsi devices, specify whether to enable (1) or disable (0) OSI Layer 2 support.

OSAHWAddr=02:00:65:00:01:09

> For Layer 2-enabled osa QDIO Ethernet devices. Either specify a MAC address manually or state OSAHWADDR= (with trailing white space) for the system default.

PortNo=<0|1>

> For osa network devices, specify the port number (provided the device supports this feature). The default value is 0.

Each of the interfaces requires certain setup options:

- Interfaces ctc and escon (CTC and ESCON are no longer officially supported):

```
ReadChannel=0.0.0600
WriteChannel=0.0.0601
```

ReadChannel specifies the READ channel to use. WriteChannel specifies the WRITE channel.

- For the ctc interface (no longer officially supported), specify the protocol that should be used for this interface:

```
CTCProtocol=<0/1/2>
```

Valid entries would be:

0	Compatibility mode, also for non-Linux peers other than OS/390 and z/OS (this is the default mode)
1	Extended mode
2	Compatibility mode with OS/390 and z/OS

- Network device type <u>osa</u> with interface <u>lcs</u>:

```
ReadChannel=0.0.0124
Portname=1
```

<u>ReadChannel</u> stands for the channel number used in this setup. A second port number can be derived from this by adding one to <u>ReadChannel</u>. <u>Portnumber</u> is used to specify the relative port.

- Interface <u>iucv</u>:

```
IUCVPeer=PEER
```

Enter the name of the peer machine.

- Network device type <u>osa</u> with interface <u>qdio</u> for OSA-Express Gigabit Ethernet:

```
ReadChannel=0.0.0700
WriteChannel=0.0.0701
DataChannel=0.0.0702
Portname=FEF400
```

For <u>ReadChannel</u>, enter the number of the READ channel. For <u>WriteChannel</u>, enter the number of the WRITE channel. <u>DataChannel</u> specifies the DATA channel. For <u>Portname</u>, enter an appropriate port name. Make sure that the READ channel carries an even device number.

- Interface <u>hsi</u> for HiperSockets and VM guest LANs:

```
ReadChannel=0.0.0800
WriteChannel=0.0.0801
DataChannel=0.0.0802
```

For <u>ReadChannel</u>, enter the appropriate number for the READ channel. For <u>WriteChan-nel</u> and <u>DataChannel</u>, enter the WRITE and DATA channel numbers.

Install=nfs://server/directory/DVD1/

> Specify the location of the installation source to use. Possible protocols are `nfs`, `smb` (Samba/CIFS), `ftp`, `tftp` `http`, and `https`.
>
> If an `ftp`, `tftp` or `smb` URL is given, specify the user name and password with the URL. These parameters are optional and anonymous or guest login is assumed if they are not given.

```
Install=ftp://user:password@server/directory/DVD1/
Install=tftp://user:password@server/directory/DVD1/
```

> If you want to install over an encrypted connection, use an `https` URL. If the certificate cannot be verified, use the `sslcerts=0` boot option to disable certificate checking.
>
> In case of a Samba or CIFS installation, you can also specify the domain that should be used:

```
Install=smb://workdomain;user:password@server/directory/DVD1/
```

ssh=1 vnc=1 Display_IP=192.168.42.42

> Depending on which parameter you give, a remote X server, SSH, or VNC will be used for installation. `ssh` enables SSH installation, `vnc` starts a VNC server on the installing machine, and `Display_IP` causes the installing system to try to connect to an X server at the given address. Only one of these parameters should be set at any time.

> **Important: X Authentication Mechanism**
>
>> The direct installation with the X Window System relies on a primitive authentication mechanism based on host names. This mechanism is disabled on current SUSE Linux Enterprise Server versions. Installation with SSH or VNC is preferred.

> To allow a connection between YaST and the remote X server, run **xhost** `<IP address>` with the address of the installing machine on the remote machine.
>
> For `VNC`, specify a password of six to eight characters to use for installation:

```
VNCPassword=<a password>
```

For `SSH`, specify a password of six to eight characters to use for installation:

```
ssh.password=<a password>
```

4.3.4   Example Parmfiles

The maximum capacity of a parmfile is 860 characters. As a rule of thumb, the parmfile should contain a maximum of 10 lines with no more than 79 characters. When reading a parmfile, all lines are concatenated without adding white spaces, therefore the last character (79) of each line needs to be a Space .

To receive potential error messages on the console, use

```
linuxrclog=/dev/console
```

EXAMPLE 4.8: PARMFILE FOR AN INSTALLATION FROM NFS WITH VNC AND AUTOYAST

```
ramdisk_size=131072 root=/dev/ram1 ro init=/linuxrc TERM=dumb
instnetdev=osa osainterface=qdio layer2=1 osahwaddr=
pointopoint=192.168.0.1
hostip=192.168.0.2
nameserver=192.168.0.3
install=nfs://192.168.0.4/SLES/SLES-12-Server/s390x/DVD1
autoyast=http://192.168.0.5/autoinst.xml
linuxrclog=/dev/console vnc=1
VNCPassword=testing
```

EXAMPLE 4.9: PARMFILE FOR INSTALLATION WITH NFS, SSH, AND HSI AND AUTOYAST WITH NFS

```
ramdisk_size=131072 root=/dev/ram1 ro init=/linuxrc TERM=dumb
AutoYast=nfs://192.168.1.1/autoinst/s390.xml
Hostname=zseries.example.com HostIP=192.168.1.2
Gateway=192.168.1.3 Nameserver=192.168.1.4
InstNetDev=hsi layer2=0
Netmask=255.255.255.128 Broadcast=192.168.1.255
readchannel=0.0.702c writechannel=0.0.702d datachannel=0.0.702e
```

```
install=nfs://192.168.1.5/SLES-12-Server/s390x/DVD1/
ssh=1 ssh.password=testing linuxrclog=/dev/console
```

4.4 Using the vt220 Terminal Emulator

Recent MicroCode Levels allow the use of an integrated vt220 terminal emulator (ASCII terminal) in addition to the standard line mode terminal. The vt220 terminal is connected to `/dev/ttysclp0`. The line mode terminal is connected to `/dev/ttysclp_line0`. For LPAR installations, the vt220 terminal emulator is activated by default.

To start the ASCII console on HMC, log in to the HMC, and select *Systems Management › Systems › IMAGE_ID* . Select the radio button for the LPAR and select *Recovery › Integrated ASCII Console*.

To redirect the kernel messages at boot time from the system console to the vt220 terminal, add the following entries to the `parameters` line in `/etc/zipl.conf`:

```
console=ttysclp0 console=ttysclp_line0
```

The resulting `parameters` line would look like the following example:

```
parameters = "root=/dev/dasda2 TERM=dumb console=ttysclp0 console=ttysclp_line0"
```

Save the changes in `/etc/zipl.conf`, run **zipl**, and reboot the system.

4.5 Further In-Depth Information about IBM z Systems

IBM has published several very interesting documents about their z Systems platform. Find them at http://www.redbooks.ibm.com.

4.5.1   IBM z Systems with SUSE Linux Enterprise Server

Find additional in-depth technical documentation about the kernel and application topics on IBM z Systems with SUSE Linux Enterprise Server at the following location:

- http://www.ibm.com/developerworks/linux/linux390/documentation_suse.html

4.5.2   Hardware

For a first glance at the technical details of some systems, refer to:

- IBM System z10 Enterprise Class Technical Introduction (SG24-7515)
- IBM System z9 Business Class Technical Introduction (SG24-7241)
- Linux on zSeries Fibre Channel Protocol Implementation Guide (SG24-6344)

4.5.3   General Documents about Linux on IBM z Systems

A general coverage of Linux on IBM z Systems can be found in the following documents:

- Linux on IBM eServer zSeries and S/390: ISP and ASP Solutions (SG24-6299)

These documents might not reflect the current state of Linux, but the principles of Linux deployment outlined there remain accurate.

4.5.4   Technical Issues of Linux on IBM z Systems

Refer to the following documents to get in-depth technical information about the Linux kernel and application topics. Refer to the Internet for up-to-date versions of these documents for the most recent code drop (http://www.ibm.com/developerworks/linux/linux390/index.html).

- Linux on System z Device Drivers, Features, and Commands
- zSeries ELF Application Binary Interface Supplement
- Linux on System z Device Drivers, Using the Dump Tools
- IBM System z9-109 Technical Introduction (SG26-6669)
- IBM System z10 Enterprise Class Technical Guide (SG24-7516)

There also is a Redbook for Linux application development on http://www.redbooks.ibm.com:

- Linux on IBM eServer zSeries and S/390: Application Development (SG24-6807)

4.5.5   Advanced Configurations for Linux on IBM z Systems

Refer to the following Redbooks, Redpapers, and links for some more complex IBM z Systems scenarios:

- Linux on IBM eServer zSeries and S/390: Large Scale Deployment (SG24-6824)

- Linux on IBM eServer zSeries and S/390: Performance Measuring and Tuning (SG24-6926)

- Linux with zSeries and ESS: Essentials (SG24-7025)

- IBM TotalStorage Enterprise Storage Server Implementing ESS Copy Services with IBM eServer zSeries (SG24-5680)

- Linux on IBM zSeries and S/390: High Availability for z/VM and Linux (REDP-0220)

- Saved Segments Planning and Administration
  http://publibz.boulder.ibm.com/epubs/pdf/hcsg4a00.pdf

- Linux on System z documentation for "Development stream"
  http://www.ibm.com/developerworks/linux/linux390/development_documentation.html

II Manual Deployment

5 Deployment Strategies

There are several different ways to deploy SUSE Linux Enterprise Server. Choose from various approaches ranging from a local installation using physical media or a network installation server to a mass deployment using a remote-controlled, highly-customized, and automated installation technique. Select the method that best matches your requirements.

5.1 Deploying up to 10 Workstations

If your deployment of SUSE Linux Enterprise Server only involves 1 to 10 workstations, the easiest and least complex way of deploying SUSE Linux Enterprise Server is a plain manual installation as featured in *Chapter 6, Installation with YaST*. Manual installation can be done in several different ways, depending on your requirements:

Installing from the SUSE Linux Enterprise Server Media

Consider this approach if you want to install a single, disconnected workstation.

Installing from a Network Server Using SLP

Consider this approach if you have a single workstation or a few workstations and if a network installation server announced via SLP is available.

Installing from a Network Server

Consider this approach if you have a single workstation or a few workstations and if a network installation server is available.

TABLE 5.1: INSTALLING FROM THE SUSE LINUX ENTERPRISE SERVER MEDIA

Installation Source	SUSE Linux Enterprise Server Media Kit
Tasks Requiring Manual Interaction	• Inserting the installation media • Booting the installation target • Changing media • Determining the YaST installation scope • Configuring the system with YaST

Remotely Controlled Tasks	None
Details	*Installing from the SUSE Linux Enterprise Server Media (DVD, USB)*

Installation Source	Network installation server holding the SUSE Linux Enterprise Server installation media
Tasks Requiring Manual Interaction	• Inserting the boot disk • Booting installation target • Determining the YaST installation scope • Configuring the system with YaST
Remotely Controlled Tasks	None, but this method can be combined with VNC
Details	*Installing from a Network Server*

Installation Source	Network installation server holding the SUSE Linux Enterprise Server installation media
Tasks Requiring Manual Interaction	• Inserting the boot disk • Providing boot options • Booting the installation target • Determining the YaST installation scope • Configuring the system with YaST
Remotely Controlled Tasks	None, but method can be combined with VNC
Details	*Installing from a Network Server*

5.2   Deploying up to 100 Workstations

With a growing number of workstations to install, you certainly do not want to install and configure each one of them manually. There are many automated or semi-automated approaches and several options for performing an installation with minimal to no physical user interaction.

Before considering a fully-automated approach, take into account that the more complex the scenario gets the longer it takes to set up. If a time limit is associated with your deployment, it might be a good idea to select a less complex approach that can be carried out much more quickly. Automation makes sense for huge deployments and those that need to be carried out remotely.

Choose from the following options:

Simple Remote Installation via VNC—Static Network Configuration

> Consider this approach in a small to medium scenario with a static network setup. A network, network installation server, and VNC viewer application are required.

Simple Remote Installation via VNC—Dynamic Network Configuration

> Consider this approach in a small to medium scenario with dynamic network setup through DHCP. A network, network installation server, and VNC viewer application are required.

Remote Installation via VNC—PXE Boot and Wake on LAN

> Consider this approach in a small to medium scenario that needs to be installed via the network and without physical interaction with the installation targets. A network, a network installation server, network boot images, network bootable target hardware, and a VNC viewer application are required.

Simple Remote Installation via SSH—Static Network Configuration

> Consider this approach in a small to medium scenario with static network setup. A network, network installation server, and SSH client application are required.

Remote Installation via SSH—Dynamic Network Configuration

> Consider this approach in a small to medium scenario with dynamic network setup through DHCP. A network, network installation server, and SSH client application are required.

Remote Installation via SSH—PXE Boot and Wake on LAN

> Consider this approach in a small to medium scenario that needs to be installed via the network and without physical interaction with the installation targets. A network, a network installation server, network boot images, network bootable target hardware, and an SSH client application are required.

Simple Mass Installation

Consider this approach for large deployments to identical machines. If configured to use network booting, physical interaction with the target systems is not needed. A network, a network installation server, a remote controlling application (such as a VNC viewer or an SSH client), and an AutoYaST configuration profile are required. If using network boot, a network boot image and network bootable hardware are required, as well.

Rule-Based Autoinstallation

Consider this approach for large deployments to various types of hardware. If configured to use network booting, physical interaction with the target systems is not needed. A network, installation server, a remote controlling application (such as a VNC viewer or an SSH client), and several AutoYaST configuration profiles as well (as a rule setup for AutoYaST) are required. If using network boot, a network boot image and network bootable hardware are required, as well.

TABLE 5.4: SIMPLE REMOTE INSTALLATION VIA VNC—STATIC NETWORK CONFIGURATION

Installation Source	Network
Preparations	• Setting up an installation source • Booting from the installation media
Control and Monitoring	Remote: VNC
Best Suited For	Small to medium scenarios with varying hardware
Drawbacks	• Each machine must be set up individually • Physical access is needed for booting
Details	*Section 13.1.1, "Simple Remote Installation via VNC—Static Network Configuration"*

TABLE 5.5: SIMPLE REMOTE INSTALLATION VIA VNC—DYNAMIC NETWORK CONFIGURATION

Installation Source	Network
Preparations	• Setting up the installation source • Booting from the installation media

Control and Monitoring	Remote: VNC
Best Suited For	Small to medium scenarios with varying hardware
Drawbacks	• Each machine must be set up individually • Physical access is needed for booting
Details	*Section 13.1.2, "Simple Remote Installation via VNC—Dynamic Network Configuration"*

TABLE 5.6: REMOTE INSTALLATION VIA VNC—PXE BOOT AND WAKE ON LAN

Installation Source	Network
Preparations	• Setting up the installation source • Configuring DHCP, TFTP, PXE boot, and WOL • Booting from the network
Control and Monitoring	Remote: VNC
Best Suited For	• Small to medium scenarios with varying hardware • Completely remote installations; cross-site deployment
Drawbacks	Each machine must be set up manually
Details	*Section 13.1.3, "Remote Installation via VNC—PXE Boot and Wake on LAN"*

TABLE 5.7: SIMPLE REMOTE INSTALLATION VIA SSH—STATIC NETWORK CONFIGURATION

Installation Source	Network
Preparations	• Setting up the installation source • Booting from the installation media

Deploying up to 100 Workstations

Control and Monitoring	Remote: SSH
Best Suited For	• Small to medium scenarios with varying hardware • Low bandwidth connections to target
Drawbacks	• Each machine must be set up individually • Physical access is needed for booting
Details	*Section 13.1.4, "Simple Remote Installation via SSH—Static Network Configuration"*

TABLE 5.8: REMOTE INSTALLATION VIA SSH—DYNAMIC NETWORK CONFIGURATION

Installation Source	Network
Preparations	• Setting up the installation source • Booting from installation media
Control and Monitoring	Remote: SSH
Best Suited For	• Small to medium scenarios with varying hardware • Low bandwidth connections to target
Drawbacks	• Each machine must be set up individually • Physical access is needed for booting
Details	*Section 13.1.5, "Simple Remote Installation via SSH—Dynamic Network Configuration"*

TABLE 5.9: REMOTE INSTALLATION VIA SSH—PXE BOOT AND WAKE ON LAN

Installation Source	Network

Preparations	• Setting up the installation source
	• Configuring DHCP, TFTP, PXE boot, and WOL
	• Booting from the network
Control and Monitoring	Remote: SSH
Best Suited For	• Small to medium scenarios with varying hardware
	• Completely remote installs; cross-site deployment
	• Low bandwidth connections to target
Drawbacks	Each machine must be set up individually
Details	*Section 13.1.6, "Remote Installation via SSH—PXE Boot and Wake on LAN"*

TABLE 5.10: SIMPLE MASS INSTALLATION

Installation Source	Preferably network
Preparations	• Gathering hardware information
	• Creating AutoYaST profile
	• Setting up the installation server
	• Distributing the profile
	• Setting up network boot (DHCP, TFTP, PXE, WOL) *or* Booting the target from installation media
Control and Monitoring	Local or remote through VNC or SSH

Best Suited For	• Large scenarios
	• Identical hardware
	• No access to system (network boot)
Drawbacks	Applies only to machines with identical hardware
Details	*Section 25.1, "Simple Mass Installation"*

Installation Source	Preferably network
Preparations	• Gathering hardware information
	• Creating AutoYaST profiles
	• Creating AutoYaST rules
	• Setting up the installation server
	• Distributing the profile
	• Setting up network boot (DHCP, TFTP, PXE, WOL) *or* Booting the target from installation media
Control and Monitoring	Local or remote through SSH or VNC
Best Suited For	• Varying hardware
	• Cross-site deployments
Drawbacks	Complex rule setup
Details	*Section 25.2, "Rule-Based Autoinstallation"*

5.3 Deploying More than 100 Workstations

Most of the considerations brought up for medium installation scenarios in *Section 5.1, "Deploying up to 10 Workstations"* still hold true for large scale deployments. However, with a growing number of installation targets, the benefits of a fully automated installation method outweigh its drawbacks.

It pays off to invest a considerable amount of time to create a sophisticated rule and class framework in AutoYaST to match the requirements of a huge deployment site. Not having to touch each target separately can save you a tremendous amount of time depending on the scope of your installation project.

As an alternative, and if user settings should be done during the first bootup, create preload images with kiwi and firstboot. Deploying such images could even be done by a PXE boot server specialized for this task. For more details, see http://doc.opensuse.org/projects/kiwi/doc/, *Chapter 27, Automated Deployment of Preload Images*, *Chapter 25, Automated Installation*, **and** *Chapter 24, Deploying Customized Preinstallations*.

6 Installation with YaST

After your hardware has been prepared for the installation of SUSE® Linux Enterprise Server as described in *Part I, "Architecture-Specific Installation Considerations"* and after the connection with the installation system has been established, you are presented with the interface of SUSE Linux Enterprise Server's system assistant YaST. YaST guides you through the entire installation.

During the installation process, YaST analyzes both your current system settings and your hardware components. Based on this analysis your system will be set up with a basic configuration including networking (provided the system could be configured using DHCP). To fine-tune the system after the installation has finished, start YaST from the installed system.

6.1   Choosing the Installation Method

After having selected the installation medium, determine the suitable installation method and boot option that best matches your needs:

Installing from the SUSE Linux Enterprise Server Media (DVD, USB)
Choose this option if you want to perform a stand-alone installation and do not want to rely on a network to provide the installation data or the boot infrastructure. The installation proceeds exactly as outlined in *Section 6.3, "The Installation Workflow"*.

Installing from a Network Server
Choose this option if you have an installation server available in your network or want to use an external server as the source of your installation data. This setup can be configured to boot from physical media (flash disk, CD/DVD, or hard disk) or configured to boot via network using PXE/BOOTP. Refer to *Section 6.2, "System Start-up for Installation"* for details. The installation program configures the network connection with DHCP and retrieves the location of the network installation source from the OpenSLP server. If no DHCP is available, choose *F4 Source › Network Config › Manual* and enter the network data. On EFI systems modify the network boot parameters as described in *Section 6.2.2.2, "The Boot Screen on Machines Equipped with UEFI"*.

Installing from an SLP Server. If your network setup supports OpenSLP and your network installation source has been configured to announce itself via SLP (described in *Section 13.2,*

"Setting Up the Server Holding the Installation Sources"), boot the system, press F4 in the boot screen and select *SLP* from the menu. On EFI systems set the `install` parameter to `install=slp:/` as described in *Section 6.2.2.2, "The Boot Screen on Machines Equipped with UEFI"*.

Installing from a Network Source without SLP.   If your network setup does not support OpenSLP for the retrieval of network installation sources, boot the system and press F4 in the boot screen to select the desired network protocol (NFS, HTTP, FTP, or SMB/CIFS) and provide the server's address and the path to the installation media. On EFI systems modify the boot parameter `install=` as described in *Section 6.2.2.2, "The Boot Screen on Machines Equipped with UEFI"*.

6.2   System Start-up for Installation

The way the system is started for the installation depends on the architecture—system start-up is different for PC (x86_64) or mainframe, for example. If you install SUSE Linux Enterprise Server as a VM Guest on a KVM or Xen hypervisor, follow the instructions for the x86_64 architecture.

6.2.1   IBM z Systems: System Start-up

For IBM z Systems platforms, the system is booted (IPL, Initial Program Load) as described in *Section 4.2.4, "IPLing the SUSE Linux Enterprise Server Installation System"*. SUSE Linux Enterprise Server does not show a splash screen on these systems. During the installation, load the kernel, initrd, and parmfile manually. YaST starts with its installation screen as soon as a connection has been established to the installation system via VNC, X, or SSH. Because there is no splash screen, kernel or boot parameters cannot be entered on screen, but must be specified in a parmfile (see *Section 4.3, "The parmfile—Automating the System Configuration"*).

6.2.2   PC (x86_64): System Start-up

SUSE Linux Enterprise Server supports several different boot options from which you can choose, depending on the hardware available and on the installation scenario you prefer. Booting from the SUSE Linux Enterprise Server media is the most straightforward option, but special requirements might call for special setups:

TABLE 6.1: BOOT OPTIONS

Boot Option	Description
DVD	This is the easiest boot option. This option can be used if the system has a local DVD-ROM drive that is supported by Linux.
| USB Mass Storage Device | In case your machine is not equipped with an optical drive, you can boot the installation image from a USB mass storage device such as a flash disk. To create a bootable USB storage device, you need to copy either the DVD or the Mini CD iso image to the device using the **dd** command (the USB device must not be mounted, all data on the device will be erased):<br><br>```
dd if=PATH_TO_ISO_IMAGE
 of=USB_STORAGE_DEVICE bs=4M
```<br><br>**❗ Important: Compatibility**<br>Note that booting from a USB Mass Storage Device is *not* supported on UEFI machines (this includes the complete ia64 architecture) and on the ppc64 architecture. |
```

Boot Option	Description
PXE or BOOTP	Booting over the network must be supported by the system's BIOS or firmware, and a boot server must be available in the network. This task can also be handled by another SUSE Linux Enterprise Server system. Refer to *Chapter 13, Remote Installation* for more information.
Hard Disk	SUSE Linux Enterprise Server installation can also be booted from the hard disk. To do this, copy the kernel (`linux`) and the installation system (`initrd`) from the directory `/boot/architecture/` on the installation media to the hard disk and add an appropriate entry to the existing boot loader of a previous SUSE Linux Enterprise Server installation.

 ## Tip: Booting from DVD on UEFI Machines

DVD1 can be used as a boot medium for machines equipped with UEFI (Unified Extensible Firmware Interface). Refer to your vendor's documentation for specific information. If booting fails, try to enable CSM (Compatibility Support Module) in your firmware.

 ## Note: Add-on Product Installation Media

Media for add-on products (extensions or third-party products) cannot be used as stand-alone installation media. They can either be embedded as additional installation sources during the installation process (see *Section 6.8, "Extension Selection"*) or be installed from the running system using the YaST Add-on Products module (see *Chapter 9, Installing Modules, Extensions, and Third Party Add-On Products* for details).

The boot screen displays several options for the installation procedure. *Boot from Hard Disk* boots the installed system and is selected by default, because the CD is often left in the drive. Select one of the other options with the arrow keys and press `Enter` to boot it. The relevant options are:

Installation

> The normal installation mode. All modern hardware functions are enabled. In case the installation fails, see `F5` *Kernel* for boot options that disable potentially problematic functions.

Upgrade

> Perform a system upgrade. For more information refer to *Chapter 17, Upgrading SUSE Linux Enterprise*.

Rescue System

> Starts a minimal Linux system without a graphical user interface. For more information, see *Book "Administration Guide", Chapter 37 "Common Problems and Their Solutions", Section 37.6.2 "Using the Rescue System"*.

Check Installation Media

> This option is only available when you install from media created from downloaded ISOs. In this case it is recommended to check the integrity of the installation medium. This option starts the installation system before automatically checking the media. In case the check was successful, the normal installation routine starts. If a corrupt media is detected, the installation routine aborts.

> **Warning: Failure of Media Check**
>
> If the media check fails, your medium is damaged. Do not continue the installation because installation may fail or you may lose your data. Replace the broken medium and restart the installation process.

Memory Test

> Tests your system RAM using repeated read and write cycles. Terminate the test by rebooting. For more information, see *Book "Administration Guide", Chapter 37 "Common Problems and Their Solutions", Section 37.2.4 "Fails to Boot"*.

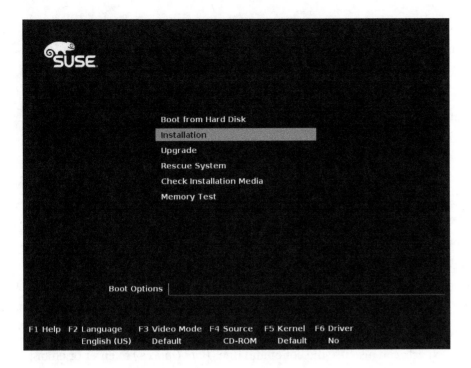

FIGURE 6.1: THE BOOT SCREEN ON MACHINES WITH A TRADITIONAL BIOS

Use the function keys indicated in the bar at the bottom of the screen to change the language, screen resolution, installation source or to add an additional driver from your hardware vendor:

F1 *Help*

Get context-sensitive help for the active element of the boot screen. Use the arrow keys to navigate, Enter to follow a link, and Esc to leave the help screen.

F2 *Language*

Select the display language and a corresponding keyboard layout for the installation. The default language is English (US).

F3 *Video Mode*

Select various graphical display modes for the installation. By *Default* the video resolution is automatically determined using KMS (Kernel Mode Settings). If this setting does not work on your system, choose *No KMS* and, optionally, specify vga=ask on the boot command line to get prompted for the video resolution. Choose *Text Mode* if the graphical installation causes problems.

PC (x86_64): System Start-up

F4 *Source*

> Normally, the installation is performed from the inserted installation medium. Here, select other sources, like FTP or NFS servers. If the installation is deployed on a network with an SLP server, select an installation source available on the server with this option. Find information about setting up an installation server with SLP at *Section 13.2, "Setting Up the Server Holding the Installation Sources"*.

F5 *Kernel*

> If you encounter problems with the regular installation, this menu offers to disable a few potentially problematic functions. If your hardware does not support ACPI (advanced configuration and power interface) select *No ACPI* to install without ACPI support. *No local APIC* disables support for APIC (Advanced Programmable Interrupt Controllers) which may cause problems with some hardware. *Safe Settings* boots the system with the DMA mode (for CD/DVD-ROM drives) and power management functions disabled.
> If you are not sure, try the following options first: *Installation—ACPI Disabled* or *Installation—Safe Settings*. Experts can also use the command line (*Boot Options*) to enter or change kernel parameters.

F6 *Driver*

> Press this key to notify the system that you have an optional driver update for SUSE Linux Enterprise Server. With *File* or *URL*, load drivers directly before the installation starts. If you select *Yes*, you are prompted to insert the update disk at the appropriate point in the installation process.

 Tip: Getting Driver Update Disks

> Driver updates for SUSE Linux Enterprise are provided at http://drivers.suse.com/. These drivers have been created via the SUSE SolidDriver Program.

6.2.2.2 The Boot Screen on Machines Equipped with UEFI

UEFI (Unified Extensible Firmware Interface) is a new industry standard which replaces and extends the traditional BIOS. The latest UEFI implementations contain the "Secure Boot" extension, which prevents booting malicious code by only allowing signed boot loaders to be executed. See *Book "Administration Guide", Chapter 12 "UEFI (Unified Extensible Firmware Interface)"* for more information.

The boot manager GRUB 2, used to boot machines with a traditional BIOS, does not support UEFI, therefore GRUB 2 is replaced with ELILO. If Secure Boot is enabled, a GRUB 2 UEFI module is used via an ELILO compatibility layer. From an administrative and user perspective, both boot manager implementations behave the same and are called `ELILO` in the following.

 Tip: UEFI and Secure Boot are Supported by Default

The installation routine of SUSE Linux Enterprise automatically detects if the machine is equipped with UEFI. All installation sources also support Secure Boot. If an EFI system partition already exists on dual boot machines (from a Microsoft Windows 8 installation, for example), it will automatically be detected and used. Partition tables will be written as GPT on UEFI systems.

 Warning: Using Non-Inbox Drivers with Secure Boot

There is no support for adding non-inbox drivers (that is, drivers that do not come with SLE) during installation with Secure Boot enabled. The signing key used for SolidDriver/PLDP is not trusted by default.

To solve this problem, it is necessary to either add the needed keys to the firmware database via firmware/system management tools before the installation or to use a bootable ISO that will enroll the needed keys in the MOK list at first boot. For more information, see *Book "Administration Guide", Chapter 12 "UEFI (Unified Extensible Firmware Interface)", Section 12.1 "Secure Boot".*

The boot screen displays several options for the installation procedure. Change the selected option with the arrow keys and press `Enter` to boot it. The relevant options are:

Installation

The normal installation mode.

Upgrade

Perform a system upgrade. For more information refer to Chapter 17, Upgrading SUSE Linux Enterprise.

Rescue System

Starts a minimal Linux system without a graphical user interface. For more information, see *Book "Administration Guide", Chapter 37 "Common Problems and Their Solutions", Section 37.6.2 "Using the Rescue System".*

Check Installation Media

This option is only available when you install from media created from downloaded ISOs. In this case it is recommended to check the integrity of the installation medium. This option starts the installation system before automatically checking the media. In case the check was successful, the normal installation routine starts. If a corrupt media is detected, the installation routine aborts.

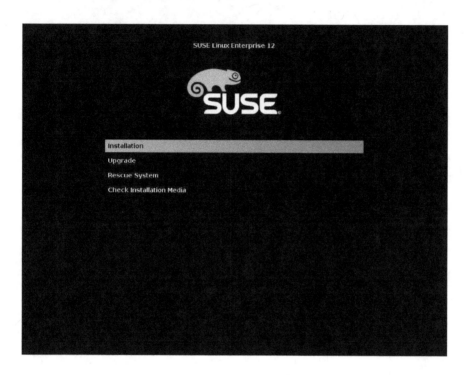

FIGURE 6.2: THE BOOT SCREEN ON MACHINES WITH UEFI

ELILO on SUSE Linux Enterprise Server does not support a boot prompt or function keys for adding boot parameters. By default, the installation will be started with American English and the boot media as the installation source. A DHCP lookup will be performed to configure the network. To change these defaults or to add additional boot parameters you need to edit the respective boot entry. Highlight it using the arrow keys and press E . See the on-screen help for editing hints (note that only an English keyboard is available now). The *Installation* entry will look similar to the following:

```
setparams 'Installation'

    set gfxpayload=keep
    echo 'Loading kernel ...'
```

```
linuxefi /boot/x86_64/loader/linux splash=slilent
echo 'Loading initial ramdisk ...'
initrdefi /boot/x86_64/loader/initrd
```

Add space-separated parameters to the end of the line starting with `linuxefi`. To boot the edited entry, press `F10`. If you access the machine via serial console, press `Esc`–`0`. A complete list of parameters is available at http://en.opensuse.org/Linuxrc. The most important ones are:

TABLE 6.2: INSTALLATION SOURCES

CD/DVD (default)	`install=cd:/`
Hard disk	`install=hd:/?device=`*sda*`/PATH_TO_ISO`
SLP	`install=slp:/`
FTP	`install=ftp://`*ftp.example.com*`/PATH_TO_ISO`
HTTP	`install=http://`*www.example.com*`/PATH_TO_ISO`
NFS	`install=nfs:/PATH_TO_ISO`
SMB / CIFS	`install=smb://PATH_TO_ISO`

TABLE 6.3: NETWORK CONFIGURATION

DHCP (default)	netsetup = dhcp
Prompt for Parameters	`netsetup=hostip,netmask,gateway,nameserver`
Host IP address	`hostip=192.168.2.100` `hostip=192.168.2.100/24`
Netmask	`netmask=255.255.255.0`
Gateway	`gateway=192.168.5.1`
Name Server	`nameserver=192.168.1.116` `nameserver=192.168.1.116,192.168.1.118`
Domain Search Path	`domain=example.com`

Driver Updates: Prompt	`dud=1`
Driver Updates: URL	`dud=ftp://ftp.example.com/PATH_TO_DRIVER` `dud=http://www.example.com/PATH_TO_DRIVER`
Installation Language	`Language=LANGUAGE` Supported values for `LANGUAGE` are, among others, `cs_CZ`, `de_DE`, `es_ES`, `fr_FR`, `ja_JP`, `pt_BR`, `pt_PT`, `ru_RU`, `zh_CN`, and `zh_TW`.
Kernel: No ACPI	`acpi=off`
Kernel: No Local APIC	`noapic`
Video: Disable KMS	`nomodeset`
Video: Start Installer in Text Mode	`Textmode=1`

6.2.3 Boot Parameters for Advanced Setups

In case you want to configure access to a local SMT or `supportconfig` server for the installation, you can specify boot parameters that will be parsed by the installation routine to set up these services. The same is also true if you need IPv6 support during the installation.

6.2.3.1 Providing Data to Access an SMT Server

By default, updates for SUSE Linux Enterprise Server are delivered by the SUSE Customer Center. If your network provides a so called SMT server to provide a local update source, you need to equip the client with the server's URL. Client and server communicate solely via HTTPS protocol, therefore you also need to enter a path to the server's certificate if the certificate was not issued by a certificate authority.

Note: Non-Interactive Installation Only

Providing parameters for accessing an SMT server is only needed for non-interactive installations. During an interactive installation the data can be provided during the installation (see *Section 6.7, "SUSE Customer Center Registration"* for details).

regurl

URL of the SMT server. This URL has a fixed format `https://FQN/center/regsvc/`. *FQN* needs to be a fully qualified host name of the SMT server. Example:

```
regurl=https://smt.example.com/center/regsvc/
```

regcert

Location of the SMT server's certificate. Specify one of the following locations:

URL

Remote location (HTTP, HTTPS or FTP) from which the certificate can be downloaded. Example:

```
regcert=http://smt.example.com/smt-ca.crt
```

local path

Absolute path to the certificate on the local machine. Example:

```
regcert=/data/inst/smt/smt-ca.cert
```

Interactive

Use `ask` to open a pop-up menu during the installation where you can specify the path to the certificate. Do not use this option with AutoYaST. Example

```
regcert=ask
```

Deactivate certificate installation

Use `done` if either the certificate will be installed by an add-on product, or if you are using a certificate issued by an official certificate authority. Example:

```
regcert=done
```

Warning: Beware of Typing Errors

Make sure the values you enter are correct. If `regurl` has not been specified correctly, the registration of the update source will fail. If a wrong value for regcert has been entered, you will be prompted for a local path to the certificate.

In case regcert is not specified, it will default to `http://FQN/smt.crt` with `FQN` being the name of the SMT server.

6.2.3.2 Configuring an Alternative Data Server for `supportconfig`

The data that supportconfig (see *Book "Administration Guide", Chapter 36 "Gathering System Information for Support"* for more information) gathers is sent to the SUSE Customer Center by default. It is also possible to set up a local server to collect this data. If such a server is available on your network, you need to set the server's URL on the client. This information needs to be entered at the boot prompt.

supporturl

URL of the server. The URL has the format `http://FQN/Path/`, `FQN` needs to be the fully qualified host name of the server, `Path` needs to be replaced with the location on the server. Example:

```
supporturl=http://support.example.com/supportconfig/data/
```

6.2.3.3 Using IPv6 During the Installation

By default you can only assign IPv4 network addresses to your machine. To enable IPv6 during installation, enter one of the following parameters at the boot prompt:

* `ipv6=1` (accept IPv4 and IPv6)

* `ipv6only=1` (accept IPv6 only).

6.2.3.4 Using a Proxy During the Installation

In networks enforcing the usage of a proxy server for accessing remote Web sites, registration during installation is only possible when configuring a proxy server.

To use a proxy during the installation, press [F4] on the boot screen and set the required parameters in the *HTTP Proxy* dialog. Alternatively provide the Kernel parameter `proxy` at the boot prompt:

- `proxy=http://USER:Password@proxy.example.com:PORT`

Specifying *USER* and *Password* is optional—if the server allows anonymous access, the following data is sufficient: `http://proxy.example.com:PORT`.

6.2.3.5 Disabling the Import of SSH Host Keys and Users from a Previous Installation

If installing on a machine hosting a previous Linux installation, the SSH host keys from that installation will automatically be imported into the SUSE Linux Enterprise Server setup by default. It is also possible to import users from that installation in the *Create New User* dialog.

To disable these features, specify the `ignore_features` parameter at the boot prompt. Adding the (optional) `ptoptions` parameter ensures that the `ignore_features` parameter is only used for the installation and not appended to the Kernel command line in the installed system:

- `ignore_features=import_ssh_keys ptoptions=ignore_features` (do not import SSH host keys)

- `ignore_features=import_users  ptoptions=ignore_features` (disable user import dialog)

- `ignore_features=import_ssh_keys,import_users    ptoptions=ignore_features` (disable user import dialog)

Boot Parameters for Advanced Setups

6.2.3.6 Enabling SELinux Support

Enabling SELinux upon installation start-up enables you to configure it after the installation has been finished without having to reboot. Use the following parameters:

- `security=selinux selinux=1`

6.3 The Installation Workflow

The interactive installation of SUSE Linux Enterprise Server split into several steps is listed below. For a description of how to perform non-interactive, automated installations, refer to *Part V, "Automated Installations"*.

After starting the installation, SUSE Linux Enterprise Server loads and configures a minimal Linux system to run the installation procedure. To view the boot messages and copyright notices during this process, press `Esc`. On completion of this process, the YaST installation program starts and displays the graphical installer.

 Tip: Installation Without a Mouse

If the installer does not detect your mouse correctly, use `→|` for navigation, arrow keys to scroll, and `Enter` to confirm a selection. Various buttons or selection fields contain a letter with an underscore. Use `Alt`-`Letter` to select a button or a selection directly instead of navigating there with `→|`.

1. *Section 6.4, "Language, Keyboard and License Agreement"*

2. *Section 6.6, "Network Settings"*

3. *Section 6.5, "IBM z Systems: Disk Activation"*

4. *Section 6.7, "SUSE Customer Center Registration"*

5. *Section 6.8, "Extension Selection"*

6. *Section 6.9, "Suggested Partitioning"*

7. *Section 6.10, "Clock and Time Zone"*

8. *Section 6.11, "Create New User"*

9. Section 6.12, "Password for the System Administrator root"

10. Section 6.13, "Installation Settings"

11. Section 6.14, "Performing the Installation"

6.4 Language, Keyboard and License Agreement

Start the installation of SUSE Linux Enterprise Server by choosing your language. Changing the language will automatically preselect a corresponding keyboard layout. Override this proposal by selecting a different keyboard layout from the drop-down box. The language selected here is also used to assume a time zone for the system clock. This setting can be modified later in the installed system as described in *Chapter 12, Changing Language and Country Settings with YaST*.

Read the license agreement that is displayed beneath the language and keyboard selection thoroughly. Use *License Translations* to access translations. If you agree to the terms, check *I Agree to the License Terms* and click *Next* to proceed with the installation. If you do not agree to the license agreement, you cannot install SUSE Linux Enterprise Server; click *Abort* to terminate the installation.

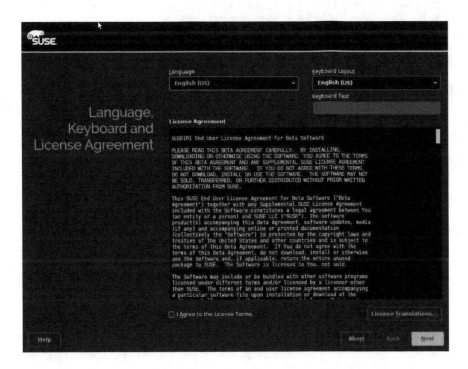

FIGURE 6.3: LANGUAGE, KEYBOARD AND LICENSE AGREEMENT

Language, Keyboard and License Agreement

6.5 IBM z Systems: Disk Activation

When installing on IBM z Systems platforms, the language selection dialog is followed by a dialog to configure the attached hard disks. Select DASD, Fibre Channel Attached SCSI Disks (zFCP), or iSCSI for installation of SUSE Linux Enterprise Server. The DASD and zFCP configuration buttons are only available if the corresponding devices are attached. For instructions on how to configure iSCSI disks, refer to *Book "Storage Administration Guide", Chapter 13 "Mass Storage over IP Networks: iSCSI"*.

You can also *Change the Network Configuration* in this screen by launching the *Network Settings* dialog. Choose a network interface from the list and click *Edit* to change its settings. Use the tabs to configure DNS and routing. See *Book "Administration Guide", Chapter 19 "Basic Networking", Section 19.4 "Configuring a Network Connection with YaST"* for more details.

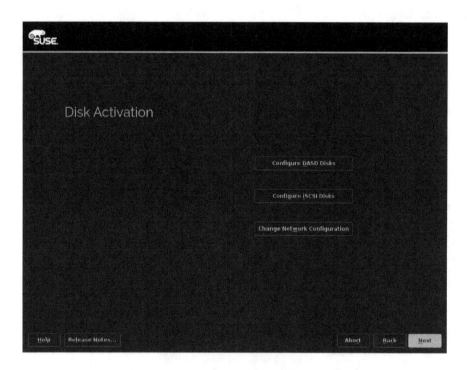

FIGURE 6.4: DISK ACTIVATION

6.5.1 Configuring DASD Disks

After selecting *Configure DASD Disks*, an overview lists all available DASDs. To get a clearer picture of the available devices, use the text box located above the list to specify a range of channels to display. To filter the list according to such a range, select *Filter*.

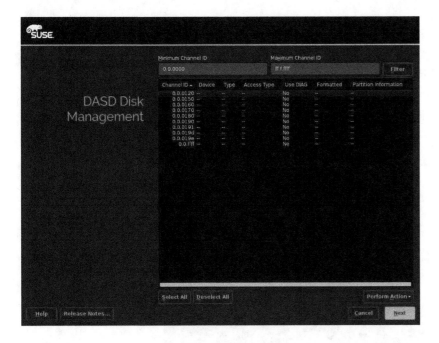

FIGURE 6.5: IBM Z SYSTEMS: SELECTING A DASD

Specify the DASDs to use for the installation by selecting the corresponding entries in the list. Use *Select All* to select all DASDs currently displayed. Activate and make the selected DASDs available for the installation by selecting *Perform Action* > *Activate*. To format the DASDs, select *Perform Action* > *Format*. Alternatively use the YaST Partitioner later as described in *Section 14.1, "Using the YaST Partitioner"*.

6.5.2 Configuring zFCP Disks

To use zFCP disks for the SUSE Linux Enterprise Server installation, select *Configure zFCP Disks* in the selection dialog. This opens a dialog with a list of the zFCP disks available on the system. In this dialog, select *Add* to open another dialog in which to enter zFCP parameters.

To make a zFCP disk available for the SUSE Linux Enterprise Server installation, choose an available *Channel Number* from the drop-down box. *Get WWPNs* (World Wide Port Number) and *Get LUNs* (Logical Unit Number) return lists with available WWPNs and FCP-LUNs, respectively, to choose from. When completed, exit the zFCP dialog with *Next* and the general hard disk configuration dialog with *Finish* to continue with the rest of the configuration.

6.6 Network Settings

After booting into the installation, the installation routine is set up. During this setup, an attempt to configure at least one network interface with DHCP is made. In case this attempt fails, the *Network Settings* dialog launches. Choose a network interface from the list and click *Edit* to change its settings. Use the tabs to configure DNS and routing. See *Book* "Administration Guide", *Chapter 19* "Basic Networking", *Section 19.4* "Configuring a Network Connection with YaST" for more details. On IBM z Systems this dialog does not start automatically. It can be started in the *Disk Activation* step.

In case DHCP was successfully configured during installation setup, you can also access this dialog by clicking *Network Configuration* at the *SUSE Customer Center Registration* step. It lets you change the automatically provided settings.

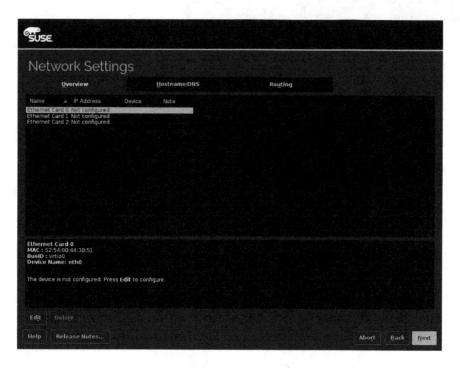

FIGURE 6.6: NETWORK SETTINGS

6.7 SUSE Customer Center Registration

To get technical support and product updates, you need to register and activate your product with the SUSE Customer Center. Registering SUSE Linux Enterprise Server now grants you immediate access to the update repository. This enables you to install the system with the latest updates and patches available. If you are offline or want to skip this step, select *Skip Registration*. You can register your system at any time later from the installed system.

 Note: Network Configuration

> After booting into the installation, the installation routine is set up. During this setup, an attempt to configure all network interfaces with DHCP is made. In case DHCP is not available or if you want to modify the network configuration, click *Network Configuration* in the upper right corner of the *SUSE Customer Center Registration* screen. The YaST module *Network Settings* opens. See *Book "Administration Guide", Chapter 19 "Basic Networking", Section 19.4 "Configuring a Network Connection with YaST"* for details.

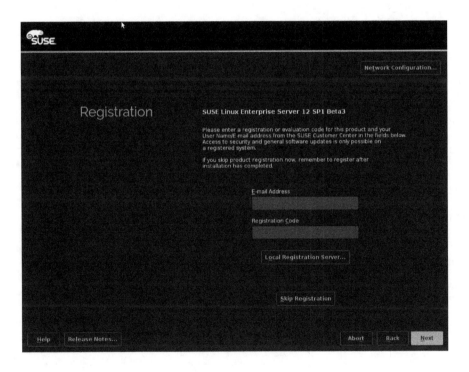

FIGURE 6.7: SUSE CUSTOMER CENTER REGISTRATION

To register your system, provide the *E-mail* address associated with the SUSE account you or your organization uses to manage subscriptions. In case you do not have a SUSE account yet, go to the SUSE Customer Center home page (https://scc.suse.com/ to create one. Also enter the registration code you received with your copy of SUSE Linux Enterprise Server.

Proceed with *Next* to start the registration process. If one or more local registration servers are available on your network, you can to choose one of them from a list—by default SUSE Linux Enterprise Server is registered at the SUSE Customer Center. If your local registration server was not discovered automatically, choose *Cancel*, select *Local Registration Server* and enter the URl of the server. Restart the registration by choosing *Next* again.

During the registration the online update channels will be added to your installation setup. When finished, you can choose whether to install the latest available package versions from the update channels. This ensures that SUSE Linux Enterprise Server is installed with the latest security updates available. If you choose *No*, all packages will be installed from the installation media. Proceed with *Next*.

6.8 Extension Selection

If you have successfully registered your system in the previous step, a list of available modules and extensions based on SUSE Linux Enterprise Server is shown. Otherwise this configuration step is skipped. It is also possible to add modules and extensions from the installed system, see *Chapter 9, Installing Modules, Extensions, and Third Party Add-On Products* for details.

The list contains free modules for SUSE Linux Enterprise Server, such as the SUSE Linux Enterprise SDK and extensions requiring a registration key that is liable for costs. Click an entry to see its description. Select a module or extension for installation by activating its check mark. This will add its repository from the SUSE Customer Center server to your installation—no additional installation sources are required. Furthermore the installation pattern for the module or extension is added to the default installation to ensure it gets installed automatically.

The amount of available extensions and modules depends on the registration server. A local registration server may only offer update repositories and no additional extensions.

Tip: Modules

Modules are fully supported parts of SUSE Linux Enterprise Server with a different life cycle. They have a clearly defined scope and are delivered via online channel only. Registering at the SUSE Customer Center is a prerequisite for being able to subscribe to these channels.

 Tip: SUSE Linux Enterprise Desktop

As of SUSE Linux Enterprise 12, SUSE Linux Enterprise Desktop is not only available as a separate product, but also as a workstation extension for SUSE Linux Enterprise Server. If you register at the SUSE Customer Center, the `SUSE Linux Enterprise Worksta-` `tion Extension` can be selected for installation. Note that installing it requires a valid registration key.

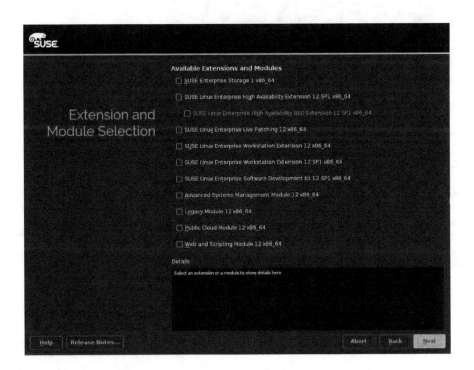

FIGURE 6.8: EXTENSION SELECTION

Proceed with *Next* to the *Add-on Product* dialog, where you can specify sources for additional add-on products not available on the registration server.

If you do not want to install add-ons, proceed with *Next*. Otherwise activate *I would like to install an additional Add-on Product*. Specify the Media Type by choosing from CD, DVD, Hard Disk, USB Mass Storage, a Local Directory or a Local ISO Image. In case network access has been configured you can choose from additional remote sources such as HTTP, SLP, FTP, etc. Alternatively you may directly specify a URL. Check *Download Repository Description Files* to download the files describing the repository now. If deactivated, they will be downloaded after the installation starts. Proceed with *Next* and insert a CD or DVD if required.

Depending on the add-on's content it may be necessary to accept additional license agreements. If you have chosen an add-on product requiring a registration key, you will be asked to enter it at the *Extension and Module Registration Codes* page. Proceed with *Next*.

FIGURE 6.9: ADD-ON PRODUCT

 Tip: "No Registration Key" Error

In case you have chosen a product in the *Extension Selection* dialog for which you do not have a valid registration key, choose *Back* until you see the *Extension Selection* dialog. Deselect the module or extension and proceed with *Next*. Modules or extensions can also be installed at any time later from the running system as described in *Chapter 9, Installing Modules, Extensions, and Third Party Add-On Products*.

6.9 Suggested Partitioning

Define a partition setup for SUSE Linux Enterprise Server in this step. The installer creates a proposal for one of the available disks containing a root partition formatted with Btrfs (with snapshots enabled), a swap partition, and a home partition formatted with XFS. On hard disks smaller than 25 GB the proposal does not include a separate home partition. If one or more swap partitions have been detected on the available hard disks, these existing ones will be used (rather than proposing a new swap partition). You have several options to proceed:

Next

> To accept the proposal without any changes, click *Next* to proceed with the installation workflow.

Edit Proposal Settings

> To adjust the proposal choose *Edit Proposal Settings*. It lets you switch to an LVM-based proposal, adjust file systems for the proposed partitions and enlarge the swap partition, to enable suspend to disk. You can also disable Btrfs snapshots here.

Create Partition Setup

> Use this option to move the proposal described above to a different disk. Select a specific disk from the list. If the chosen hard disk does not contain any partitions yet, the whole hard disk will be used for the proposal. Otherwise, you can choose which existing partition(s) to use. *Edit Proposal Settings* lets you fine-tune the proposal.

Expert Partitioner

> To create a custom partition setup choose *Expert Partitioner*. The Expert Partitioner opens, displaying the current partition setup for all hard disks, including the proposal suggested by the installer. You can *Add, Edit, Resize,* or *Delete* partitions.
>
> You can also set up Logical Volumes (LVM), configure software RAID and device mapping (DM), encrypt Partitions, mount NFS shares and manage tmpfs volumes with the Expert Partitioner. To fine-tune settings such as the subvolume and snapshot handling for each Btrfs partition, choose *Btrfs*. For more information about custom partitioning and configuring advanced features, refer to *Section 14.1, "Using the YaST Partitioner"*.

! Important: Btrfs on an Encrypted Root Partition

The default partitioning setup suggests the root partition as Btrfs with `/boot` being a directory. If you need to have the root partition encrypted in this setup, make sure to use the GPT partition table type instead of the default MSDOS type. Otherwise the GRUB2 boot loader may not have enough space for the second stage loader.

Warning: Custom Partitioning on UEFI machines

A UEFI machine *requires* an EFI system partition that must be mounted to `/boot/efi`. This partition must be formatted with the `FAT` file system.

If an EFI system partition is already present on your system (for example from a previous Windows installation) use it by mounting it to `/boot/efi` without formatting it.

Warning: Custom Partitioning and Snapper

By default, SUSE Linux Enterprise Server is set up to support snapshots which provide the ability to do rollbacks of system changes. SUSE Linux Enterprise Server uses Snapper in conjunction with Btrfs for this feature. Refer to *Book "Administration Guide", Chapter 3 "System Recovery and Snapshot Management with Snapper"* for details.

Being able to create system snapshots that enable rollbacks requires most of the system directories to be mounted on a single partition. Refer to *Book "Administration Guide", Chapter 3 "System Recovery and Snapshot Management with Snapper", Section 3.1 "Default Setup"* for more information. This also includes `/usr` and `/var`. Only directories that are excluded from snapshots (see *Book "Administration Guide", Chapter 3 "System Recovery and Snapshot Management with Snapper", Section 3.1.2 "Directories That Are Excluded from Snapshots"* for a list) may reside on separate partitions. Among others, this list includes `/usr/local`, `/var/log`, and `/tmp`.

If you do not plan use Snapper for system rollbacks, the partitioning restrictions mentioned above do not apply.

Note: IBM z Systems Using Minidisks in z/VM

If SUSE Linux Enterprise Server is installed on minidisks in z/VM, which reside on the same physical disk, the access path of the minidisks (/dev/disk/by-id/) is not unique, because it represents the ID of the physical disk. So if two or more minidisks are on the same physical disk, they all have the same ID.

To avoid problems when mounting minidisks, always mount them either *by path* or *by UUID*.

Note: Supported Software RAID Volumes

Installing to and booting from existing software RAID volumes is supported for Disk Data Format (DDF) volumes and Intel Matrix Storage Manager (IMSM) volumes. IMSM is also known by the following names:

- Intel Rapid Storage Technology

- Intel Matrix Storage Technology

- Intel Application Accelerator / Intel Application Accelerator RAID Edition

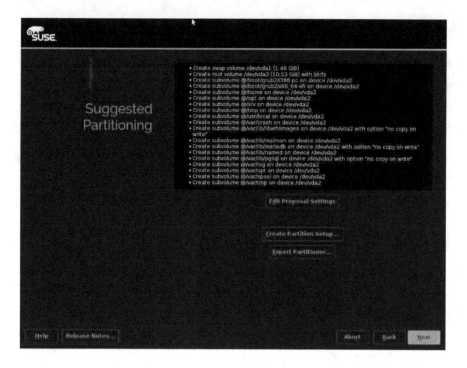

FIGURE 6.10: PARTITIONING

6.10 Clock and Time Zone

In this dialog, select your region and time zone. Both are preselected according to the installation language. To change the preselected values, either use the map or the drop-down boxes for *Region* and *Time Zone*. When using the map, point the cursor at the rough direction of your region and left-click to zoom. Now choose your country or region by left-clicking. Right-click to return to the world map.

To set up the clock, choose whether the *Hardware Clock is Set to UTC*. If you run another operating system on your machine, such as Microsoft Windows, it is likely your system uses local time instead. If you only run Linux on your machine, set the hardware clock to UTC and have the switch from standard time to daylight saving time performed automatically.

ⓘ Important: Set the Hardware Clock to UTC

The switch from standard time to daylight saving time (and vice versa) can only be performed automatically when the hardware clock (CMOS clock) is set to UTC. This also applies if you use automatic time synchronization with NTP, because automatic synchronization will only be performed if the time difference between the hardware and system clock is less than 15 minutes.

Since a wrong system time can cause severe problems (missed backups, dropped mail messages, mount failures on remote file systems, etc.) it is strongly recommended to *always* set the hardware clock to UTC.

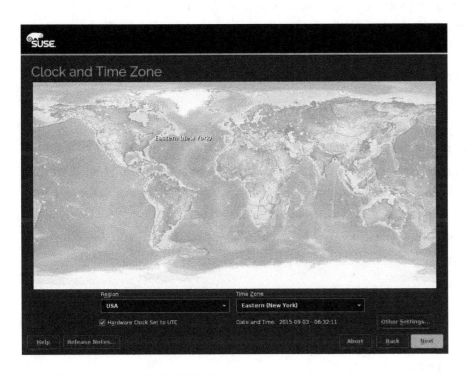

FIGURE 6.11: CLOCK AND TIME ZONE

`POWER, x86_64` If a network is already configured, you can configure time synchronization with an NTP server. Click *Other Settings* to either alter the NTP settings or to *Manually* set the time. See *Book "Administration Guide", Chapter 21 "Time Synchronization with NTP"* for more information on configuring the NTP service. When finished, click *Accept* to continue the installation. ◁

`POWER, x86_64` If running without NTP configured, consider setting `SYSTOHC=no` (`sysconfig` variable) to avoid saving unsynchronized time into the hardware clock. ◁

Note: Time Cannot be Changed on IBM z Systems

Since the operating system is not allowed to change time and date directly, the *Other Settings* option is not available on IBM z Systems.

6.11 Create New User

Create a local user in this step. In case you do not want to configure any local users, for example when setting up a client on a network with centralized user authentication, skip this step by choosing *Next* and confirming the warning. Network user authentication can be configured at any time later in the installed system, refer to *Chapter 11, Managing Users with YaST* for instructions.

After entering the first name and last name, either accept the proposal or specify a new *User name* that will be used to log in. Only use lowercase letters (a-z), digits (0-9) and the characters . (dot), - (hyphen) and _ (underscore). Special characters, umlauts and accented characters are not allowed.

Finally, enter a password for the user. Re-enter it for confirmation (to ensure that you did not type something else by mistake). To provide effective security, a password should be at least six characters long and consist of uppercase and lowercase letters, digits and special characters (7-bit ASCII). Umlauts or accented characters are not allowed. Passwords you enter are checked for weakness. When entering a password that is easy to guess (such as a dictionary word or a name) you will see a warning. It is a good security practice to use strong passwords.

Important: User Name and Password

Remember both your user name and the password because they are needed each time you log in to the system.

FIGURE 6.12: CREATE NEW USER

Three additional options are available:

Use this Password for System Administrator

> If checked, the same password you have entered for the user will be used for the system administrator `root`. This option is suitable for stand-alone workstations or machines in a home network that are administrated by a single user. When not checked, you are prompted for a system administrator password in the next step of the installation workflow (see *Section 6.12, "Password for the System Administrator `root`"*).

Receive System Mail

> Checking this box sends messages created by the system services to the user. These are usually only sent to `root`, the system administrator. This option is useful for the most frequently used account, because it is highly recommended to log in as `root` only in special cases.
>
> The mails sent by system services are stored in the local mailbox `/var/spool/mail/` *username*, where *username* is the login name of the selected user. To read e-mails after installation, you can use any e-mail client, for example KMail or Evolution.

Automatic Login

This option automatically logs the current user in to the system when it starts. This is mainly useful if the computer is operated by only one user. For automatic login to work, the option must be explicitly enabled.

6.11.1   Expert Settings

Click *Change* in the Create User dialog to import users from a previous installation (if present). Also change the password encryption type in this dialog.

The default authentication method is *Local (/etc/passwd)*. If a former version of SUSE Linux Enterprise Server or another system using `/etc/passwd` is detected, you may import local users. To do so, check *Read User Data from a Previous Installation* and click *Choose*. In the next dialog, select the users to import and finish with *OK*.

By default the passwords are encrypted with the SHA-512 hash function. Changing this method is not recommended unless needed for compatibility reasons.

6.12   Password for the System Administrator root

If you have not chosen *Use this Password for System Administrator* in the previous step, you will be prompted to enter a password for the System Administrator `root`. Otherwise this configuration step is skipped.

`root` is the name of the superuser, or the administrator of the system. Unlike regular users (who may or may not have permission to access certain areas or execute certain commands on the system), `root` has unlimited access to change the system configuration, install programs, and set up new hardware. If users forget their passwords or have other problems with the system, `root` can help. The `root` account should only be used for system administration, maintenance, and repair. Logging in as `root` for daily work is rather risky: a single mistake could lead to irretrievable loss of system files.

For verification purposes, the password for `root` must be entered twice. Do not forget the `root` password. After having been entered, this password cannot be retrieved.

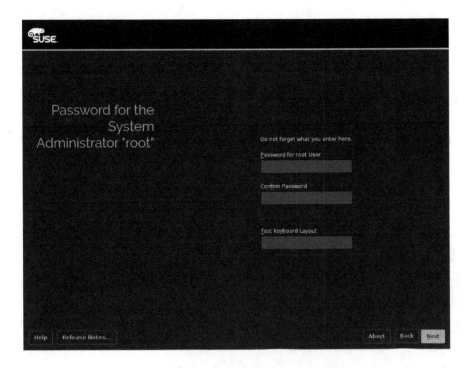

FIGURE 6.13: PASSWORD FOR THE SYSTEM ADMINISTRATOR root

 Tip: Passwords and Keyboard Layout

It is recommended to only use characters that are available on an English keyboard. In case of a system error or when you need to start your system in rescue mode a localized keyboard might not be available.

The `root` password can be changed any time later in the installed system. To do so run YaST and start *Security and Users* › *User and Group Management.*

 Warning: The root User

The user `root` has all the permissions needed to make changes to the system. To carry out such tasks, the `root` password is required. You cannot carry out any administrative tasks without this password.

Password for the System Administrator root

6.13   Installation Settings

On the last step before the real installation takes place, you can alter installation settings suggested by the installer. To modify the suggestions, click the respective headline. After having made changes to a particular setting, you are always returned to the Installation Settings window, which is updated accordingly.

The *Export Configuration* option lets you save the current configuration to an XML file which can be used by AutoYaST for the automated installation of other machines.

FIGURE 6.14: INSTALLATION SETTINGS

 Tip: Existing SSH Host Keys

If you install SUSE Linux Enterprise Server on a machine with one or more existing Linux installations, the installation routine automatically imports the SSH host key with the most recent access time from an existing installation.

6.13.1 Software

SUSE Linux Enterprise Server contains several software patterns for various application purposes. Click *Software* to open the *Software Selection and System Tasks* screen where you can modify the pattern selection according to your needs. Select a pattern from the list and see a description in the right-hand part of the window. Each pattern contains several software packages needed for specific functions (for example Web and LAMP server or a print server). For a more detailed selection based on software packages to install, select *Details* to switch to the YaST Software Manager.

You can also install additional software packages or remove software packages from your system at any later time with the YaST Software Manager. For more information, refer to *Chapter 8, Installing or Removing Software*.

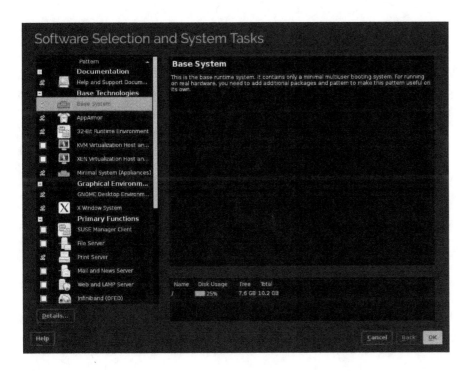

FIGURE 6.15: SOFTWARE SELECTION AND SYSTEM TASKS

Note: Graphical Desktop

By default SUSE Linux Enterprise Server is installed with X Window and the GNOME desktop environment. If you do not need X Window, deselect the two respective patterns in the *Software Selection and System Tasks* screen. As an alternative to GNOME, the lightweight window manager IceWM can be installed. Select *Details* from the *Software Selection and System Tasks* screen and search for `icewm`.

Tip: IBM z Systems: HW crypto support

The HW crypto stack is not installed by default. To install it, select *System z HW crypto support* in the *Software Selection and System Tasks* screen.

Tip: Adding Secondary Languages

The language you selected with the first step of the installation will be used as the primary (default) language for the system. You can add secondary languages from within the *Software* dialog by choosing *Details > View > Languages*.

6.13.2 *Booting*

The installer proposes a boot configuration for your system. Other operating systems found on your computer, such as Microsoft Windows or other Linux installations, will automatically be detected and added to the boot loader. However, SUSE Linux Enterprise Server will be booted by default. Normally, you can leave these settings unchanged. If you need a custom setup, modify the proposal according to your needs. For information, see *Book "Administration Guide", Chapter 11 "The Boot Loader GRUB 2", Section 11.3 "Configuring the Boot Loader with YaST"*.

Important: Software RAID 1

Booting a configuration where `/boot` resides on a software RAID 1 device is supported, but it requires to install the boot loader into the MBR (*Boot Loader Location > Boot from Master Boot Record*). Having `/boot` on software RAID devices with a level other than RAID 1 is not supported. Also see *Book "Storage Administration Guide", Chapter 7 "Configuring Software RAID 1 for the Root Partition"*.

6.13.3 *Firewall and SSH*

By default SuSEFirewall2 is enabled on all configured network interfaces. To globally disable the firewall for this computer, click *Disable* (not recommended).

To enable remote access via the secure shell (SSH), make sure the `SSH service` is enabled and the `SSH port` is open.

 Note: Firewall Settings

> If the firewall is activated, all interfaces are configured to be in the "External Zone", where all ports are closed by default, ensuring maximum security. The only port you can open during the installation is port 22 (SSH), to allow remote access. All other services requiring network access (such as FTP, Samba, Web server, etc.) will only work after having adjusted the firewall settings. Refer to *Book "Security Guide", Chapter 15 "Masquerading and Firewalls"* for more information.

In case you are performing a remote administration over VNC, you can also configure whether the machine should be accessible via VNC even after the installation. Note that enabling VNC also requires you to set the *Default systemd Target* to *graphical*.

6.13.4 *Kdump*

Using Kdump, you can save a dump of the kernel (in case of a crash) to analyze what went wrong. Use this dialog to enable and configure Kdump. Find detailed information at *Book "System Analysis and Tuning Guide", Chapter 17 "Kexec and Kdump"*.

6.13.5 IBM z Systems: Blacklist Devices

To save memory, all channels for devices currently not in use are blacklisted by default (each channel that is not blacklisted occupies approximately 50 kB of memory). To configure additional hardware in the installed system using channels that are currently blacklisted, run the respective YaST module to enable the respective channels first.

To disable blacklisting, click *disable*.

6.13.6 Default systemd Target

SUSE Linux Enterprise Server can boot into two different targets (formerly known as "run-levels"). The *graphical* target starts a display manager, whereas the *multi-user* target starts the command line interface.

The default target is *graphical*. In case you have not installed the *X Window System* patterns, you need to change it to *multi-user*. If the system should be accessible via VNC, you need to choose *graphical*.

6.13.7 System

This screen lists all the hardware information the installer could obtain about your computer. When opened for the first time, the hardware detection is started. Depending on your system, this may take some time. Select any item in the list and click *Details* to see detailed information about the selected item. Use *Save to File* to save a detailed list to either the local file system or a removable device.

Advanced users can also change the *PCI ID Setup* and Kernel Settings by choosing *Kernel Settings*. A screen with two tabs opens:

PCI ID Setup

Each kernel driver contains a list of device IDs of all devices it supports. If a new device is not in any driver's database, the device is treated as unsupported, even if it can be used with an existing driver. You can add PCI IDs to a device driver here. Only advanced users should attempt to do so.

To add an ID, click *Add* and select whether to *Manually* enter the data, or whether to choose from a list. Enter the required data. The *SysFS Dir* is the directory name from `/sys/bus/pci/drivers`—if empty, the *driver* name is used as the directory name. Existing entries can be managed with *Edit* and *Delete*.

Kernel Settings

Change the *Global I/O Scheduler* here. If *Not Configured* is chosen, the default setting for the respective architecture will be used. This setting can also be changed at any time later from the installed system. Refer to *Book "System Analysis and Tuning Guide", Chapter 12 "Tuning I/O Performance"* for details on I/O tuning.

Also activate the *Enable SysRq Keys* here. These keys will let you issue basic commands (such as rebooting the system or writing kernel dumps) in case the system crashes. Enabling these keys is recommended when doing kernel development. Refer to http://www.kernel.org/doc/Documentation/sysrq.txt for details.

6.14 Performing the Installation

After configuring all installation settings, click *Install* in the Installation Settings window to start the installation. Some software may require a license confirmation. If your software selection includes such software, license confirmation dialogs are displayed. Click *Accept* to install the software package. When not agreeing to the license, click *I Disagree* and the software package will not be installed. In the dialog that follows, confirm with *Install* again.

The installation usually takes between 15 and 30 minutes, depending on the system performance and the selected software scope. After having prepared the hard disk and having saved and restored the user settings, the software installation starts. During this procedure a slide show introduces the features of SUSE Linux Enterprise Server. Choose *Details* to switch to the installation log or *Release Notes* to read important up-to-date information that was not available when the manuals were printed.

After the software installation has completed, the system reboots into the new installation where you can log in. To customize the system configuration or to install additional software packages, start YaST.

 Note: The Second Installation Stage is Gone

SUSE Linux Enterprise versions prior to 12 installed the system in two stages: the base system installation was done in stage one, the system configuration in stage two after having rebooted into the newly installed system. Starting with SUSE Linux Enterprise Server 12 the system installation and basic configuration including the network setup is done in a single stage. After having rebooted into the installed system, you can log in and start using the system. To fine-tune the setup, to configure services or to install additional software, start YaST.

6.14.1   IBM z Systems: IPLing the Installed System

YaST usually reboots into the installed system on the IBM z Systems platform. Known exceptions to this are installations where the boot loader resides on an FCP device in environments with LPAR on a machine older than z196 or with z/VM older than release 5.4. The boot loader gets written to a separate partition mounted as `/boot/zipl/`.

In cases where an automatic reboot is not possible, YaST will show a dialog containing information about from which device to do an IPL. Accept the shutdown option and perform an IPL after the shutdown. The procedure varies according to the type of installation:

LPAR Installation

In the IBM z Systems HMC, select *Load*, select *Clear*, then enter the loading address (the address of the device containing the `/boot/zipl` directory with the boot loader). If using a zFCP disk as the boot device, choose *Load from SCSI* and specify the load address of your FCP adapter plus WWPN and LUN of the boot device. Now start the loading process.

z/VM Installation

Log in to the VM guest (see *Example 4.1, "Configuration of a z/VM Directory"* for the configuration) as `LINUX1` and proceed to IPL the installed system:

```
IPL 151 CLEAR
```

`151` is an example address of the DASD boot device, replace this value with the correct address.

If using a zFCP disk as the boot device, specify both the zFCP WWPN and LUN of the boot device before initiating the IPL. The parameter length is limited to eight characters. Longer numbers must be separated by spaces:

```
SET LOADDEV PORT 50050763 00C590A9 LUN 50010000 00000000
```

Finally, initiate the IPL:

```
IPL FC00
```

`FC00` is an example address of the zFCP adapter, replace this value with the correct address.

KVM Guest Installation

Afer the installation has finished, the system restarts and once again IPLs into the installation system. At this point, log in to the KVM host and shut down the virtual machine, edit its description file and restart it to IPL into the installed system:

1. Log in to the KVM host.

2. Shut down the VM Guest:

```
tux > virsh list
 Id    Name                           State
----------------------------------------------------
  1     s12-1                          running

tux > virsh shutdown s12-1
tux > virsh list --all
 Id    Name                           State
----------------------------------------------------
  -     s12-1                          shut off
```

3. Edit the domain XML file by running

```
virsh edit s12-1
```

and remove the following lines:

```
<!-- Boot kernel - remove 3 lines after successfull installation -->
<kernel>/var/lib/libvirt/images/s12-kernel.boot</kernel>
<initrd>/var/lib/libvirt/images/s12-initrd.boot</initrd>
<cmdline>linuxrcstderr=/dev/console</cmdline>
```

4. Restart the VM Guest to IPL into the installed system:

```
virsh start s12-1 --console
```

IBM z Systems: IPLing the Installed System

6.14.2 IBM z Systems: Connecting to the Installed System

After IPLing the system, establish a connection via VNC, SSH, or X to log in to the installed system. Using either VNC or SSH is recommended. To customize the system configuration or to install additional software packages, start YaST.

6.14.2.1 Using VNC to Connect

A message in the 3270 terminal asks you to connect to the Linux system using a VNC client. This message is easily missed, however, because it is mixed with kernel messages and the terminal process might quit before you become aware of the message. If nothing happens for five minutes, try to initiate a connection to the Linux system using a VNC viewer.

If you connect using a Java-capable browser, enter the complete URL, consisting of the IP address of the installed system along with the port number, in the following fashion:

```
http://<IP of installed system>:5801/
```

6.14.2.2 Using SSH to Connect

A message in the 3270 terminal asks you to connect to the Linux system with an SSH client. This message is easily missed, however, because it is mixed with kernel messages and the terminal process might quit before you become aware of the message.

When the message appears, use SSH to log in to the Linux system as `root`. If the connection is denied or times out, wait for the login timeout to expire, then try again (this time may vary depending on server settings).

6.14.2.3 Using X to Connect

When IPLing the installed system, make sure that the X server used for the first phase of the installation is up and still available before booting from the DASD. YaST opens on this X server to finish the installation. Complications may arise if the system is booted up but unable to connect to the X server in a timely fashion.

7 Setting Up Hardware Components with YaST

YaST allows you to configure hardware items such as audio hardware, your system keyboard layout or printers.

 Note: Graphics Card, Monitor, Mouse and Keyboard Settings
Graphics card, monitor, mouse and keyboard can be configured with GNOME tools.

7.1 Setting Up Your System Keyboard Layout

The YaST *System Keyboard Layout* module lets you define the default keyboard layout for the system (also used for the console). Users can modify the keyboard layout in their individual X sessions, using the desktop's tools.

1. Start the YaST *System Keyboard Configuration* dialog by clicking *Hardware* > *System Keyboard Layout* in YaST. Alternatively, start the module from the command line with **sudo yast2 keyboard**.

2. Select the desired *Keyboard Layout* from the list.

3. Optionally, you can also define the keyboard repeat rate or keyboard delay rate in the *Expert Settings*.

4. Try the selected settings in the *Test* text box.

5. If the result is as expected, confirm your changes and close the dialog. The settings are written to `/etc/sysconfig/keyboard`.

7.2 Setting Up Sound Cards

YaST detects most sound cards automatically and configures them with the appropriate values. If you want to change the default settings, or need to set up a sound card that could not be configured automatically, use the YaST sound module. There, you can also set up additional sound cards or switch their order.

To start the sound module, start YaST and click *Hardware › Sound*. Alternatively, start the *Sound Configuration* dialog directly by running `yast2 sound &` as user `root` from a command line.

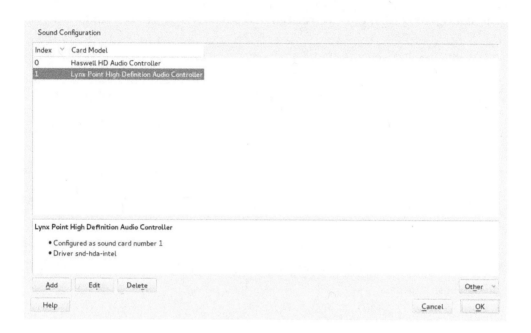

The dialog shows all sound cards that could be detected.

PROCEDURE 7.1: CONFIGURING SOUND CARDS

> If you have added a new sound card or YaST could not automatically configure an existing sound card, follow the steps below. For configuring a new sound card, you need to know your sound card vendor and model. If in doubt, refer to your sound card documentation for the required information. For a reference list of sound cards supported by ALSA with their corresponding sound modules, see http://www.alsa-project.org/main/index.php/Matrix:Main.
>
> During configuration, you can choose between the following setup options:
>
> *Quick Automatic Setup*
>
> > You are not required to go through any of the further configuration steps—the sound card is configured automatically. You can set the volume or any options you want to change later.
>
> *Normal Setup*
>
> > Allows you to adjust the output volume and play a test sound during the configuration.

Setting Up Sound Cards

Advanced setup with possibility to change options

For experts only. Allows you to customize all parameters of the sound card.

 Important: Advanced Configuration

Only use this option if you know exactly what your are doing. Otherwise leave the parameters untouched and use the normal or the automatic setup options.

1. Start the YaST sound module.

2. To configure a detected, but *Not Configured* sound card, select the respective entry from the list and click *Edit*.
   To configure a new sound card, click *Add*. Select your sound card vendor and model and click *Next*.

3. Choose one of the setup options and click *Next*.

4. If you have chosen *Normal Setup*, you can now *Test* your sound configuration and make adjustments to the volume. You should start at about ten percent volume to avoid damage to your hearing or the speakers.

5. If all options are set according to your wishes, click *Next*.
   The *Sound Configuration* dialog shows the newly configured or modified sound card.

6. To remove a sound card configuration that you no longer need, select the respective entry and click *Delete*.

7. Click *OK* to save the changes and leave the YaST sound module.

PROCEDURE 7.2: MODIFYING SOUND CARD CONFIGURATIONS

1. To change the configuration of an individual sound card (for experts only!), select the sound card entry in the *Sound Configuration* dialog and click *Edit*.
   This takes you to the *Sound Card Advanced Options* where you can fine-tune several parameters. For more information, click *Help*.

2. To adjust the volume of an already configured sound card or to test the sound card, select the sound card entry in the *Sound Configuration* dialog and click *Other*. Select the respective menu item.

Setting Up Sound Cards

Note: YaST Mixer

The YaST mixer settings provide only basic options. They are intended for troubleshooting (for example, if the test sound is not audible). Access the YaST mixer settings from *Other > Volume*. For everyday use and fine-tuning of sound options, use the mixer applet provided by your desktop or the **alsasound** command line tool.

3. For playback of MIDI files, select *Other > Start Sequencer*.

4. When a supported sound card is detected (like a Creative `Soundblaster Live`, `Audigy` or `AWE` sound card), you can also install SoundFonts for playback of MIDI files:

    a. Insert the original driver CD-ROM into your CD or DVD drive.

    b. Select *Other > Install SoundFonts* to copy SF2 SoundFonts™ to your hard disk. The SoundFonts are saved in the directory `/usr/share/sfbank/creative/`.

5. If you have configured more than one sound card in your system you can adjust the order of your sound cards. To set a sound card as primary device, select the sound card in the *Sound Configuration* and click *Other > Set as the Primary Card*. The sound device with index `0` is the default device and thus used by the system and the applications.

6. By default, SUSE Linux Enterprise Server uses the PulseAudio sound system. It is an abstraction layer that helps to mix multiple audio streams, bypassing any restrictions the hardware may have. To enable or disable the PulseAudio sound system, click *Other > PulseAudio Configuration*. If enabled, PulseAudio daemon is used to play sounds. Disable *PulseAudio Support* in case you want to use something else system-wide.

The volume and configuration of all sound cards are saved when you click *OK* and leave the YaST sound module. The mixer settings are saved to the file `/etc/asound.state`. The ALSA configuration data is appended to the end of the file `/etc/modprobe.d/sound` and written to `/etc/sysconfig/sound`.

7.3 Setting Up a Printer

YaST can be used to configure a local printer that is directly connected to your machine via USB and to set up printing with network printers. It is also possible to share printers over the network. Further information about printing (general information, technical details, and troubleshooting) is available in *Book "Administration Guide", Chapter 14 "Printer Operation"*.

In YaST, click *Hardware › Printer* to start the printer module. By default it opens in the *Printer Configurations* view, displaying a list of all printers that are available and configured. This is especially useful when having access to a lot of printers via the network. From here you can also *Print a Test Page* and configure printers.

 Note: Starting CUPS

> To be able to print from your system, CUPS must run. In case it is not running, you are asked to start it. Answer with *Yes*, or you cannot configure printing. In case CUPS is not started at boot time, you will also be asked to enable this feature. It is recommended to say *Yes*, otherwise CUPS would need to be started manually after each reboot.

7.3.1 Configuring Printers

Usually a USB printer is automatically detected. There are two possible reasons it is not automatically detected:

- The USB printer is switched off.

- The communication between printer and computer is not possible. Check the cable and the plugs to make sure that the printer is properly connected. If this is the case, the problem may not be printer-related, but rather a USB-related problem.

Configuring a printer is a three-step process: specify the connection type, choose a driver, and name the print queue for this setup.

For many printer models, several drivers are available. When configuring the printer, YaST defaults to those marked `recommended` as a general rule. Normally it is not necessary to change the driver. However, if you want a color printer to print only in black and white, it is most convenient to use a driver that does not support color printing, for example. If you experience performance problems with a PostScript printer when printing graphics, it may help to switch from a PostScript driver to a PCL driver (provided your printer understands PCL).

If no driver for your printer is listed, try to select a generic driver with an appropriate standard language from the list. Refer to your printer's documentation to find out which language (the set of commands controlling the printer) your printer understands. If this does not work, refer to *Section 7.3.1.1, "Adding Drivers with YaST"* for another possible solution.

A printer is never used directly, but always through a print queue. This ensures that simultaneous jobs can be queued and processed one after the other. Each print queue is assigned to a specific driver, and a printer can have multiple queues. This makes it possible to set up a second queue on a color printer that prints black and white only, for example. Refer to *Book "Administration Guide", Chapter 14 "Printer Operation", Section 14.1 "The CUPS Workflow"* for more information about print queues.

PROCEDURE 7.3: ADDING A NEW PRINTER

1. Start the YaST printer module with *Hardware > Printer*.

2. In the *Printer Configurations* screen click *Add*.

3. If your printer is already listed under `Specify the Connection`, proceed with the next step. Otherwise, try to *Detect More* or start the *Connection Wizard*.

4. In the text box under `Find and Assign a Driver` enter the vendor name and the model name and click *Search for*.

5. Choose a driver that matches your printer. It is recommended to choose the driver listed first. If no suitable driver is displayed:

   a. Check your search term

   b. Broaden your search by clicking *Find More*

   c. Add a driver as described in *Section 7.3.1.1, "Adding Drivers with YaST"*

6. Specify the `Default paper size`.

7. In the *Set Arbitrary Name* field, enter a unique name for the print queue.

8. The printer is now configured with the default settings and ready to use. Click *OK* to return to the *Printer Configurations* view. The newly configured printer is now visible in the list of printers.

7.3.1.1   Adding Drivers with YaST

Not all printer drivers available for SUSE Linux Enterprise Server are installed by default. If no suitable driver is available in the *Find and Assign a Driver* dialog when adding a new printer install a driver package containing drivers for your printers:

PROCEDURE 7.4: INSTALLING ADDITIONAL DRIVER PACKAGES

1. Start the YaST printer module with *Hardware › Printer*.

2. In the *Printer Configurations* screen, click *Add*.

3. In the `Find and Assign a Driver` section, click *Driver Packages*.

4. Choose one or more suitable driver packages from the list. Do *not* specify the path to a printer description file.

5. Choose *OK* and confirm the package installation.

6. To directly use these drivers, proceed as described in *Procedure 7.3, "Adding a New Printer"*.

PostScript printers do not need printer driver software. PostScript printers need only a PostScript Printer Description (PPD) file which matches the particular model. PPD files are provided by the printer manufacturer.

If no suitable PPD file is available in the *Find and Assign a Driver* dialog when adding a PostScript printer install a PPD file for your printer:

Several sources for PPD files are available. It is recommended to first try additional driver packages that are shipped with SUSE Linux Enterprise Server but not installed by default (see below for installation instructions). If these packages do not contain suitable drivers for your printer, get PPD files directly from your printer vendor or from the driver CD of a PostScript printer. For details, see *Book "Administration Guide", Chapter 14 "Printer Operation", Section 14.8.2 "No Suitable PPD File Available for a PostScript Printer"*. Alternatively, find PPD files at http://www.linuxfoundation.org/collaborate/workgroups/openprinting/database/databaseintro, the "OpenPrinting.org printer database". When downloading PPD files from OpenPrinting, keep in mind that it always shows the latest Linux support status, which is not necessarily met by SUSE Linux Enterprise Server.

1. Start the YaST printer module with *Hardware* › *Printer*.

2. In the *Printer Configurations* screen, click *Add*.

3. In the `Find and Assign a Driver` section, click *Driver Packages*.

4. Enter the full path to the PPD file into the text box under `Make a Printer Description File Available`.

5. Click *OK* to return to the `Add New Printer Configuration` screen.

6. To directly use this PPD file, proceed as described in *Procedure 7.3, "Adding a New Printer"*.

7.3.1.2   Editing a Local Printer Configuration

By editing an existing configuration for a printer you can change basic settings such as connection type and driver. It is also possible to adjust the default settings for paper size, resolution, media source, etc. You can change identifiers of the printer by altering the printer description or location.

1. Start the YaST printer module with *Hardware* › *Printer*.

2. In the *Printer Configurations* screen, choose a local printer configuration from the list and click *Edit*.

3. Change the connection type or the driver as described in *Procedure 7.3, "Adding a New Printer"*. This should only be necessary in case you have problems with the current configuration.

4. Optionally, make this printer the default by checking *Default Printer*.

5. Adjust the default settings by clicking *All Options for the Current Driver*. To change a setting, expand the list of options by clicking the relative + sign. Change the default by clicking an option. Apply your changes with *OK*.

7.3.2 Configuring Printing via the Network with YaST

Network printers are not detected automatically. They must be configured manually using the YaST printer module. Depending on your network setup, you can print to a print server (CUPS, LPD, SMB, or IPX) or directly to a network printer (preferably via TCP). Access the configuration view for network printing by choosing *Printing via Network* from the left pane in the YaST printer module.

7.3.2.1 Using CUPS

In a Linux environment CUPS is usually used to print via the network. The simplest setup is to only print via a single CUPS server which can directly be accessed by all clients. Printing via more than one CUPS server requires a running local CUPS daemon that communicates with the remote CUPS servers.

> ## ⓘ Important: Browsing Network Print Queues
>
> CUPS servers announce their print queues over the network either via the traditional CUPS browsing protocol or via Bonjour/DND-SD. Clients need to be able to browse these lists, so users can select specific printers to send their print jobs to. To be able to browse network print queues, the service `cups-browsed` provided by the package `cups-filters-cups-browsed` needs to run on all clients that print via CUPS servers. `cups-browsed` is started automatically when configuring network printing with YaST.
>
> In case browsing does not work after having started `cups-browsed`, the CUPS server(s) probably announce the network print queues via Bonjour/DND-SD. In this case you need to additionally install the package `avahi` and start the associated service with **sudo systemctl start avahi-daemon** on all clients.

PROCEDURE 7.6: PRINTING VIA A SINGLE CUPS SERVER

1. Start the YaST printer module with *Hardware > Printer*.

2. From the left pane, launch the *Print via Network* screen.

3. Check *Do All Your Printing Directly via One Single CUPS Server* and specify the name or IP address of the server.

4. Click *Test Server* to make sure you have chosen the correct name or IP address.

5. Click OK to return to the *Printer Configurations* screen. All printers available via the CUPS server are now listed.

PROCEDURE 7.7: PRINTING VIA MULTIPLE CUPS SERVERS

1. Start the YaST printer module with *Hardware › Printer*.

2. From the left pane, launch the *Print via Network* screen.

3. Check *Accept Printer Announcements from CUPS Servers*.

4. Under `General Settings` specify which servers to use. You may accept connections from all networks available or from specific hosts. If you choose the latter option, you need to specify the host names or IP addresses.

5. Confirm by clicking *OK* and then *Yes* when asked to start a local CUPS server. After the server has started YaST will return to the *Printer Configurations* screen. Click *Refresh list* to see the printers detected by now. Click this button again, in case more printer are to be available.

7.3.2.2 Using Print Servers other than CUPS

If your network offers print services via print servers other than CUPS, start the YaST printer module with *Hardware › Printer* and launch the *Print via Network* screen from the left pane. Start the *Connection Wizard* and choose the appropriate *Connection Type*. Ask your network administrator for details on configuring a network printer in your environment.

7.3.3 Sharing Printers Over the Network

Printers managed by a local CUPS daemon can be shared over the network and so turn your machine into a CUPS server. Usually you share a printer by enabling CUPS' so-called "browsing mode". If browsing is enabled, the local print queues are made available on the network for listening to remote CUPS daemons. It is also possible to set up a dedicated CUPS server that manages all print queues and can directly be accessed by remote clients. In this case it is not necessary to enable browsing.

PROCEDURE 7.8: SHARING PRINTERS

1. Start the YaST printer module with *Hardware › Printer*.

2. Launch the *Share Printers* screen from the left pane.

3. Select *Allow Remote Access*. Also check *For computers within the local network* and enable browsing mode by also checking *Publish printers by default within the local network*.

4. Click *OK* to restart the CUPS server and to return to the *Printer Configurations* screen.

5. Regarding CUPS and firewall settings, see http://en.opensuse.org/ SDB:CUPS_and_SANE_Firewall_settings.

8 Installing or Removing Software

Use YaST's software management module to search for software components you want to add or remove. YaST resolves all dependencies for you. To install packages not shipped with the installation media, add additional software repositories to your setup and let YaST manage them. Keep your system up-to-date by managing software updates with the update applet.

Change the software collection of your system with the YaST Software Manager. This YaST module is available in two flavors: a graphical variant for X Window and a text-based variant to be used on the command line. The graphical flavor is described here—for details on the text-based YaST, see *Book "Administration Guide", Chapter 2 "YaST in Text Mode"*.

 Note: Confirmation and Review of Changes

When installing, updating or removing packages, any changes in the Software Manager are not applied immediately but only after confirming them with *Accept* or *Apply* respectively. YaST maintains a list with all actions, allowing you to review and modify your changes before applying them to the system.

8.1 Definition of Terms

Repository

A local or remote directory containing packages, plus additional information about these packages (package metadata).

(Repository) Alias/Repository Name

A short name for a repository (called `Alias` within Zypper and *Repository Name* within YaST). It can be chosen by the user when adding a repository and must be unique.

Repository Description Files

Each repository provides files describing content of the repository (package names, versions, etc.). These repository description files are downloaded to a local cache that is used by YaST.

Product

Represents a whole product, for example SUSE® Linux Enterprise Server.

Pattern

A pattern is an installable group of packages dedicated to a certain purpose. For example, the `Laptop` pattern contains all packages that are needed in a mobile computing environment. Patterns define package dependencies (such as required or recommended packages) and come with a preselection of packages marked for installation. This ensures that the most important packages needed for a certain purpose are available on your system after installation of the pattern. However, not necessarily all packages in a pattern are preselected for installation and you can manually select or deselect packages within a pattern according to your needs and wishes.

Package

A package is a compressed file in `rpm` format that contains the files for a particular program.

Patch

A patch consists of one or more packages and may be applied by means of delta RPMs. It may also introduce dependencies to packages that are not installed yet.

Resolvable

A generic term for product, pattern, package or patch. The most commonly used type of resolvable is a package or a patch.

Delta RPM

A delta RPM consists only of the binary diff between two defined versions of a package, and therefore has the smallest download size. Before being installed, the full RPM package is rebuilt on the local machine.

Package Dependencies

Certain packages are dependent on other packages, such as shared libraries. In other terms, a package may `require` other packages—if the required packages are not available, the package cannot be installed. In addition to dependencies (package requirements) that must be fulfilled, some packages `recommend` other packages. These recommended packages are only installed if they are actually available, otherwise they are ignored and the package recommending them is installed nevertheless.

8.2 Using the YaST Software Manager

Start the software manager from the *YaST Control Center* by choosing *Software* › *Software Management*.

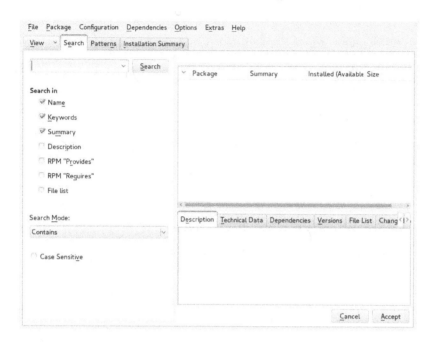

8.2.1 Views for Searching Packages or Patterns

The YaST software manager can install packages or patterns from all currently enabled repositories. It offers different views and filters to make it easier to find the software you are searching for. The *Search* view is the default view of the window. To change view, click *View* and select one of the following entries from the drop-down box. The selected view opens in a new tab.

Patterns

Lists all patterns available for installation on your system.

Package Groups

Lists all packages sorted by groups such as *Graphics*, *Programming*, or *Security*.

RPM Groups

Lists all packages sorted by functionality with groups and subgroups. For example *Networking* › *Email* › *Clients*.

Languages

A filter to list all packages needed to add a new system language.

Repositories

A filter to list packages by repository. To select more than one repository, hold the `Ctrl` key while clicking repository names. The "pseudo repository" *@System* lists all packages currently installed.

Search

Lets you search for a package according to certain criteria. Enter a search term and press `Enter`. Refine your search by specifying where to *Search In* and by changing the *Search Mode*. For example, if you do not know the package name but only the name of the application that you are searching for, try including the package *Description* in the search process.

Installation Summary

If you have already selected packages for installation, update or removal, this view shows the changes that will be applied to your system as soon as you click *Accept*. To filter for packages with a certain status in this view, activate or deactivate the respective check boxes. Press `Shift`-`F1` for details on the status flags.

 Tip: Finding Packages Not Belonging to an Active Repository

To list all packages that do not belong to an active repository, choose *View > Repositories > @System* and then choose *Secondary Filter > Unmaintained Packages*. This is useful, for example, if you have deleted a repository and want to make sure no packages from that repository remain installed.

8.2.2 Installing and Removing Packages or Patterns

Certain packages are dependent on other packages, such as shared libraries. On the other hand, some packages cannot coexist with others on the system. If possible, YaST automatically resolves these dependencies or conflicts. If your choice results in a dependency conflict that cannot be automatically solved, you need to solve it manually as described in *Section 8.2.4, "Checking Software Dependencies"*.

Note: Removal of Packages

When removing any packages, by default YaST only removes the selected packages. If you want YaST to also remove any other packages that become unneeded after removal of the specified package, select *Options* › *Cleanup when deleting packages* from the main menu.

1. Search for packages as described in *Section 8.2.1, "Views for Searching Packages or Patterns"*.

2. The packages found are listed in the right pane. To install a package or remove it, right-click it and choose *Install* or *Delete*. If the relevant option is not available, check the package status indicated by the symbol in front of the package name—press Shift-F1 for help.

    Tip: Applying an Action to All Packages Listed

   To apply an action to all packages listed in the right pane, go to the main menu and choose an action from *Package* › *All in This List*.

3. To install a pattern, right-click the pattern name and choose *Install*.

4. It is not possible to remove a pattern per se. Instead, select the packages of a pattern you want to remove and mark them for removal.

5. To select more packages, repeat the steps mentioned above.

6. Before applying your changes, you can review or modify them by clicking *View* › *Installation Summary*. By default, all packages that will change status, are listed.

7. to: To revert the status for a package, right-click the package and select one of the following entries: *Keep* if the package was scheduled to be deleted or updated, or *Do Not Install* if it was scheduled for installation. To abandon all changes and quit the Software Manager, click *Cancel* and *Abandon*.

8. When you are finished, click *Accept* to apply your changes.

9. In case YaST found dependencies on other packages, a list of packages that have additionally been chosen for installation, update or removal is presented. Click *Continue* to accept them.

   After all selected packages are installed, updated or removed, the YaST Software Manager automatically terminates.

Note: Installing Source Packages

Installing source packages with YaST Software Manager is not possible at the moment. Use the command line tool **zypper** for this purpose. For more information, see *Book "Administration Guide", Chapter 4 "Managing Software with Command Line Tools", Section 4.1.2.1 "Installing or Downloading Source Packages"*.

8.2.3 Updating Packages

Instead of updating individual packages, you can also update all installed packages or all packages from a certain repository. When mass updating packages, the following aspects are generally considered:

- priorities of the repositories that provide the package,

- architecture of the package (for example, x86_64),

- version number of the package,

- package vendor.

Which of the aspects has the highest importance for choosing the update candidates depends on the respective update option you choose.

1. To update all installed packages to the latest version, choose *Package > All Packages > Update if Newer Version Available* from the main menu.

   All repositories are checked for possible update candidates, using the following policy: YaST first tries to restrict the search to packages with the same architecture and vendor like the installed one. If the search is positive, the "best" update candidate from those is selected according to the process below. However, if no comparable package of the same vendor can be found, the search is expanded to all packages with the same architecture. If still no comparable package can be found, all packages are considered and the "best" update candidate is selected according to the following criteria:

   1. Repository priority: Prefer the package from the repository with the highest priority.

   2. If more than one package results from this selection, choose the one with the "best" architecture (best choice: matching the architecture of the installed one).

If the resulting package has a higher version number than the installed one, the installed package will be updated and replaced with the selected update candidate.

This option tries to avoid changes in architecture and vendor for the installed packages, but under certain circumstances, they are tolerated.

 Note: Update Unconditionally

If you choose *Package › All Packages › Update Unconditionally* instead, the same criteria apply but any candidate package found is installed unconditionally. Thus, choosing this option might actually lead to downgrading some packages.

2. To make sure that the packages for a mass update derive from a certain repository:

   a. Choose the repository from which to update as described in *Section 8.2.1, "Views for Searching Packages or Patterns"* .

   b. On the right hand side of the window, click *Switch system packages to the versions in this repository*. This explicitly allows YaST to change the package vendor when replacing the packages.

      As soon as you proceed with *Accept*, all installed packages will be replaced by packages deriving from this repository, if available. This may lead to changes in vendor and architecture and even to downgrading some packages.

   c. To refrain from this, click *Cancel switching system packages to the versions in this repository*. Note that you can only cancel this until you press the *Accept* button.

3. Before applying your changes, you can review or modify them by clicking *View › Installation Summary*. By default, all packages that will change status, are listed.

4. If all options are set according to your wishes, confirm your changes with *Accept* to start the mass update.

8.2.4   Checking Software Dependencies

Most packages are dependent on other packages. If a package, for example, uses a shared library, it is dependent on the package providing this library. On the other hand some packages cannot coexist with each other, causing a conflict (for example, you can only install one mail transfer agent: sendmail or postfix). When installing or removing software, the Software Manager makes sure no dependencies or conflicts remain unsolved to ensure system integrity.

In case there exists only one solution to resolve a dependency or a conflict, it is resolved automatically. Multiple solutions always cause a conflict which needs to be resolved manually. If solving a conflict involves a vendor or architecture change, it also needs to be solved manually. When clicking *Accept* to apply any changes in the Software Manager, you get an overview of all actions triggered by the automatic resolver which you need to confirm.

By default, dependencies are automatically checked. A check is performed every time you change a package status (for example, by marking a package for installation or removal). This is generally useful, but can become exhausting when manually resolving a dependency conflict. To disable this function, go to the main menu and deactivate *Dependencies* › *Autocheck*. Manually perform a dependency check with *Dependencies* › *Check Now*. A consistency check is always performed when you confirm your selection with *Accept*.

To review a package's dependencies, right-click it and choose *Show Solver Information*. A map showing the dependencies opens. Packages that are already installed are displayed in a green frame.

 Note: Manually Solving Package Conflicts

Unless you are very experienced, follow the suggestions YaST makes when handling package conflicts, otherwise you may not be able to resolve them. Keep in mind that every change you make, potentially triggers other conflicts, so you can easily end up with a steadily increasing number of conflicts. In case this happens, *Cancel* the Software Manager, *Abandon* all your changes and start again.

⚠ sendmail-8.14.9-2.26.x86_64 conflicts with postfix provided by postfi

Conflict Resolution:
  1: deinstallation of postfix-2.11.0-2.3.x86_64
  2: do not install sendmail-8.14.9-2.26.x86_64

OK -- Try Again   Expert ∨   Cancel

FIGURE 8.1: CONFLICT MANAGEMENT OF THE SOFTWARE MANAGER

8.2.4.1 Handling of Package Recommendations

In addition to the hard dependencies required to run a program (for example a certain library), a package can also have weak dependencies, that add for example extra functionality or translations. These weak dependencies are called package recommendations.

The way package recommendations are handled has slightly changed with SUSE Linux Enterprise Server 12 SP1. Nothing has changed when installing a new package—recommended packages are still installed by default.

Prior to SLES 12 SP1, missing recommendations for already installed packages were installed automatically. Starting with SLES 12 SP1, these packages will no longer be installed automatically. To switch to the old default, set `PKGMGR_REEVALUATE_RECOMMENDED="yes"` in `/etc/sysconfig/yast2`. To install all missing recommendations for already installed packages, start *YaST › Software Manager* and choose *Extras › Install All Matching Recommended Packages*.

To disable the installation of recommended packages when installing new packages, deactivate *Dependencies › Install Recommended Packages* in the YaST Software Manager. If using the command line tool Zypper to install packages, use the option `--no-recommends`.

8.3 Managing Software Repositories and Services

If you want to install third-party software, add additional software repositories to your system. By default, the product repositories such as SUSE Linux Enterprise Server-DVD 12 SP1 and a matching update repository are automatically configured after you have registered your system. For more information about registration, see *Section 6.7, "SUSE Customer Center Registration"* or *Section 17.8, "Registering Your System"*. Depending on the initially selected product, an additional repository containing translations, dictionaries, etc. might also be configured.

To manage repositories, start YaST and select *Software* > *Software Repositories*. The *Configured Software Repositories* dialog opens. Here, you can also manage subscriptions to so-called *Services* by changing the *View* at the right corner of the dialog to *All Services*. A Service in this context is a *Repository Index Service* (RIS) that can offer one or more software repositories. Such a Service can be changed dynamically by its administrator or vendor.

Each repository provides files describing content of the repository (package names, versions, etc.). These repository description files are downloaded to a local cache that is used by YaST. To ensure their integrity, software repositories can be signed with the GPG Key of the repository maintainer. Whenever you add a new repository, YaST offers the ability to import its key.

 Warning: Trusting External Software Sources

> Before adding external software repositories to your list of repositories, make sure this repository can be trusted. SUSE is not responsible for any problems arising from software installed from third-party software repositories.

8.3.1 Adding Software Repositories

You can either add repositories from DVD/CD, removable mass storage devices (such as flash disks), or a local directory or ISO image.

To add repositories from the *Configured Software Repositories* dialog in YaST proceed as follows:

1. Click *Add*.

2. Select one of the options listed in the dialog:

Add On Product

- Scan Using SLP...
- Extensions and Modules from Registration Server...
- Specify URL...
- FTP...
- HTTP...
- HTTPS...
- SMB/CIFS
- NFS...
- CD...
- DVD...
- Hard Disk...
- USB Mass Storage (USB Stick, Disk)...
- Local Directory...
- Local ISO Image...

☑ Download repository description files

Help   Abort   Back   Next

FIGURE 8.2: ADDING A SOFTWARE REPOSITORY

- To scan your network for installation servers announcing their services via SLP, select *Scan Using SLP* and click *Next*.

- To add a repository from a removable medium, choose the relevant option and insert the medium or connect the USB device to the machine, respectively. Click *Next* to start the installation.

- For the majority of repositories, you will be asked to specify the path (or URL) to the media after selecting the respective option and clicking *Next*. Specifying a *Repository Name* is optional. If none is specified, YaST will use the product name or the URL as repository name.

The option *Download Repository Description Files* is activated by default. If you deactivate the option, YaST will automatically download the files later, if needed.

3. Depending on the repository you have added, you may be asked if you want to import the GPG key with which it is signed or asked to agree to a license.
   After confirming these messages, YaST will download and parse the metadata. It will add the repository to the list of *Configured Repositories*.

4. If needed, adjust the repository *Properties* as described in *Section 8.3.2, "Managing Repository Properties"*.

5. Confirm your changes with *OK* to close the configuration dialog.

6. After having successfully added the repository, the software manager starts and you can install packages from this repository. For details, refer to *Chapter 8, Installing or Removing Software.*

8.3.2   Managing Repository Properties

The *Configured Software Repositories* overview of the *Software Repositories* lets you change the following repository properties:

Status

The repository status can either be *Enabled* or *Disabled*. You can only install packages from repositories that are enabled. To turn a repository off temporarily, select it and deactivate *Enable*. You can also double-click a repository name to toggle its status. If you want to remove a repository completely, click *Delete*.

Refresh

When refreshing a repository, its content description (package names, versions, etc.) is downloaded to a local cache that is used by YaST. It is sufficient to do this once for static repositories such as CDs or DVDs, whereas repositories whose content changes often should be refreshed frequently. The easiest way to keep a repository's cache up-to-date is to choose *Automatically Refresh*. To do a manual refresh click *Refresh* and select one of the options.

Keep Downloaded Packages

Packages from remote repositories are downloaded before being installed. By default, they are deleted upon a successful installation. Activating *Keep Downloaded Packages* prevents the deletion of downloaded packages. The download location is configured in `/etc/zypp/zypp.conf`, by default it is `/var/cache/zypp/packages`.

Priority

The *Priority* of a repository is a value between `1` and `200`, with `1` being the highest priority and `200` the lowest priority. Any new repositories that are added with YaST get a priority of `99` by default. If you do not care about a priority value for a certain repository, you can also set the value to `0` to apply the default priority to that repository (`99`). If a package is available in more than one repository, then the repository with the highest priority takes precedence. This is useful if you want to avoid downloading packages unnecessarily from the Internet by giving a local repository (for example, a DVD) a higher priority.

Important: Priority vs. Version

The repository with the highest priority takes precedence in any case. Therefore, make sure that the update repository always has the highest priority, otherwise you might install an outdated version that will not be updated until the next online update.

Name and URL

To change a repository name or its URL, select it from the list with a single-click and then click *Edit*.

8.3.3   Managing Repository Keys

To ensure their integrity, software repositories can be signed with the GPG Key of the repository maintainer. Whenever you add a new repository, YaST offers to import its key. Verify it as you would do with any other GPG key and make sure it does not change. If you detect a key change, something might be wrong with the repository. Disable the repository as an installation source until you know the cause of the key change.

To manage all imported keys, click *GPG Keys* in the *Configured Software Repositories* dialog. Select an entry with the mouse to show the key properties at the bottom of the window. *Add*, *Edit* or *Delete* keys with a click on the respective buttons.

8.4   Keeping the System Up-to-date

SUSE offers a continuous stream of software security patches for your product. They can be installed using the *Book* "Administration Guide", *Chapter 1* "YaST Online Update" module. It also offers advanced features to customize the patch installation.

The GNOME desktop also provides a tool for installing patches, and, additionally, for installing package updates of packages that are already installed. In contrast to a *Patch*, a package update is only related to *one* package and provides a newer version of a package. The GNOME tool lets you install both patches and package updates with a few clicks as described in *Section 8.4.2, "Installing Patches and Package Updates".*

8.4.1 The GNOME Software Updater

Whenever new patches or package updates are available, GNOME shows a notification about this at the bottom of the desktop (or on the locked screen).

FIGURE 8.3: UPDATE NOTIFICATION ON GNOME LOCK SCREEN

8.4.2 Installing Patches and Package Updates

Whenever new patches or package updates are available, GNOME shows a notification about this at the bottom of the desktop (or on the locked screen).

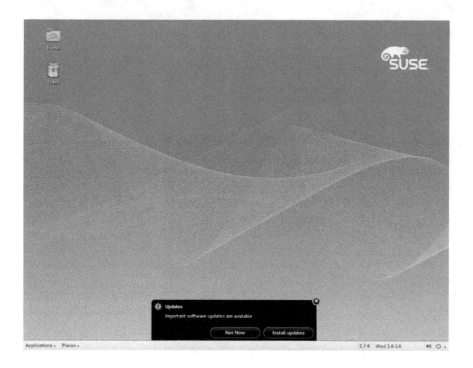

FIGURE 8.4: UPDATE NOTIFICATION ON GNOME DESKTOP

1. To install the patches and updates, click *Install updates* in the notification message. This opens the GNOME update viewer. Alternatively, open the update viewer from *Applications › System Tools › Software Update* or press `Alt`–`F2` and enter **gpk-update-viewer**.

2. All *Security Updates* and *Important Updates* are preselected. It is strongly recommended to install these patches. *Other Updates* can be manually selected by activating the respective check boxes. Get detailed information on a patch or package update by clicking its title.

3. Click *Install Updates* to start the installation. You will be prompted for the `root` password.

4. Enter the `root` password in the authentication dialog and proceed.

Installing Patches and Package Updates

There are **9 updates available**

Software updates correct errors, eliminate security vulnerabilities and provide new features.

Security updates

openssl: Update to OpenSSL 1.0.1g
SUSE-2014-8-1   1.4 MB

Important updates

plymouth: Update to recent git snapshot
SUSE-2014-16-1   353.9 kB

timezone: Update to 2014c
SUSE-2014-22-1   347.9 kB

samba: Fix printer job purging
SUSE-2014-23-1   9.4 MB

Fixes a regression in timezone-2014c.
SUSE-2014-26-1   350.2 kB

plymouth: fix a crash in some rare cases in serial consoles
SUSE-2014-32-1   360.7 kB

fipscheck: added baselibs.conf
SUSE-2014-33-1   19.4 kB

Other updates

SUSE Linux Enterprise Server 12 (Beta8)
sles-release-12-1.191 (64-bit)   12.2 kB

SUSE Linux Enterprise Server 12
sles-release-DVD-12-1.191 (64-bit)   3.5 kB

▶ Details

9 updates selected (12.2 MB)   Quit   Install Updates

FIGURE 8.5: GNOME UPDATE VIEWER

8.4.3   Configuring the GNOME Software Updater

To define the appearance of the notification (where it appears on the screen, whether to display it on the lock screen), select *Applications › System Settings › Notification › Software Update* and change the settings according to your wishes.

To configure how often to check for updates or to activate or deactivate repositories, select *Applications › System Tools › Settings › Software Settings*. The tabs of the configuration dialog let you modify the following settings:

UPDATE SETTINGS

Check for Updates

Choose how often a check for updates is performed: *Hourly, Daily, Weekly,* or *Never.*

Check for Major Upgrades

Choose how often a check for major upgrades is performed: *Daily*, *Weekly*, or *Never*.

Check for updates when using mobile broadband

This configuration option is only available on mobile computers. Turned off by default.

Check for updates on battery power

This configuration option is only available on mobile computers. Turned off by default.

SOFTWARE SOURCES

Repositories

Lists the repositories that will be checked for available patches and package updates. You can enable or disable certain repositories.

 Important: Keep Update **Repository Enabled**

To make sure that you are notified about any patches that are security-relevant, keep the Updates repository for your product enabled.

More options are configurable using **gconf-editor**: *apps* › *gnome-packagekit*.

9 Installing Modules, Extensions, and Third Party Add-On Products

Modules and extensions add additional parts or functionality to the system. Modules are fully supported parts of SUSE Linux Enterprise Server with a different life cycle and update timeline. They are a set of packages, have a clearly defined scope and are delivered via online channel only. Extensions, such as the Work Station Extension or the High Availability Extension, add extra functionality to the system and require a registration key that is liable for costs. Extensions are delivered via online channel or physical media. Registering at the SUSE Customer Center or a local registration server is a prerequisite for being able to subscribe to the online channels.

A list of available modules and extensions for your product is available after having registered your system at SUSE Customer Center or a local registration server. If you skipped the registration step during the installation, you can register your system at any time using the *SUSE Customer Center Configuration* module in YaST. For details, refer to *Section 17.8, "Registering Your System"*.

Some add-on products are also provided by third parties, for example, binary-only drivers that are needed by certain hardware to function properly. If you have such hardware, refer to the release notes for more information about availability of binary drivers for your system. The release notes are available from http://www.suse.com/releasenotes/, from YaST or from `/usr/share/doc/release-notes/` in your installed system.

9.1 Installing Modules and Extensions from Online Channels

The following procedure requires that you have registered your system with SUSE Customer Center, or a local registration server. If you are in the process of registering your system, you will see a list of extensions and modules immediately after having completed *Step 4* of *Section 17.8, "Registering Your System"*. In that case, skip the next steps and proceed with *Step 3*.

PROCEDURE 9.1: INSTALLING ADD-ONS AND EXTENSIONS FROM ONLINE CHANNELS WITH YAST

1. Start YaST and select *Software* › *Add-On Products*. Alternatively, start the YaST *Add-On Products* module from the command line with **sudo yast2 add-on**.

The dialog will show an overview of already installed add-on products, modules and extensions.

2. To add repositories from SUSE Customer Center (or a local registration server), select *Add › Extensions and Modules from Registration Server*.

   YaST connects to the registration server and displays a list of *Available Extensions and Modules*.

 Note: Available Extensions and Modules

> The amount of available extensions and modules depends on the registration server. A local registration server may only offer update repositories and no additional extensions.

3. Click an entry to see its description.

4. Select one or multiple entries for installation by activating their check marks.

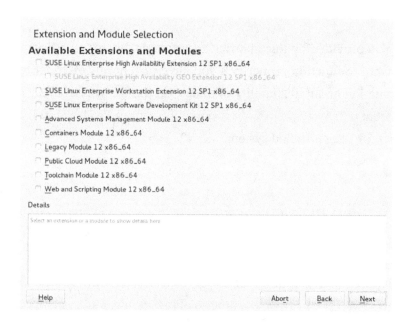

FIGURE 9.1: INSTALLATION OF SYSTEM EXTENSIONS

5. Click *Next* to proceed.

6. Depending on the repositories to be added for the extension or module, you may be asked if you want to import the GPG key with which the repository is signed or asked to agree to a license.

After confirming these messages, YaST will download and parse the metadata. The repositories for the selected extensions will be added to your system—no additional installation sources are required.

7. If needed, adjust the repository *Properties* as described in *Section 8.3.2, "Managing Repository Properties"*.

 Note: For More Information

White paper SUSE Linux Enterprise Server 12 Modules [https://www.suse.com/docrep/documents/huz0a6bf9a/suse_linux_enterprise_server_12_modules_white_paper.pdf].

9.2   Installing Extensions and Third Party Add-On Products from Media

When installing an extension or add-on product from media, you can select various types of product media, like DVD/CD, removable mass storage devices (such as flash disks), or a local directory or ISO image. The media can also be provided by a network server, for example, via HTTP, FTP, NFS, or Samba.

1. Start YaST and select *Software › Add-On Products*. Alternatively, start the YaST *Add-On Products* module from the command line with `sudo yast2 add-on`.
   The dialog will show an overview of already installed add-on products, modules and extensions.

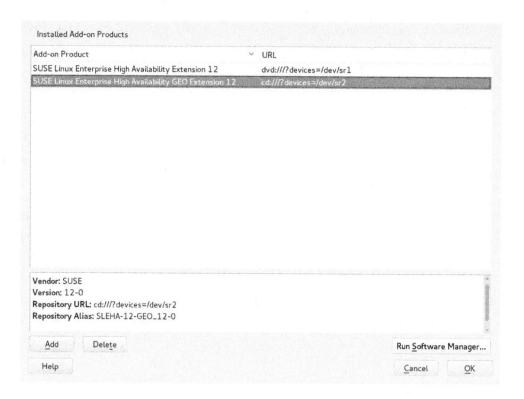

Installed Add-on Products

Add-on Product	URL
SUSE Linux Enterprise High Availability Extension 12	dvd:///?devices=/dev/sr1
SUSE Linux Enterprise High Availability GEO Extension 12	cd:///?devices=/dev/sr2

Vendor: SUSE
Version: 12-0
Repository URL: cd:///?devices=/dev/sr2
Repository Alias: SLEHA-12-GEO_12-0

Add   Delete   Run Software Manager...

Help   Cancel   OK

FIGURE 9.2: LIST OF INSTALLED ADD-ON PRODUCTS, MODULES AND EXTENSIONS

2. Choose *Add* to install a new add-on product.

3. In the *Add-On Product* dialog, select the option that matches the type of medium from which you want to install:

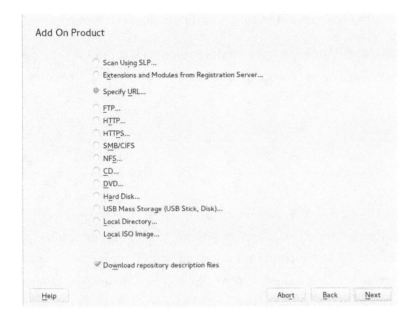

Add On Product

Scan Using SLP...
Extensions and Modules from Registration Server...
Specify URL...
FTP...
HTTP...
HTTPS...
SMB/CIFS
NFS...
CD...
DVD...
Hard Disk...
USB Mass Storage (USB Stick, Disk)...
Local Directory...
Local ISO Image...

Download repository description files

Help   Abort   Back   Next

FIGURE 9.3: INSTALLATION OF AN ADD-ON PRODUCT OR AN EXTENSION

- To scan your network for installation servers announcing their services via SLP, select *Scan Using SLP* and click *Next*.

- To add a repository from a removable medium, choose the relevant option and insert the medium or connect the USB device to the machine, respectively. Click *Next* to start the installation.

- For the majority of media types, you will be asked to specify the path (or URL) to the media after selecting the respective option and clicking *Next*. Specifying a *Repository Name* is optional. If none is specified, YaST will use the product name or the URL as the repository name.

The option *Download Repository Description Files* is activated by default. If you deactivate the option, YaST will automatically download the files later, if needed.

4. Depending on the repository you have added, you may be asked if you want to import the GPG key with which it is signed or asked to agree to a license.
After confirming these messages, YaST will download and parse the metadata. It will add the repository to the list of *Configured Repositories*.

5. If needed, adjust the repository *Properties* as described in *Section 8.3.2, "Managing Repository Properties"*.

6. Confirm your changes with *OK* to close the configuration dialog.

7. After having successfully added the repository for the add-on media, the software manager starts and you can install packages. For details, refer to *Chapter 8, Installing or Removing Software*.

9.3 SUSE Software Development Kit (SDK) 12 SP1

SUSE Software Development Kit 12 SP1 is a module for SUSE Linux Enterprise 12 SP1. It is a complete tool kit for application development. In fact, to provide a comprehensive build system, SUSE Software Development Kit 12 SP1 includes all the open source tools that were used to build the SUSE Linux Enterprise Server product. It provides you as a developer, independent software vendor (ISV), or independent hardware vendor (IHV) with all the tools needed to port applications to all the platforms supported by SUSE Linux Enterprise Desktop and SUSE Linux Enterprise Server.

SUSE Software Development Kit also contains integrated development environments (IDEs), debuggers, code editors, and other related tools. It supports most major programming languages, including C, C++, Java, and most scripting languages. For your convenience, SUSE Software Development Kit includes multiple Perl packages that are not included in SUSE Linux Enterprise.

The SDK is a module for SUSE Linux Enterprise and is available via an online channel from the SUSE Customer Center. Alternatively, go to http://download.suse.com/, search for SUSE Linux Enterprise Software Development Kit and download it from there. Refer to *Chapter 9, Installing Modules, Extensions, and Third Party Add-On Products* for details.

10 Installing Multiple Kernel Versions

SUSE Linux Enterprise Server supports the parallel installation of multiple kernel versions. When installing a second kernel, a boot entry and an initrd are automatically created, so no further manual configuration is needed. When rebooting the machine, the newly added kernel is available as an additional boot option.

Using this functionality, you can safely test kernel updates while being able to always fall back to the proven former kernel. To do so, do not use the update tools (such as the YaST Online Update or the updater applet), but instead follow the process described in this chapter.

 Warning: Support Entitlement

Be aware that you lose your entire support entitlement for the machine when installing a self-compiled or a third-party kernel. Only kernels shipped with SUSE Linux Enterprise Server and kernels delivered via the official update channels for SUSE Linux Enterprise Server are supported.

 Tip: Check Your Boot Loader Configuration Kernel

It is recommended to check your boot loader configuration after having installed another kernel to set the default boot entry of your choice. See *Book "Administration Guide", Chapter 11 "The Boot Loader GRUB 2", Section 11.3 "Configuring the Boot Loader with YaST"* for more information.

10.1 Enabling and Configuring Multiversion Support

Installing multiple versions of a software package (multiversion support) is enabled by default on SUSE Linux Enterprise 12. To verify this setting, proceed as follows:

1. Open `/etc/zypp/zypp.conf` with the editor of your choice as `root`.

2. Search for the string `multiversion`. If multiversion is enabled for all kernel packages capable of this feature, the following line appears uncommented:

```
multiversion = provides:multiversion(kernel)
```

3. To restrict multiversion support to certain kernel flavors, add the package names as a comma-separated list to the `multiversion` option in `/etc/zypp/zypp.conf` —for example

```
multiversion = kernel-default,kernel-default-base,kernel-source
```

4. Save your changes.

 Warning: Kernel Module Packages (KMP)

> Make sure that required vendor provided kernel modules (Kernel Module Packages) are also installed for the new updated kernel. The kernel update process will not warn about eventually missing kernel modules because package requirements are still fulfilled by the old kernel that is kept on the system.

10.1.1 Automatically Deleting Unused Kernels

When frequently testing new kernels with multiversion support enabled, the boot menu quickly becomes confusing. Since a `/boot` partition usually has limited space you also might run into trouble with `/boot` overflowing. While you may delete unused kernel versions manually with YaST or Zypper (as described below), you can also configure `libzypp` to automatically delete kernels no longer used. By default no kernels are deleted.

1. Open `/etc/zypp/zypp.conf` with the editor of your choice as `root`.

2. Search for the string `multiversion.kernels` and activate this option by uncommenting the line. This option takes a comma-separated list of the following values:

   `3.12.24-7.1`: keep the kernel with the specified version number

   `latest`: keep the kernel with the highest version number

   `latest-N`: keep the kernel with the Nth highest version number

   `running`: keep the running kernel

Automatically Deleting Unused Kernels

`oldest`: keep the kernel with the lowest version number (the one that was originally shipped with SUSE Linux Enterprise Server)

`oldest+N`. keep the kernel with the Nth lowest version number
Here are some examples

`multiversion.kernels = latest,running`
> Keep the latest kernel and the one currently running. This is similar to not enabling the multiversion feature, except that the old kernel is removed *after the next reboot* and not immediately after the installation.

`multiversion.kernels = latest,latest-1,running`
> Keep the last two kernels and the one currently running.

`multiversion.kernels = latest,running,3.12.25.rc7-test`
> Keep the latest kernel, the one currently running, and `3.12.25.rc7-test`.

💡 **Tip: Keep the `running` Kernel**
> Unless using special setups, you probably always want to keep the `running` Kernel. If not keeping the running Kernel, it will be deleted in case of a Kernel update. This in turn makes it necessary to immediately reboot the system after the update, since modules for the Kernel that is currently running can no longer be loaded since they have been deleted.

10.2   Installing/Removing Multiple Kernel Versions with YaST

1. Start YaST and open the software manager via *Software › Software Management.*

2. List all packages capable of providing multiple versions by choosing *View › Package Groups › Multiversion Packages.*

FIGURE 10.1: THE YAST SOFTWARE MANAGER: MULTIVERSION VIEW

3. Select a package and open its *Version* tab in the bottom pane on the left.

4. To install a package, click its check box. A green check mark indicates it is selected for installation.

   To remove an already installed package (marked with a white check mark), click its check box until a red X indicates it is selected for removal.

5. Click *Accept* to start the installation.

10.3 Installing/Removing Multiple Kernel Versions with Zypper

1. Use the command **zypper se -s 'kernel*'** to display a list of all kernel packages available:

```
S | Name           | Type       | Version        | Arch   | Repository
--+----------------+------------+----------------+--------+-------------------
v | kernel-default | package    | 2.6.32.10-0.4.1 | x86_64 | Alternative Kernel
i | kernel-default | package    | 2.6.32.9-0.5.1 | x86_64 | (System Packages)
  | kernel-default | srcpackage | 2.6.32.10-0.4.1 | noarch | Alternative Kernel
i | kernel-default | package    | 2.6.32.9-0.5.1 | x86_64 | (System Packages)
...
```

2. Specify the exact version when installing:

```
zypper in kernel-default-2.6.32.10-0.4.1
```

3. When uninstalling a kernel, use the commands **zypper se -si 'kernel*'** to list all kernels installed and **zypper rm** *PACKAGENAME-VERSION* to remove the package.

11 Managing Users with YaST

During installation, you were able to create a local user for your system. With the YaST module *User and Group Management* you can add more users or edit existing ones. It also lets you configure your system to authenticate users with a network server.

11.1 User and Group Administration Dialog

To administer users or groups, start YaST and click *Security and Users › User and Group Management*. Alternatively, start the *User and Group Administration* dialog directly by running **sudo yast2 users &** from a command line.

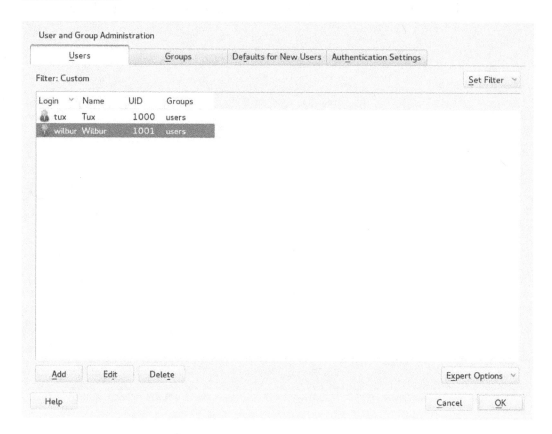

FIGURE 11.1: YAST USER AND GROUP ADMINISTRATION

Every user is assigned a system-wide user ID (UID). Apart from the users which can log in to your machine, there are also several *system users* for internal use only. Each user is assigned to one or more groups. Similar to *system users*, there are also *system groups* for internal use.

Depending on the set of users you choose to view and modify with, the dialog (local users, network users, system users), the main window shows several tabs. These allow you to execute the following tasks:

Managing User Accounts

From the *Users* tab create, modify, delete or temporarily disable user accounts as described in *Section 11.2, "Managing User Accounts"*. Learn about advanced options like enforcing password policies, using encrypted home directories, or managing disk quotas in *Section 11.3, "Additional Options for User Accounts"*.

Changing Default Settings

Local users accounts are created according to the settings defined on the *Defaults for New Users* tab. Learn how to change the default group assignment, or the default path and access permissions for home directories in *Section 11.4, "Changing Default Settings for Local Users"*.

Assigning Users to Groups

Learn how to change the group assignment for individual users in *Section 11.5, "Assigning Users to Groups"*.

Managing Groups

From the *Groups* tab, you can add, modify or delete existing groups. Refer to *Section 11.6, "Managing Groups"* for information on how to do this.

Changing the User Authentication Method

When your machine is connected to a network that provides user authentication methods like NIS or LDAP, you can choose between several authentication methods on the *Authentication Settings* tab. For more information, refer to *Section 11.7, "Changing the User Authentication Method"*.

For user and group management, the dialog provides similar functionality. You can easily switch between the user and group administration view by choosing the appropriate tab at the top of the dialog.

Filter options allow you to define the set of users or groups you want to modify: On the *Users* or *Group* tab, click *Set Filter* to view and edit users or groups according to certain categories, such as *Local Users* or *LDAP Users*, for instance (if you are part of a network which uses LDAP). With *Set Filter > Customize Filter* you can also set up and use a custom filter.

Depending on the filter you choose, not all of the following options and functions will be available from the dialog.

User and Group Administration Dialog

11.2 Managing User Accounts

YaST offers to create, modify, delete or temporarily disable user accounts. Do not modify user accounts unless you are an experienced user or administrator.

 Note: Changing User IDs of Existing Users

> File ownership is bound to the user ID, not to the user name. After a user ID change, the files in the user's home directory are automatically adjusted to reflect this change. However, after an ID change, the user no longer owns the files he created elsewhere in the file system unless the file ownership for those files are manually modified.

In the following, learn how to set up default user accounts. For some further options, such as auto login, login without password, setting up encrypted home directories or managing quotas for users and groups, refer to *Section 11.3, "Additional Options for User Accounts"*.

PROCEDURE 11.1: ADDING OR MODIFYING USER ACCOUNTS

1. Open the YaST *User and Group Administration* dialog and click the *Users* tab.

2. With *Set Filter* define the set of users you want to manage. The dialog lists users in the system and the groups the users belong to.

3. To modify options for an existing user, select an entry and click *Edit*.
   To create a new user account, click *Add*.

4. Enter the appropriate user data on the first tab, such as *Username* (which is used for login) and *Password*. This data is sufficient to create a new user. If you click *OK* now, the system will automatically assign a user ID and set all other values according to the default.

5. If you want to adjust further details such as the user ID or the path to the user's home directory, do so on the *Details* tab.
   If you need to relocate the home directory of an existing user, enter the path to the new home directory there and move the contents of the current home directory with *Move to New Location*. Otherwise, a new home directory is created without any of the existing data.

6. To force users to regularly change their password or set other password options, switch to *Password Settings* and adjust the options. For more details, refer to *Section 11.3.2, "Enforcing Password Policies"*.

7. If all options are set according to your wishes, click *OK*.

8. Click *OK* to close the administration dialog and to save the changes. A newly added user can now log in to the system using the login name and password you created. Alternatively, if you want to save all changes without exiting the *User and Group Administration* dialog, click *Expert Options* › *Write Changes Now*.

 Tip: Matching User IDs

For a new (local) user on a laptop which also needs to integrate into a network environment where this user already has a user ID, it is useful to match the (local) user ID to the ID in the network. This ensures that the file ownership of the files the user creates "offline" is the same as if he had created them directly on the network.

PROCEDURE 11.2: DISABLING OR DELETING USER ACCOUNTS

1. Open the YaST *User and Group Administration* dialog and click the *Users* tab.

2. To temporarily disable a user account without deleting it, select the user from the list and click *Edit*. Activate *Disable User Login*. The user cannot log in to your machine until you enable the account again.

3. To delete a user account, select the user from the list and click *Delete*. Choose if you also want to delete the user's home directory or if you want to retain the data.

11.3   Additional Options for User Accounts

In addition to the settings for a default user account, SUSE® Linux Enterprise Server offers further options, such as options to enforce password policies, use encrypted home directories or define disk quotas for users and groups.

11.3.1   Automatic Login and Passwordless Login

If you use the GNOME desktop environment you can configure *Auto Login* for a certain user and *Passwordless Login* for all users. Auto login causes a user to become automatically logged in to the desktop environment on boot. This functionality can only be activated for one user at a time. Login without password allows all users to log in to the system after they have entered their user name in the login manager.

Warning: Security Risk

Enabling *Auto Login* or *Passwordless Login* on a machine that can be accessed by more than one person is a security risk. Without the need to authenticate, any user can gain access to your system and your data. If your system contains confidential data, do not use this functionality.

If you want to activate auto login or login without password, access these functions in the YaST *User and Group Administration* with *Expert Options* › *Login Settings*.

11.3.2 Enforcing Password Policies

On any system with multiple users, it is a good idea to enforce at least basic password security policies. Users should change their passwords regularly and use strong passwords that cannot easily be exploited. For local users, proceed as follows:

PROCEDURE 11.3: CONFIGURING PASSWORD SETTINGS

1. Open the YaST *User and Group Administration* dialog and select the *Users* tab.

2. Select the user for which to change the password options and click *Edit*.

3. Switch to the *Password Settings* tab. The user's last password change is displayed on the tab.

4. To make the user change his password at next login, activate *Force Password Change*.

5. To enforce password rotation, set a *Maximum Number of Days for the Same Password* and a *Minimum Number of Days for the Same Password*.

6. To remind the user to change his password before it expires, set a number of *Days before Password Expiration to Issue Warning*.

7. To restrict the period of time the user can log in after his password has expired, change the value in *Days after Password Expires with Usable Login*.

8. You can also specify a certain expiration date for the complete account. Enter the *Expiration Date* in `YYYY-MM-DD` format. Note that this setting is not password-related but rather applies to the account itself.

9. For more information about the options and about the default values, click *Help*.

10. Apply your changes with *OK*.

11.3.3   Managing Encrypted Home Directories

To protect data in home directories against theft and hard disk removal, you can create encrypted home directories for users. These are encrypted with LUKS (Linux Unified Key Setup), which results in an image and an image key being generated for the user. The image key is protected with the user's login password. When the user logs in to the system, the encrypted home directory is mounted and the contents are made available to the user.

With YaST, you can create encrypted home directories for new or existing users. To encrypt or modify encrypted home directories of already existing users, you need to know the user's current login password. By default, all existing user data is copied to the new encrypted home directory, but it is not deleted from the unencrypted directory.

 Warning: Security Restrictions

Encrypting a user's home directory does not provide strong security from other users. If strong security is required, the system should not be physically shared.

Find background information about encrypted home directories and which actions to take for stronger security in *Book "Security Guide", Chapter 11 "Encrypting Partitions and Files", Section 11.2 "Using Encrypted Home Directories"*.

PROCEDURE 11.4: CREATING ENCRYPTED HOME DIRECTORIES

1. Open the YaST *User and Group Management* dialog and click the *Users* tab.

2. To encrypt the home directory of an existing user, select the user and click *Edit*. Otherwise, click *Add* to create a new user account and enter the appropriate user data on the first tab.

3. In the *Details* tab, activate *Use Encrypted Home Directory*. With *Directory Size in MB*, specify the size of the encrypted image file to be created for this user.

4. Apply your settings with *OK*.

5. Enter the user's current login password to proceed if YaST prompts for it.

6. Click *OK* to close the administration dialog and save the changes.
   Alternatively, if you want to save all changes without exiting the *User and Group Administration* dialog, click *Expert Options > Write Changes Now*.

PROCEDURE 11.5: MODIFYING OR DISABLING ENCRYPTED HOME DIRECTORIES

Of course, you can also disable the encryption of a home directory or change the size of the image file at any time.

1. Open the YaST *User and Group Administration* dialog in the *Users* view.

2. Select a user from the list and click *Edit*.

3. If you want to disable the encryption, switch to the *Details* tab and disable *Use Encrypted Home Directory*.
   If you need to enlarge or reduce the size of the encrypted image file for this user, change the *Directory Size in MB*.

4. Apply your settings with *OK*.

5. Enter the user's current login password to proceed if YaST prompts for it.

6. Click *OK* to close the administration dialog and save the changes.
   Alternatively, if you want to save all changes without exiting the *User and Group Administration* dialog, click *Expert Options* › *Write Changes Now*.

11.3.4 Managing Quotas

To prevent system capacities from being exhausted without notification, system administrators can set up quotas for users or groups. Quotas can be defined for one or more file systems and restrict the amount of disk space that can be used and the number of inodes (index nodes) that can be created there. Inodes are data structures on a file system that store basic information about a regular file, directory, or other file system object. They store all attributes of a file system object (like user and group ownership, read, write, or execute permissions), except file name and contents.

SUSE Linux Enterprise Server allows usage of `soft` and `hard` quotas. Additionally, grace intervals can be defined that allow users or groups to temporarily violate their quotas by certain amounts.

Soft Quota

Defines a warning level at which users are informed that they are nearing their limit. Administrators will urge the users to clean up and reduce their data on the partition. The soft quota limit is usually lower than the hard quota limit.

Hard Quota

Defines the limit at which write requests are denied. When the hard quota is reached, no more data can be stored and applications may crash.

Grace Period

Defines the time between the overflow of the soft quota and a warning being issued. Usually set to a rather low value of one or several hours.

PROCEDURE 11.6: ENABLING QUOTA SUPPORT FOR A PARTITION

To configure quotas for certain users and groups, you need to enable quota support for the respective partition in the YaST Expert Partitioner first.

Note: Quotas Btrfs Partitions

Quotas for Btrfs partitions are handled differently. For more information, see *Book "Storage Administration Guide", Chapter 1 "Overview of File Systems in Linux", Section 1.2.1.5 "Btrfs Quota Support for Subvolumes"*.

1. In YaST, select *System › Partitioner* and click *Yes* to proceed.

2. In the *Expert Partitioner*, select the partition for which to enable quotas and click *Edit*.

3. Click *Fstab Options* and activate *Enable Quota Support*. If the `quota` package is not already installed, it will be installed once you confirm the respective message with *Yes*.

4. Confirm your changes and leave the *Expert Partitioner*.

5. Make sure the service `quotaon` is running by entering the following command:

```
systemctl status quotaon
```

It should be marked as being `active`. If this is not the case, start it with the command **`systemctl start quotaon`**.

PROCEDURE 11.7: SETTING UP QUOTAS FOR USERS OR GROUPS

Now you can define soft or hard quotas for specific users or groups and set time periods as grace intervals.

1. In the YaST *User and Group Administration*, select the user or the group you want to set the quotas for and click *Edit*.

2. On the *Plug-Ins* tab, select the *Manage User Quota* entry and click *Launch* to open the *Quota Configuration* dialog.

3. From *File System*, select the partition to which the quota should apply.

Quota Configuration

File System
/dev/vdd3 ⌄

Size Limits
Soft limit
5000

Hard limit
8000

Days   Hours   Minutes   Seconds
0   0   0   0

I-nodes Limit
Soft limit
0

Hard limit
0

Days   Hours   Minutes   Seconds
0   0   0   0

Help   Cancel   OK

4. Below *Size Limits*, restrict the amount of disk space. Enter the number of 1 KB blocks the user or group may have on this partition. Specify a *Soft Limit* and a *Hard Limit* value.

5. Additionally, you can restrict the number of inodes the user or group may have on the partition. Below *Inodes Limits*, enter a *Soft Limit* and *Hard Limit*.

6. You can only define grace intervals if the user or group has already exceeded the soft limit specified for size or inodes. Otherwise, the time-related text boxes are not activated. Specify the time period for which the user or group is allowed to exceed the limits set above.

7. Confirm your settings with *OK*.

8. Click *OK* to close the administration dialog and save the changes.
   Alternatively, if you want to save all changes without exiting the *User and Group Administration* dialog, click *Expert Options ᐳ Write Changes Now*.

SUSE Linux Enterprise Server also ships command line tools like `repquota` or `warnquota` with which system administrators can control the disk usage or send e-mail notifications to users exceeding their quota. With **quota_nld**, administrators can also forward kernel messages about exceeded quotas to D-BUS. For more information, refer to the `repquota`, the `warnquota` and the **quota_nld** man page.

163   Managing Quotas

11.4 Changing Default Settings for Local Users

When creating new local users, several default settings are used by YaST. These include, for example, the primary group and the secondary groups the user belongs to, or the access permissions of the user's home directory. You can change these default settings to meet your requirements:

1. Open the YaST *User and Group Administration* dialog and select the *Defaults for New Users* tab.

2. To change the primary group the new users should automatically belong to, select another group from *Default Group*.

3. To modify the secondary groups for new users, add or change groups in *Secondary Groups*. The group names must be separated by commas.

4. If you do not want to use `/home/username` as default path for new users' home directories, modify the *Path Prefix for Home Directory*.

5. To change the default permission modes for newly created home directories, adjust the umask value in *Umask for Home Directory*. For more information about umask, refer to *Book "Security Guide", Chapter 10 "Access Control Lists in Linux"* and to the `umask` man page.

6. For information about the individual options, click *Help*.

7. Apply your changes with *OK*.

11.5 Assigning Users to Groups

Local users are assigned to several groups according to the default settings which you can access from the *User and Group Administration* dialog on the *Defaults for New Users* tab. In the following, learn how to modify an individual user's group assignment. If you need to change the default group assignments for new users, refer to *Section 11.4, "Changing Default Settings for Local Users"*.

PROCEDURE 11.8: CHANGING A USER'S GROUP ASSIGNMENT

1. Open the YaST *User and Group Administration* dialog and click the *Users* tab. It lists users and of the groups the users belong to.

2. Click *Edit* and switch to the *Details* tab.

3. To change the primary group the user belongs to, click *Default Group* and select the group from the list.

4. To assign the user additional secondary groups, activate the corresponding check boxes in the *Additional Groups* list.

5. Click *OK* to apply your changes.

6. Click *OK* to close the administration dialog and save the changes.
   Alternatively, if you want to save all changes without exiting the *User and Group Administration* dialog, click *Expert Options* › *Write Changes Now*.

11.6 Managing Groups

With YaST you can also easily add, modify or delete groups.

PROCEDURE 11.9: CREATING AND MODIFYING GROUPS

1. Open the YaST *User and Group Management* dialog and click the *Groups* tab.

2. With *Set Filter* define the set of groups you want to manage. The dialog lists groups in the system.

3. To create a new group, click *Add*.

4. To modify an existing group, select the group and click *Edit*.

5. In the following dialog, enter or change the data. The list on the right shows an overview of all available users and system users which can be members of the group.

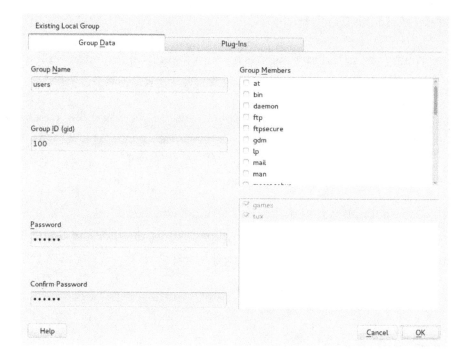

6. To add existing users to a new group select them from the list of possible *Group Members* by checking the corresponding box. To remove them from the group deactivate the box.

7. Click *OK* to apply your changes.

8. Click *OK* to close the administration dialog and save the changes.
   Alternatively, if you want to save all changes without exiting the *User and Group Administration* dialog, click *Expert Options* › *Write Changes Now*.

To delete a group, it must not contain any group members. To delete a group, select it from the list and click *Delete*. Click *OK* to close the administration dialog and save the changes. Alternatively, if you want to save all changes without exiting the *User and Group Administration* dialog, click *Expert Options* › *Write Changes Now*.

11.7 Changing the User Authentication Method

When your machine is connected to a network, you can change the authentication method. The following options are available:

NIS

>   Users are administered centrally on a NIS server for all systems in the network. For details, see *Book "Security Guide", Chapter 3 "Using NIS"*.

LDAP

>   Users are administered centrally on an LDAP server for all systems in the network. For details about LDAP, see *Book "Security Guide", Chapter 5 "LDAP—A Directory Service"*. You can manage LDAP users with the YaST user module. All other LDAP settings, including the default settings for LDAP users, need to be defined with the YaST LDAP client module as described in *Book "Security Guide", Chapter 4 "Authentication Server and Client", Section 4.2 "Configuring an Authentication Client with YaST (SSSD)"*.

Kerberos

>   With Kerberos, a user registers once and then is trusted in the entire network for the rest of the session.

Samba

>   SMB authentication is often used in mixed Linux and Windows networks. For details, see *Book "Administration Guide", Chapter 25 "Samba"*.

To change the authentication method, proceed as follows:

1. Open the *User and Group Administration* dialog in YaST.

2. Click the *Authentication Settings* tab to show an overview of the available authentication methods and the current settings.

3. To change the authentication method, click *Configure* and select the authentication method you want to modify. This takes you directly to the client configuration modules in YaST. For information about the configuration of the appropriate client, refer to the following sections:

    NIS: *Book "Security Guide", Chapter 3 "Using NIS", Section 3.2 "Configuring NIS Clients"*

LDAP: *Book "Security Guide", Chapter 4 "Authentication Server and Client", Section 4.2 "Configuring an Authentication Client with YaST (SSSD)"*

Samba: *Book "Administration Guide", Chapter 25 "Samba", Section 25.5.1 "Configuring a Samba Client with YaST"*

4. After accepting the configuration, return to the *User and Group Administration* overview.

5. Click *OK* to close the administration dialog.

Changing the User Authentication Method

12 Changing Language and Country Settings with YaST

Working in different countries or having to work in a multilingual environment requires your computer to be set up to support this. SUSE® Linux Enterprise Server can handle different locales in parallel. A locale is a set of parameters that defines the language and country settings reflected in the user interface.

The main system language was selected during installation and keyboard and time zone settings were adjusted. However, you can install additional languages on your system and determine which of the installed languages should be the default.

For those tasks, use the YaST language module as described in *Section 12.1, "Changing the System Language"*. Install secondary languages to get optional localizations if you need to start applications or desktops in languages other than the primary one.

Apart from that, the YaST timezone module allows you to adjust your country and timezone settings accordingly. It also lets you synchronize your system clock against a time server. For details, refer to *Section 12.2, "Changing the Country and Time Settings"*.

12.1 Changing the System Language

Depending on how you use your desktop and whether you want to switch the entire system to another language or only the desktop environment itself, there are several ways to achieve this:

Changing the System Language Globally

Proceed as described in *Section 12.1.1, "Modifying System Languages with YaST"* and *Section 12.1.2, "Switching the Default System Language"* to install additional localized packages with YaST and to set the default language. Changes are effective after the next login. To ensure that the entire system reflects the change, reboot the system or close and restart all running services, applications, and programs.

Changing the Language for the Desktop Only

Provided you have previously installed the desired language packages for your desktop environment with YaST as described below, you can switch the language of your desktop using the desktop's control center. After the X server has been restarted, your entire desktop reflects your new choice of language. Applications not belonging to your desktop framework are not affected by this change and may still appear in the language that was set in YaST.

Temporarily Switching Languages for One Application Only

You can also run a single application in another language (that has already been installed with YaST). To do so, start it from the command line by specifying the language code as described in *Section 12.1.3, "Switching Languages for Standard X and GNOME Applications"*.

12.1.1   Modifying System Languages with YaST

YaST knows two different language categories:

Primary Language

The primary language set in YaST applies to the entire system, including YaST and the desktop environment. This language is used whenever available unless you manually specify another language.

Secondary Languages

Install secondary languages to make your system multilingual. Languages installed as secondary languages can be selected manually for a specific situation. For example, use a secondary language to start an application in a certain language to do word processing in this language.

Before installing additional languages, determine which of them should be the default system language (primary language).

To access the YaST language module, start YaST and click *System* > *Language*. Alternatively, start the *Languages* dialog directly by running `sudo yast2 language &` from a command line.

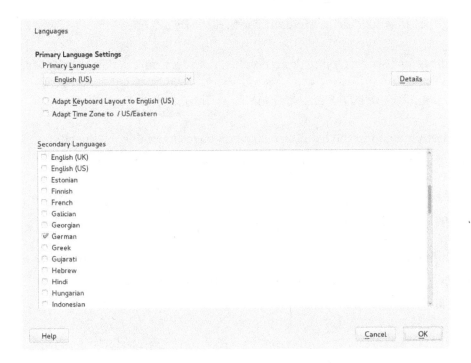

PROCEDURE 12.1: INSTALLING ADDITIONAL LANGUAGES

When installing additional languages, YaST also allows you to set different locale settings for the user `root`, see *Step 4*. The option *Locale Settings for User root* determines how the locale variables (`LC_*`) in the file `/etc/sysconfig/language` are set for `root`. You can either set them to the same locale as for normal users, keep it unaffected by any language changes or only set the variable `RC_LC_CTYPE` to the same values as for the normal users. This variable sets the localization for language-specific function calls.

1. To add additional languages in the YaST language module, select the *Secondary Languages* you want to install.

2. To make a language the default language, set it as *Primary Language*.

3. Additionally, adapt the keyboard to the new primary language and adjust the time zone, if appropriate.

 Tip: Advanced Settings

For advanced keyboard or time zone settings, select *Hardware* › *System Keyboard Layout* or *System* › *Date and Time* in YaST to start the respective dialogs. For more information, refer to *Section 7.1, "Setting Up Your System Keyboard Layout"* and *Section 12.2, "Changing the Country and Time Settings"*.

Modifying System Languages with YaST

4. To change language settings specific to the user `root`, click *Details*.

    a. Set *Locale Settings for User root* to the desired value. For more information, click *Help*.

    b. Decide if you want to *Use UTF-8 Encoding* for `root` or not.

5. If your locale was not included in the list of primary languages available, try specifying it with *Detailed Locale Setting*. However, some localizations may be incomplete.

6. Confirm your changes in the dialogs with *OK*. If you have selected secondary languages, YaST installs the localized software packages for the additional languages.

The system is now multilingual. However, to start an application in a language other than the primary one, you need to set the desired language explicitly as explained in *Section 12.1.3, "Switching Languages for Standard X and GNOME Applications"*.

12.1.2 Switching the Default System Language

1. To globally switch the default system language, start the YaST language module.

2. Select the desired new system language as *Primary Language*.

 Important: Deleting Former System Languages

If you switch to a different primary language, the localized software packages for the former primary language will be removed from the system. If you want to switch the default system language but want to keep the former primary language as additional language, add it as *Secondary Language* by enabling the respective check box.

3. Adjust the keyboard and time zone options as desired.

4. Confirm your changes with *OK*.

5. After YaST has applied the changes, restart any X sessions (for example, by logging out and logging in again) to make YaST and the desktop applications reflect your new language settings.

12.1.3 Switching Languages for Standard X and GNOME Applications

After you have installed the respective language with YaST, you can run a single application in another language.

Start the application from the command line by using the following command:

```
LANG=language application
```

For example, to start f-spot in German, run **LANG=de_DE f-spot**. For other languages, use the appropriate language code. Get a list of all language codes available with the **locale -av** command.

12.2 Changing the Country and Time Settings

Using the YaST date and time module, adjust your system date, clock and time zone information to the area you are working in. To access the YaST module, start YaST and click *System › Date and Time*. Alternatively, start the *Clock and Time Zone* dialog directly by running **sudo yast2 timezone &** from a command line.

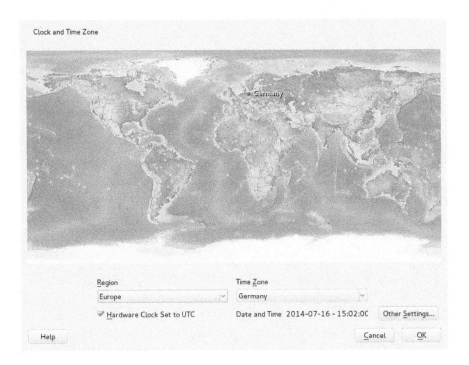

First, select a general region, such as *Europe*. Choose an appropriate country that matches the one you are working in, for example, *Germany*.

Depending on which operating systems run on your workstation, adjust the hardware clock settings accordingly:

- If you run another operating system on your machine, such as Microsoft Windows*, it is likely your system does not use UTC, but local time. In this case, deactivate *Hardware Clock Set To UTC*.

- If you only run Linux on your machine, set the hardware clock to UTC and have the switch from standard time to daylight saving time performed automatically.

> ### Important: Set the Hardware Clock to UTC
>
> The switch from standard time to daylight saving time (and vice versa) can only be performed automatically when the hardware clock (CMOS clock) is set to UTC. This also applies if you use automatic time synchronization with NTP, because automatic synchronization will only be performed if the time difference between the hardware and system clock is less than 15 minutes.
>
> Since a wrong system time can cause severe problems (missed backups, dropped mail messages, mount failures on remote file systems, etc.) it is strongly recommended to *always* set the hardware clock to UTC.

You can change the date and time manually or opt for synchronizing your machine against an NTP server, either permanently or only for adjusting your hardware clock.

PROCEDURE 12.2: MANUALLY ADJUSTING TIME AND DATE

1. In the YaST timezone module, click *Other Settings* to set date and time.

2. Select *Manually* and enter date and time values.

3. Confirm your changes.

PROCEDURE 12.3: SETTING DATE AND TIME WITH NTP SERVER

1. Click *Other Settings* to set date and time.

2. Select *Synchronize with NTP Server*.

3. Enter the address of an NTP server, if not already populated.

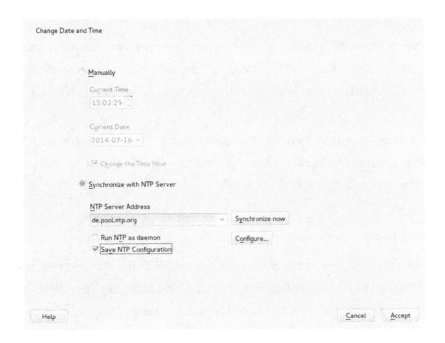

4. Click *Synchronize Now* to get your system time set correctly.

5. If you want to use NTP permanently, enable *Save NTP Configuration*.

6. With the *Configure* button, you can open the advanced NTP configuration. For details, see Book *"Administration Guide", Chapter 21 "Time Synchronization with NTP", Section 21.1 "Configuring an NTP Client with YaST"*.

7. Confirm your changes.

13 Remote Installation

SUSE® Linux Enterprise Server can be installed in different ways. Apart from the usual media installation covered in *Chapter 6, Installation with YaST*, you can choose from various network-based approaches or even take a completely hands-off approach to the installation of SUSE Linux Enterprise Server.

Each method is introduced by means of two short checklists: one listing the prerequisites for this method and the other illustrating the basic procedure. More detail is then provided for all the techniques used in these installation scenarios.

 Note: Terminology

In the following sections, the system to hold your new SUSE Linux Enterprise Server installation is called *target system* or *installation target*. The term *repository* (previously called "installation source") is used for all sources of installation data. This includes physical media, such as CD and DVD, and network servers distributing the installation data in your network.

13.1 Installation Scenarios for Remote Installation

This section introduces the most common installation scenarios for remote installations. For each scenario, carefully check the list of prerequisites and follow the procedure outlined for this scenario. If in need of detailed instructions for a particular step, follow the links provided for each one of them.

13.1.1 Simple Remote Installation via VNC—Static Network Configuration

This type of installation still requires some degree of physical access to the target system to boot for installation. The installation itself is entirely controlled by a remote workstation using VNC to connect to the installation program. User interaction is required as with the manual installation in *Chapter 6, Installation with YaST*.

For this type of installation, make sure that the following requirements are met:

- A repository, either remote or local:

    - Remote repository: NFS, HTTP, FTP, TFTP, or SMB with working network connection.

    - Local repository: DVD without the parameter `install=`

- Target system with working network connection.

- Controlling system with working network connection and VNC viewer software or Java-enabled browser (Firefox, Chromium, Internet Explorer, Opera, etc.).

- Physical boot medium (CD, DVD, or flash disk) for booting the target system.

- Valid static IP addresses already assigned to the repository and the controlling system.

- Valid static IP address to assign to the target system.

To perform this kind of installation, proceed as follows:

1. Set up the repository as described in *Section 13.2, "Setting Up the Server Holding the Installation Sources"*. Choose an NFS, HTTP, FTP, or TFTP network server. For an SMB repository, refer to *Section 13.2.5, "Managing an SMB Repository"*.

2. Boot the target system using DVD1 of the SUSE Linux Enterprise Server media kit.

3. When the boot screen of the target system appears, use the boot options prompt to set the appropriate VNC options and the address of the repository. This is described in detail in *Section 13.4, "Booting the Target System for Installation"*.
The target system boots to a text-based environment, giving the network address and display number under which the graphical installation environment can be addressed by any VNC viewer application or browser. VNC installations announce themselves over OpenSLP and if the firewall settings permit. They can be found using **slptool** as described at *Procedure 13.1, "Locating VNC installations via OpenSLP"*.

4. On the controlling workstation, open a VNC viewing application or Web browser and connect to the target system as described in *Section 13.5.1, "VNC Installation"*.

5. Perform the installation as described in *Chapter 6, Installation with YaST*. Reconnect to the target system after it reboots for the final part of the installation.

6. Finish the installation.

13.1.2 Simple Remote Installation via VNC—Dynamic Network Configuration

This type of installation still requires some degree of physical access to the target system to boot for installation. The network configuration is made with DHCP. The installation itself is entirely controlled from a remote workstation using VNC to connect to the installer, but still requires user interaction for the actual configuration efforts.

For this type of installation, make sure that the following requirements are met:

- Remote repository: NFS, HTTP, FTP, or SMB with working network connection.

- Target system with working network connection.

- Controlling system with working network connection and VNC viewer software or Java-enabled browser (Firefox, Chromium, Internet Explorer, or Opera).

- Boot the target system using DVD1 of the SUSE Linux Enterprise Server media kit.

- Running DHCP server providing IP addresses.

  To perform this kind of installation, proceed as follows:

1. Set up the repository as described in *Section 13.2, "Setting Up the Server Holding the Installation Sources"*. Choose an NFS, HTTP, or FTP network server. For an SMB repository, refer to *Section 13.2.5, "Managing an SMB Repository"*.

2. Boot the target system using DVD1 of the SUSE Linux Enterprise Server media kit.

3. When the boot screen of the target system appears, use the boot options prompt to set the appropriate VNC options and the address of the repository. This is described in detail in *Section 13.4, "Booting the Target System for Installation"*.

   The target system boots to a text-based environment, giving the network address and display number under which the graphical installation environment can be addressed by any VNC viewer application or browser. VNC installations announce themselves over OpenSLP and if the firewall settings permit. They can be found using **slptool** as described at *Procedure 13.1, "Locating VNC installations via OpenSLP"*.

4. On the controlling workstation, open a VNC viewing application or Web browser and connect to the target system as described in *Section 13.5.1, "VNC Installation"*.

5. Perform the installation as described in *Chapter 6, Installation with YaST*. Reconnect to the target system after it reboots for the final part of the installation.

6. Finish the installation.

13.1.3 Remote Installation via VNC—PXE Boot and Wake on LAN

This type of installation is completely hands-off. The target machine is started and booted remotely. User interaction is only needed for the actual installation. This approach is suitable for cross-site deployments.

To perform this type of installation, make sure that the following requirements are met:

* Remote repository: NFS, HTTP, FTP, or SMB with working network connection.

* TFTP server.

* Running DHCP server for your network.

* Target system capable of PXE boot, networking, and Wake on LAN, plugged in and connected to the network.

* Controlling system with working network connection and VNC viewer software or Java-enabled browser (Firefox, Chromium, Internet Explorer, or Opera).

   To perform this type of installation, proceed as follows:

1. Set up the repository as described in *Section 13.2, "Setting Up the Server Holding the Installation Sources"*. Choose an NFS, HTTP, or FTP network server or configure an SMB repository as described in *Section 13.2.5, "Managing an SMB Repository"*.

2. Set up a TFTP server to hold a boot image that can be pulled by the target system. This is described in *Section 13.3.2, "Setting Up a TFTP Server"*.

3. Set up a DHCP server to provide IP addresses to all machines and reveal the location of the TFTP server to the target system. This is described in *Section 13.3.1, "Setting Up a DHCP Server"*.

4. Prepare the target system for PXE boot. This is described in further detail in *Section 13.3.5, "Preparing the Target System for PXE Boot"*.

5. Initiate the boot process of the target system using Wake on LAN. This is described in *Section 13.3.7, "Wake on LAN"*.

6. On the controlling workstation, open a VNC viewing application or Web browser and connect to the target system as described in *Section 13.5.1, "VNC Installation"*.

7. Perform the installation as described in *Chapter 6, Installation with YaST*. Reconnect to the target system after it reboots for the final part of the installation.

8. Finish the installation.

13.1.4 Simple Remote Installation via SSH—Static Network Configuration

This type of installation still requires some degree of physical access to the target system to boot for installation and to determine the IP address of the installation target. The installation itself is entirely controlled from a remote workstation using SSH to connect to the installer. User interaction is required as with the regular installation described in *Chapter 6, Installation with YaST*.

For this type of installation, make sure that the following requirements are met:

- Remote repository: NFS, HTTP, FTP, or SMB with working network connection.

- Target system with working network connection.

- Controlling system with working network connection and working SSH client software.

- Boot the target system using DVD1 of the SUSE Linux Enterprise Server media kit.

- Valid static IP addresses already assigned to the repository and the controlling system.

- Valid static IP address to assign to the target system.

  To perform this kind of installation, proceed as follows:

1. Set up the repository as described in *Section 13.2, "Setting Up the Server Holding the Installation Sources"*. Choose an NFS, HTTP, or FTP network server. For an SMB repository, refer to *Section 13.2.5, "Managing an SMB Repository"*.

2. Boot the target system using DVD1 of the SUSE Linux Enterprise Server media kit.

3. When the boot screen of the target system appears, use the boot options prompt to set the appropriate parameters for network connection, address of the repository, and SSH enablement. This is described in detail in *Section 13.4.2, "Using Custom Boot Options"*.

   The target system boots to a text-based environment, giving the network address under which the graphical installation environment can be addressed by any SSH client.

4. On the controlling workstation, open a terminal window and connect to the target system as described in *Section 13.5.2.2, "Connecting to the Installation Program"*.

5. Perform the installation as described in *Chapter 6, Installation with YaST*. Reconnect to the target system after it reboots for the final part of the installation.

6. Finish the installation.

13.1.5   Simple Remote Installation via SSH—Dynamic Network Configuration

This type of installation still requires some degree of physical access to the target system to boot for installation and determine the IP address of the installation target. The installation itself is entirely controlled from a remote workstation using SSH to connect to the installer, but still requires user interaction for the actual configuration efforts.

 Note: Avoid Lost Connections After the Second Step (Installation)

> In the network settings dialog, check the *Traditional Method with ifup* and avoid Network-Manager. If not, your SSH connection will be lost during installation. Reset the settings to *User Controlled with NetworkManager* after your installation has finished.

For this type of installation, make sure that the following requirements are met:

- A repository, either remote or local:

  - Remote repository: NFS, HTTP, FTP, TFTP, or SMB with working network connection.

  - Local repository: DVD without the parameter `install=`.

- Target system with working network connection.

- Controlling system with working network connection and working SSH client software.

- Physical boot medium (CD, DVD, or flash disk) for booting the target system.

- Running DHCP server providing IP addresses.

  To perform this kind of installation, proceed as follows:

1. Set up the repository source as described in *Section 13.2, "Setting Up the Server Holding the Installation Sources"*. Choose an NFS, HTTP, or FTP network server. For an SMB repository, refer to *Section 13.2.5, "Managing an SMB Repository"*.

2. Boot the target system using DVD1 of the SUSE Linux Enterprise Server media kit.

3. When the boot screen of the target system appears, use the boot options prompt to pass the appropriate parameters for network connection, location of the installation source, and SSH enablement. See *Section 13.4.2, "Using Custom Boot Options"* for detailed instructions on the use of these parameters.
   The target system boots to a text-based environment, giving you the network address under which the graphical installation environment can be addressed by any SSH client.

4. On the controlling workstation, open a terminal window and connect to the target system as described in *Section 13.5.2.2, "Connecting to the Installation Program"*.

5. Perform the installation as described in *Chapter 6, Installation with YaST*. Reconnect to the target system after it reboots for the final part of the installation.

6. Finish the installation.

13.1.6   Remote Installation via SSH—PXE Boot and Wake on LAN

This type of installation is completely hands-off. The target machine is started and booted remotely.

To perform this type of installation, make sure that the following requirements are met:

- Remote repository: NFS, HTTP, FTP, or SMB with working network connection.

- TFTP server.

- Running DHCP server for your network, providing a static IP to the host to install.

- Target system capable of PXE boot, networking, and Wake on LAN, plugged in and connected to the network.

- Controlling system with working network connection and SSH client software.

To perform this type of installation, proceed as follows:

1. Set up the repository as described in *Section 13.2, "Setting Up the Server Holding the Installation Sources"*. Choose an NFS, HTTP, or FTP network server. For the configuration of an SMB repository, refer to *Section 13.2.5, "Managing an SMB Repository"*.

2. Set up a TFTP server to hold a boot image that can be pulled by the target system. This is described in *Section 13.3.2, "Setting Up a TFTP Server"*.

3. Set up a DHCP server to provide IP addresses to all machines and reveal the location of the TFTP server to the target system. This is described in *Section 13.3.1, "Setting Up a DHCP Server"*.

4. Prepare the target system for PXE boot. This is described in further detail in *Section 13.3.5, "Preparing the Target System for PXE Boot"*.

5. Initiate the boot process of the target system using Wake on LAN. This is described in *Section 13.3.7, "Wake on LAN"*.

6. On the controlling workstation, start an SSH client and connect to the target system as described in *Section 13.5.2, "SSH Installation"*.

7. Perform the installation as described in *Chapter 6, Installation with YaST*. Reconnect to the target system after it reboots for the final part of the installation.

8. Finish the installation.

13.2 Setting Up the Server Holding the Installation Sources

Depending on the operating system running on the machine to use as the network installation source for SUSE Linux Enterprise Server, there are several options for the server configuration. The easiest way to set up an installation server is to use YaST on SUSE Linux Enterprise Server 11/opensuse; 11.1 or higher.

Tip: Installation Server Operating System

> You can even use a Microsoft Windows machine as the installation server for your Linux
> deployment. See *Section 13.2.5, "Managing an SMB Repository"* for details.

13.2.1   Setting Up an Installation Server Using YaST

YaST offers a graphical tool for creating network repositories. It supports HTTP, FTP, and NFS
network installation servers.

1. Log in as `root` to the machine that should act as installation server.

2. Start *YaST › Miscellaneous › Installation Server*.

3. Select the repository type (HTTP, FTP, or NFS). The selected service is started automatically every time the system starts. If a service of the selected type is already running on
your system and you want to configure it manually for the server, deactivate the automatic configuration of the server service with *Do Not Configure Any Network Services*. In
both cases, define the directory in which the installation data should be made available
on the server.

4. Configure the required repository type. This step relates to the automatic configuration
of server services. It is skipped when automatic configuration is deactivated.
Define an alias for the root directory of the FTP or HTTP server on which the installation data should be found. The repository will later be located under `ftp://Serv-
er-IP/Alias/Name` (FTP) or under `http://Server-IP/Alias/Name` (HTTP). `Name`
stands for the name of the repository, which is defined in the following step. If you selected NFS in the previous step, define wild cards and export options. The NFS server will
be accessible under `nfs://Server-IP/Name`. Details of NFS and exports can be found in
Book "Administration Guide", *Chapter 26 "Sharing File Systems with NFS"*.

 Tip: Firewall Settings

> Make sure that the firewall settings of your server system allow traffic on the ports
> for HTTP, NFS, and FTP. If they currently do not, enable *Open Port in Firewall* or
> check *Firewall Details* first.

5. Configure the repository. Before the installation media are copied to their destination, define the name of the repository (ideally, an easily remembered abbreviation of the product and version). YaST allows providing ISO images of the media instead of copies of the installation DVDs. If you want this, activate the relevant check box and specify the directory path under which the ISO files can be found locally. Depending on the product to distribute using this installation server, it might be necessary to add additional media, such as service pack DVDs as extra repositories. To announce your installation server in the network via OpenSLP, activate the appropriate option.

 Tip: Announcing the Repository

Consider announcing your repository via OpenSLP if your network setup supports this option. This saves you from entering the network installation path on every target machine. The target systems are booted using the SLP boot option and find the network repository without any further configuration. For details on this option, refer to *Section 13.4, "Booting the Target System for Installation"*.

6. Configuring extra repositories. YaST follows a specific naming convention to configure add-on CDs or service pack CDs repositories. Configuration is accepted only if the repository name of the add-on CDs is preceded with the repository name of the installation media, In other words, if you chose SLES12SP1 as repository name for DVD1 than you should chose SLES12SP1addon repository name for DVD2. Same applies to SDK CDs.

7. Upload the installation data. The most lengthy step in configuring an installation server is copying the actual installation media. Insert the media in the sequence requested by YaST and wait for the copying procedure to end. When the sources have been fully copied, return to the overview of existing repositories and close the configuration by selecting *Finish*.

Your installation server is now fully configured and ready for service. It is automatically started every time the system is started. No further intervention is required. You only need to configure and start this service correctly by hand if you have deactivated the automatic configuration of the selected network service with YaST as an initial step.

To deactivate a repository, select the repository to remove then select *Delete*. The installation data are removed from the system. To deactivate the network service, use the respective YaST module.

If your installation server needs to provide the installation data for more than one product of the product version, start the YaST installation server module and select *Add* in the overview of existing repositories to configure the new repository.

13.2.2   Setting Up an NFS Repository Manually

Setting up an NFS source for installation is done in two main steps. In the first step, create the directory structure holding the installation data and copy the installation media over to this structure. Second, export the directory holding the installation data to the network.

To create a directory to hold the installation data, proceed as follows:

1. Log in as `root`.

2. Create a directory that will later hold all installation data and change into this directory. For example:

```
mkdir install/product/productversion
cd install/product/productversion
```

Replace *product* with an abbreviation of the product name and *product_version* with a string that contains the product name and version.

3. For each DVD contained in the media kit execute the following commands:

   a. Copy the entire content of the installation DVD into the installation server directory:

   ```
   cp -a /media/path_to_your_DVD_drive .
   ```

   Replace *path_to_your_DVD_drive* with the actual path under which your DVD drive is addressed. Depending on the type of drive used in your system, this can be `cdrom`, `cdrecorder`, `dvd`, or `dvdrecorder`.

   b. Rename the directory to the DVD number:

   ```
   mv path_to_your_DVD_drive DVDx
   ```

   Replace *x* with the actual number of your DVD.

On SUSE Linux Enterprise Server, you can export the repository with NFS using YaST. Proceed as follows:

1. Log in as `root`.

2. Start *YaST* › *Network Services* › *NFS Server*.

3. Select *Start* and *Open Port in Firewall* and click *Next*.

4. Select *Add Directory* and browse for the directory containing the installation sources, in this case, `productversion`.

5. Select *Add Host* and enter the host names of the machines to which to export the installation data. Instead of specifying host names here, you could also use wild cards, ranges of network addresses, or the domain name of your network. Enter the appropriate export options or leave the default, which works fine in most setups. For more information about the syntax used in exporting NFS shares, read the `exports` man page.

6. Click *Finish*. The NFS server holding the SUSE Linux Enterprise Server repository is automatically started and integrated into the boot process.

If you prefer manually exporting the repository via NFS instead of using the YaST NFS Server module, proceed as follows:

1. Log in as `root`.

2. Open the file `/etc/exports` and enter the following line:

```
/productversion *(ro,root_squash,sync)
```

This exports the directory `/productversion` to any host that is part of this network or to any host that can connect to this server. To limit the access to this server, use netmasks or domain names instead of the general wild card `*`. Refer to the `export` man page for details. Save and exit this configuration file.

3. To add the NFS service to the list of servers started during system boot, execute the following commands:

```
systemctl enable nfsserver
```

4. Start the NFS server with **systemctl start nfsserver**. If you need to change the configuration of your NFS server later, modify the configuration file and restart the NFS daemon with **systemctl restart nfsserver**.

Announcing the NFS server via OpenSLP makes its address known to all clients in your network.

1. Log in as root.

2. Create the /etc/slp.reg.d/install.suse.nfs.reg configuration file with the following lines:

```
# Register the NFS Installation Server

service:install.suse:nfs://$HOSTNAME/path_to_repository/DVD1,en,65535

description=NFS Repository
```

Replace *path_to_repository* with the actual path to the installation source on your server.

3. Start the OpenSLP daemon with **systemctl start slpd**.

For more information about OpenSLP, refer to the package documentation located under /usr/share/doc/packages/openslp/ or refer to *Book "Administration Guide", Chapter 20 "SLP"*. More Information about NFS, refer to *Book "Administration Guide", Chapter 26 "Sharing File Systems with NFS"*.

13.2.3 Setting Up an FTP Repository Manually

Creating an FTP repository is very similar to creating an NFS repository. An FTP repository can be announced over the network using OpenSLP as well.

1. Create a directory holding the installation sources as described in *Section 13.2.2, "Setting Up an NFS Repository Manually"*.

2. Configure the FTP server to distribute the contents of your installation directory:

   a. Log in as root and install the package vsftpd using the YaST software management.

b. Enter the FTP server root directory:

```
cd /srv/ftp
```

c. Create a subdirectory holding the installation sources in the FTP root directory:

```
mkdir repository
```

Replace *repository* with the product name.

d. Mount the contents of the installation repository into the change root environment of the FTP server:

```
mount --bind path_to_repository /srv/ftp/repository
```

Replace *path_to_repository* and *repository* with values matching your setup. If you need to make this permanent, add it to /etc/fstab.

e. Start vsftpd with **vsftpd**.

3. Announce the repository via OpenSLP, if this is supported by your network setup:

a. Create the /etc/slp.reg.d/install.suse.ftp.reg configuration file with the following lines:

```
# Register the FTP Installation Server
service:install.suse:ftp://$HOSTNAME/repository/DVD1,en,65535
description=FTP Repository
```

Replace *repository* with the actual name to the repository directory on your server. The service: line should be entered as one continuous line.

b. Start the OpenSLP daemon with **systemctl start slpd**.

 Tip: Configuring an FTP Server with YaST

If you prefer using YaST over manually configuring the FTP installation server, refer to *Book "Administration Guide", Chapter 30 "Setting up an FTP Server with YaST"* for more information on how to use the YaST FTP server module.

13.2.4　Setting Up an HTTP Repository Manually

Creating an HTTP repository is very similar to creating an NFS repository. An HTTP repository can be announced over the network using OpenSLP as well.

1. Create a directory holding the installation sources as described in *Section 13.2.2, "Setting Up an NFS Repository Manually"*.

2. Configure the HTTP server to distribute the contents of your installation directory:

   a. Install the Web server Apache as described in *Book "Administration Guide", Chapter 29 "The Apache HTTP Server", Section 29.1.2 "Installation"*.

   b. Enter the root directory of the HTTP server (`/srv/www/htdocs`) and create the subdirectory that will hold the installation sources:

   ```
   mkdir repository
   ```

   Replace `repository` with the product name.

   c. Create a symbolic link from the location of the installation sources to the root directory of the Web server (`/srv/www/htdocs`):

   ```
   ln -s /path_to_repository /srv/www/htdocs/repository
   ```

   d. Modify the configuration file of the HTTP server (`/etc/apache2/default-server.conf`) to make it follow symbolic links. Replace the following line:

   ```
   Options None
   ```

   with

   ```
   Options Indexes FollowSymLinks
   ```

   e. Reload the HTTP server configuration using **systemctl reload apache2**.

3. Announce the repository via OpenSLP, if this is supported by your network setup:

   a. Create the `/etc/slp.reg.d/install.suse.http.reg` configuration file with the following lines:

```
# Register the HTTP Installation Server

service:install.suse:http://$HOSTNAME/repository/DVD1/,en,65535

description=HTTP Repository
```

Replace *repository* with the actual path to the repository on your server. The <u>service:</u> line should be entered as one continuous line.

b. Start the OpenSLP daemon using **systemctl start slpd**.

13.2.5   Managing an SMB Repository

Using SMB, you can import the installation sources from a Microsoft Windows server and start your Linux deployment even with no Linux machine around.

To set up an exported Windows Share holding your SUSE Linux Enterprise Server repository, proceed as follows:

1. Log in to your Windows machine.

2. Create a new directory that will hold the entire installation tree and name it <u>INSTALL</u>, for example.

3. Export this share according the procedure outlined in your Windows documentation.

4. Enter this share and create a subdirectory, called *product*. Replace *product* with the actual product name.

5. Enter the <u>INSTALL/*product*</u> directory and copy each DVD to a separate directory, such as <u>DVD1</u> and <u>DVD2</u>.

To use an SMB mounted share as a repository, proceed as follows:

1. Boot the installation target.

2. Select *Installation*.

3. Press F4 for a selection of the repository.

4. Choose SMB and enter the Windows machine's name or IP address, the share name (INS-TALL/*product*/DVD1, in this example), user name, and password. The syntax looks like this:

```
smb://workdomain;user:password@server/INSTALL/DVD1
```

After you press Enter , YaST starts and you can perform the installation.

13.2.6   Using ISO Images of the Installation Media on the Server

Instead of copying physical media into your server directory manually, you can also mount the ISO images of the installation media into your installation server and use them as a repository. To set up an HTTP, NFS or FTP server that uses ISO images instead of media copies, proceed as follows:

1. Download the ISO images and save them to the machine to use as the installation server.

2. Log in as root.

3. Choose and create an appropriate location for the installation data, as described in *Section 13.2.2, "Setting Up an NFS Repository Manually", Section 13.2.3, "Setting Up an FTP Repository Manually", or Section 13.2.4, "Setting Up an HTTP Repository Manually".*

4. Create subdirectories for each DVD.

5. To mount and unpack each ISO image to the final location, issue the following command:

```
mount -o loop path_to_isopath_to_repository/product/mediumx
```

Replace *path_to_iso* with the path to your local copy of the ISO image, *path_to_repository* with the source directory of your server, *product* with the product name, and *mediumx* with the type (CD or DVD) and number of media you are using.

6. Repeat the previous step to mount all ISO images needed for your product.

7. Start your installation server as usual, as described in *Section 13.2.2, "Setting Up an NFS Repository Manually", Section 13.2.3, "Setting Up an FTP Repository Manually", or Section 13.2.4, "Setting Up an HTTP Repository Manually".*

To automatically mount the ISO images at boot time, add the respective mount entries to `/etc/fstab`. An entry according to the previous example would look like the following:

```
path_to_iso path_to_repository/productmedium auto loop
```

13.3   Preparing the Boot of the Target System

This section covers the configuration tasks needed in complex boot scenarios. It contains ready-to-apply configuration examples for DHCP, PXE boot, TFTP, and Wake on LAN.

13.3.1   Setting Up a DHCP Server

There are two ways to set up a DHCP server. For SUSE Linux Enterprise Server, YaST provides a graphical interface to the process. Users can also manually edit the configuration files. For more information about DHCP servers, see also *Book "Administration Guide", Chapter 23 "DHCP"*.

13.3.1.1   Setting Up a DHCP Server with YaST

To announce the TFTP server's location to the network clients and specify the boot image file the installation target should use, add two declarations to your DHCP server configuration.

1. Log in as `root` to the machine hosting the DHCP server.

2. Start *YaST* › *Network Services* › *DHCP Server*.

3. Complete the setup wizard for basic DHCP server setup.

4. Select *Expert Settings* and select *Yes* when warned about leaving the start-up dialog.

5. In the *Configured Declarations* dialog, select the subnet in which the new system should be located and click *Edit*.

6. In the *Subnet Configuration* dialog select *Add* to add a new option to the subnet's configuration.

7. Select `filename` and enter `pxelinux.0` as the value.

8. Add another option (`next-server`) and set its value to the address of the TFTP server.

9. Select *OK* and *Finish* to complete the DHCP server configuration.

To configure DHCP to provide a static IP address to a specific host, enter the *Expert Settings* of the DHCP server configuration module (*Step 4*) and add a new declaration of the host type. Add the options `hardware` and `fixed-address` to this host declaration and provide the appropriate values.

13.3.1.2   Setting Up a DHCP Server Manually

All the DHCP server needs to do, apart from providing automatic address allocation to your network clients, is to announce the IP address of the TFTP server and the file that needs to be pulled in by the installation routines on the target machine.

1. Log in as `root` to the machine hosting the DHCP server.

2. Append the following lines to a subnet configuration of your DHCP server's configuration file located under `/etc/dhcpd.conf`:

```
subnet 192.168.1.0 netmask 255.255.255.0 {
  range dynamic-bootp 192.168.1.200 192.168.1.228;
  # PXE related settings
  #
  # "next-server" defines the TFTP server that will be used
  next-server ip_tftp_server;
  #
  # "filename" specifies the pxelinux image on the TFTP server
  # the server runs in chroot under /srv/tftpboot
  filename  "pxelinux.0";
}
```

Replace *ip_of_the_tftp_server* with the actual IP address of the TFTP server. For more information about the options available in `dhcpd.conf`, refer to the `dhcpd.conf` manual page.

3. Restart the DHCP server by executing **systemctl restart dhcpd**.

If you plan on using SSH for the remote control of a PXE and Wake on LAN installation, explicitly specify the IP address DHCP should provide to the installation target. To achieve this, modify the above mentioned DHCP configuration according to the following example:

```
group {
  # PXE related settings
  #
  # "next-server" defines the TFTP server that will be used
  next-server ip_tftp_server:
  #
  # "filename" specifies the pxelinux image on the TFTP server
  # the server runs in chroot under /srv/tftpboot
  filename "pxelinux.0";
  host test {
    hardware ethernet mac_address;
    fixed-address some_ip_address;
    }
}
```

The host statement introduces the host name of the installation target. To bind the host name and IP address to a specific host, you must know and specify the system's hardware (MAC) address. Replace all the variables used in this example with the actual values that match your environment.

After restarting the DHCP server, it provides a static IP to the host specified, enabling you to connect to the system via SSH.

13.3.2   Setting Up a TFTP Server

If using a SUSE based installation, you may use YaST to set up a TFTP Server. Alternatively, set it up manually. The TFTP server delivers the boot image to the target system after it boots and sends a request for it.

13.3.2.1   Setting Up a TFTP Server Using YaST

1. Log in as root.

2. Start *YaST* › *Network Services* › *TFTP Server* and install the requested package.

3. Click *Enable* to make sure that the server is started and included in the boot routines. No further action from your side is required to secure this. xinetd starts tftpd at boot time.

4. Click *Open Port in Firewall* to open the appropriate port in the firewall running on your machine. If there is no firewall running on your server, this option is not available.

5. Click *Browse* to browse for the boot image directory. The default directory `/tftpboot` is created and selected automatically.

6. Click *Finish* to apply your settings and start the server.

13.3.2.2   Setting Up a TFTP Server Manually

1. Log in as `root` and install the packages `tftp` and `xinetd`.

2. If unavailable, create `/srv/tftpboot` and `/srv/tftpboot/pxelinux.cfg` directories.

3. Add the appropriate files needed for the boot image as described in *Section 13.3.3, "Using PXE Boot"*.

4. Modify the configuration of xinetd located under `/etc/xinetd.d` to make sure that the TFTP server is started on boot:

   a. If it does not exist, create a file called `tftp` under this directory with **touch tftp**. Then run **chmod 755 tftp**.

   b. Open the file `tftp` and add the following lines:

```
service tftp
{
        socket_type             = dgram
        protocol                = udp
        wait                    = yes
        user                    = root
        server                  = /usr/sbin/in.tftpd
        server_args             = -s /srv/tftpboot
        disable                 = no
}
```

c. Save the file and restart xinetd with **rcxinetd restart**.

13.3.3 Using PXE Boot

Some technical background information and PXE's complete specifications are available in the Preboot Execution Environment (PXE) Specification (http://www.pix.net/software/pxe-boot/archive/pxespec.pdf).

1. Change to the directory `boot/<architecture>/loader` of your installation repository and copy the `linux`, `initrd`, `message`, `biostest`, and `memtest` files to the `/srv/tftpboot` directory by entering the following:

```
cp -a linux initrd message biostest memtest /srv/tftpboot
```

2. Install the `syslinux` package directly from your installation DVDs with YaST.

3. Copy the `/usr/share/syslinux/pxelinux.0` file to the `/srv/tftpboot` directory by entering the following:

```
cp -a /usr/share/syslinux/pxelinux.0 /srv/tftpboot
```

4. Change to the directory of your installation repository and copy the `isolinux.cfg` file to `/srv/tftpboot/pxelinux.cfg/default` by entering the following:

```
cp -a boot/<architecture>/loader/isolinux.cfg /srv/tftpboot/pxelinux.cfg/
default
```

5. Edit the `/srv/tftpboot/pxelinux.cfg/default` file and remove the lines beginning with `readinfo` and `framebuffer`.

6. Insert the following entries in the append lines of the default `failsafe` and `apic` labels:

`insmod=kernel module`

By means of this entry, enter the network Kernel module needed to support network installation on the PXE client. Replace `kernel module` with the appropriate module name for your network device.

`netdevice=`*`interface`*

> This entry defines the client's network interface that must be used for the network installation. It is only necessary if the client is equipped with several network cards and must be adapted accordingly. In case of a single network card, this entry can be omitted.

`install=nfs://`*`ip_instserver/path_to_repository`*`/DVD1`

> This entry defines the NFS server and the repository for the client installation. Replace *`ip_instserver`* with the actual IP address of your installation server. *`path_to_repository`* should be replaced with the actual path to the repository. HTTP, FTP, or SMB repositories are addressed in a similar manner, except for the protocol prefix, which should read `http`, `ftp`, or `smb`.

> ### ❗ Important: Adding Boot Options
>
> If you need to pass other boot options to the installation routines, such as SSH or VNC boot parameters, append them to the `install` entry. An overview of parameters and some examples are given in *Section 13.4, "Booting the Target System for Installation"*.

> ### 💡 Tip: Changing Kernel and initrd File Names
>
> It is possible to use different file names for Kernel and initrd images. This is useful if you want to provide different operating systems from the same boot server. However, you should be aware that only one dot is permitted in the file names that are provided by TFTP for the PXE boot.

An example `/srv/tftpboot/pxelinux.cfg/default` file follows. Adjust the protocol prefix for the repository to match your network setup and specify your preferred method of connecting to the installer by adding the `vnc` and `VNCPassword` or the `ssh` and `ssh.password` options to the `install` entry. The lines separated by `\` must be entered as one continuous line without a line break and without the `\`.

```
default harddisk

# default
```

```
label linux
  kernel linux
  append initrd=initrd ramdisk_size=65536 \
    install=nfs://ip_instserver/path_to_repository/product/DVD1

# repair
label repair
  kernel linux
  append initrd=initrd splash=silent repair=1 showopts

# rescue
label rescue
  kernel linux
  append initrd=initrd ramdisk_size=65536 rescue=1

# bios test
label firmware
  kernel linux
  append initrd=biostest,initrd splash=silent install=exec:/bin/run_biostest
  showopts

#  memory test
label memtest
  kernel memtest

#  hard disk
label harddisk
  localboot 0

implicit     0
display      message
prompt       1
timeout      100
```

7. Replace *ip_instserver* and *path_to_repository* with the values used in your setup.

The following section serves as a short reference to the PXELINUX options used in this setup. Find more information about the options available in the documentation of the `syslinux` package located under `/usr/share/doc/packages/syslinux/`.

13.3.4   PXELINUX Configuration Options

The options listed here are a subset of all the options available for the PXELINUX configuration file.

APPEND *options...*

Add one or more options to the Kernel command line. These are added for both automatic and manual boots. The options are added at the very beginning of the Kernel command line, usually permitting explicitly entered Kernel options to override them.

APPEND -

Append nothing. `APPEND` with a single hyphen as argument in a `LABEL` section can be used to override a global `APPEND`.

DEFAULT *kernel options...*

Sets the default Kernel command line. If PXELINUX boots automatically, it acts as if the entries after DEFAULT had been typed in at the boot prompt, except the auto option is automatically added, indicating an automatic boot.

If no configuration file exists or no DEFAULT entry is defined in the configuration file, the default is the Kernel name "linux" with no options.

IFAPPEND *FLAG*

Adds a specific option to the kernel command line depending on the *FLAG* value. The `IFAPPEND` option is available only on PXELINUX. *FLAG* expects a value, described in *Table 13.1, "Generated and Added Kernel Command Line Options from* `IFAPPEND`*":*

TABLE 13.1: GENERATED AND ADDED KERNEL COMMAND LINE OPTIONS FROM `IFAPPEND`

Argument	Generated Kernel Command Line / Description
1	`ip=CLIENT_IP:BOOT_SERVER_IP:GW_IP:NETMASK`
	The placeholders are replaced based on the input from the DHCP/ BOOTP or PXE boot server.

Argument	Generated Kernel Command Line / Description
	Note, this option is not a substitute for running a DHCP client in the booted system. Without regular renewals, the lease acquired by the PXE BIOS will expire, making the IP address available for reuse by the DHCP server.
2	`BOOTIF=MAC_ADDRESS_OF_BOOT_INTERFACE` This option is useful if you want to avoid timeouts when the installation server probes one LAN interface after the other until it gets a reply from a DHCP server. Using this option allows an initrd program to determine from which interface the system has been booted. linuxrc reads this option and uses this network interface.
4	`SYSUUID=SYSTEM_UUID` Adds UUIDs in lowercase hexadecimals, see `/usr/share/doc/packages/syslinux/pxelinux.txt`

`LABEL label KERNEL image APPEND options...`

Indicates that if `label` is entered as the Kernel to boot, PXELINUX should instead boot `image` and the specified `APPEND` options should be used instead of the ones specified in the global section of the file (before the first `LABEL` command). The default for `image` is the same as `label` and, if no `APPEND` is given, the default is to use the global entry (if any). Up to 128 `LABEL` entries are permitted.

PXELINUX uses the following syntax:

```
label mylabel
  kernel mykernel
  append myoptions
```

Labels are mangled as if they were file names and they must be unique after mangling. For example, the two labels "v2.6.30" and "v2.6.31" would not be distinguishable under PXELINUX because both mangle to the same DOS file name.

The Kernel does not need to be a Linux Kernel; it can be a boot sector or a COMBOOT file.

LOCALBOOT *type*

On PXELINUX, specifying `LOCALBOOT 0` instead of a `KERNEL` option means invoking this particular label and causes a local disk boot instead of a Kernel boot.

Argument	Description
0	Perform a normal boot
4	Perform a local boot with the Universal Network Driver Interface (UNDI) driver still resident in memory
5	Perform a local boot with the entire PXE stack, including the UNDI driver, still resident in memory

All other values are undefined. If you do not know what the UNDI or PXE stacks are, specify `0`.

TIMEOUT *time-out*

Indicates how long to wait at the boot prompt until booting automatically, in units of 1/10 second. The time-out is canceled as soon as the user types anything on the keyboard, assuming the user will complete the command begun. A time-out of zero disables the time-out completely (this is also the default). The maximum possible time-out value is 35996 (just less than one hour).

PROMPT *flag_val*

If `flag_val` is 0, displays the boot prompt only if `Shift` or `Alt` is pressed or `Caps Lock` or `Scroll Lock` is set (this is the default). If `flag_val` is 1, always displays the boot prompt.

```
F2  filename
F1  filename
..etc...
F9  filename
F10 filename
```

Displays the indicated file on the screen when a function key is pressed at the boot prompt. This can be used to implement preboot online help (presumably for the Kernel command line options). For backward compatibility with earlier releases, `F10` can be also entered as `F0`. Note that there is currently no way to bind file names to `F11` and `F12`.

13.3.5   Preparing the Target System for PXE Boot

Prepare the system's BIOS for PXE boot by including the PXE option in the BIOS boot order.

 Warning: BIOS Boot Order

Do not place the PXE option ahead of the hard disk boot option in the BIOS. Otherwise this system would try to re-install itself every time you boot it.

13.3.6   Preparing the Target System for Wake on LAN

Wake on LAN (WOL) requires the appropriate BIOS option to be enabled prior to the installation. Also, note down the MAC address of the target system. This data is needed to initiate Wake on LAN.

13.3.7   Wake on LAN

Wake on LAN allows a machine to be turned on by a special network packet containing the machine's MAC address. Because every machine in the world has a unique MAC identifier, you do not need to worry about accidentally turning on the wrong machine.

 Important: Wake on LAN across Different Network Segments

If the controlling machine is not located in the same network segment as the installation target that should be awakened, either configure the WOL requests to be sent as multicasts or remotely control a machine on that network segment to act as the sender of these requests.

Users of SUSE Linux Enterprise Server can use a YaST module called WOL to easily configure Wake on LAN. Users of other versions of SUSE Linux-based operating systems can use a command line tool.

13.3.8 Wake on LAN with YaST

1. Log in as `root`.

2. Start *YaST* > *Network Services* > *WOL*.

3. Click *Add* and enter the host name and MAC address of the target system.

4. To turn on this machine, select the appropriate entry and click *Wake up*.

13.4 Booting the Target System for Installation

There are two different ways to customize the boot process for installation apart from those mentioned under *Section 13.3.7, "Wake on LAN"* and *Section 13.3.3, "Using PXE Boot"*. You can either use the default boot options and function keys or use the boot options prompt of the installation boot screen to pass any boot options that the installation Kernel might need on this particular hardware.

13.4.1 Using the Default Boot Options

The boot options are described in detail in *Chapter 6, Installation with YaST*. Generally, selecting *Installation* starts the installation boot process.

If problems occur, use *Installation—ACPI Disabled* or *Installation—Safe Settings*. For more information about troubleshooting the installation process, refer to *Book "Administration Guide", Chapter 37 "Common Problems and Their Solutions", Section 37.2 "Installation Problems"*.

The menu bar at the bottom screen offers some advanced functionality needed in some setups. Using the F keys, you can specify additional options to pass to the installation routines without having to know the detailed syntax of these parameters (see *Section 13.4.2, "Using Custom Boot Options"*). A detailed description of the available function keys is available at *Section 6.2.2.1, "The Boot Screen on Machines Equipped with Traditional BIOS"*.

13.4.2 Using Custom Boot Options

Using the appropriate set of boot options helps simplify your installation procedure. Many parameters can also be configured later using the linuxrc routines, but using the boot options is easier. In some automated setups, the boot options can be provided with `initrd` or an `info` file.

The following table lists all installation scenarios mentioned in this chapter with the required parameters for booting and the corresponding boot options. Append all of them in the order they appear in this table to get one boot option string that is handed to the installation routines. For example (all in one line):

```
install=xxx netdevice=xxx hostip=xxx netmask=xxx vnc=xxx VNCPassword=xxx
```

Replace all the values *xxx* in this string with the values appropriate for your setup.

Chapter 6, Installation with YaST

Parameters Needed for Booting. None

Boot Options. None needed

Section 13.1.1, "Simple Remote Installation via VNC—Static Network Configuration"

PARAMETERS NEEDED FOR BOOTING

- Location of the installation server
- Network device
- IP address
- Netmask
- Gateway
- VNC enablement
- VNC password

BOOT OPTIONS

- `install=(nfs,http,ftp,smb)://path_to_instmedia`
- `netdevice=some_netdevice` (only needed if several network devices are available)
- `hostip=some_ip`
- `netmask=some_netmask`
- `gateway=ip_gateway`
- `vnc=1`
- `VNCPassword=some_password`

Section 13.1.2, "Simple Remote Installation via VNC—Dynamic Network Configuration"

- Location of the installation server
- VNC enablement
- VNC password

- `install=(nfs,http,ftp,smb)://`*`path_to_instmedia`*
- `vnc=1`
- `VNCPassword=`*`some_password`*

Section 13.1.3, "Remote Installation via VNC—PXE Boot and Wake on LAN"

- Location of the installation server
- Location of the TFTP server
- VNC enablement
- VNC password

Boot Options.   Not applicable; process managed through PXE and DHCP

Section 13.1.4, "Simple Remote Installation via SSH—Static Network Configuration"

- Location of the installation server
- Network device
- IP address
- Netmask
- Gateway
- SSH enablement
- SSH password

- `install=(nfs,http,ftp,smb)://`*`path_to_instmedia`*
- `netdevice=`*`some_netdevice`* (only needed if several network devices are available)
- `hostip=`*`some_ip`*
- `netmask=`*`some_netmask`*

- `gateway=ip_gateway`
- `ssh=1`
- `ssh.password=some_password`

Section 13.1.5, "Simple Remote Installation via SSH—Dynamic Network Configuration"

PARAMETERS NEEDED FOR BOOTING

- Location of the installation server
- SSH enablement
- SSH password

BOOT OPTIONS

- `install=(nfs,http,ftp,smb)://path_to_instmedia`
- `ssh=1`
- `ssh.password=some_password`

Section 13.1.6, "Remote Installation via SSH—PXE Boot and Wake on LAN"

- Location of the installation server
- Location of the TFTP server
- SSH enablement
- SSH password

Boot Options. Not applicable; process managed through PXE and DHCP

 Tip: More Information about linuxrc Boot Options

Find more information about the linuxrc boot options used for booting a Linux system at http://en.opensuse.org/SDB:Linuxrc.

13.4.2.1 Installing Add-On Products and Driver Updates

SUSE Linux Enterprise Server supports the installation of add-on products providing extensions (for example the SUSE Linux Enterprise High Availability Extension), third-party products and drivers or additional software. To automatically install an add-on product when deploying SUSE Linux Enterprise Server remotely, specify the `addon=REPOSITORY` parameter.

REPOSITORY needs to be a hosted repository that can be read by YaST (YaST2 or YUM (rpm-md)). ISO images are currently not supported.

Tip: Driver Updates

Driver Updates can be found at http://drivers.suse.com/. Not all driver updates are provided as repositories—some are only available as iso images and therefore cannot be installed with the addon parameter. Instructions on how to install driver updates via iso image are available at http://drivers.suse.com/doc/SolidDriver/Driver_Kits.html.

13.5   Monitoring the Installation Process

There are several options for remotely monitoring the installation process. If the proper boot options have been specified while booting for installation, either VNC or SSH can be used to control the installation and system configuration from a remote workstation.

13.5.1   VNC Installation

Using any VNC viewer software, you can remotely control the installation of SUSE Linux Enterprise Server from virtually any operating system. This section introduces the setup using a VNC viewer application or a Web browser.

13.5.1.1   Preparing for VNC Installation

All you need to do on the installation target to prepare for a VNC installation is to provide the appropriate boot options at the initial boot for installation (see *Section 13.4.2, "Using Custom Boot Options"*). The target system boots into a text-based environment and waits for a VNC client to connect to the installation program.

The installation program announces the IP address and display number needed to connect for installation. If you have physical access to the target system, this information is provided right after the system booted for installation. Enter this data when your VNC client software prompts for it and provide your VNC password.

Because the installation target announces itself via OpenSLP, you can retrieve the address information of the installation target via an SLP browser without the need for any physical contact to the installation itself, provided your network setup and all machines support OpenSLP:

PROCEDURE 13.1: LOCATING VNC INSTALLATIONS VIA OPENSLP

1. Run **slptool findsrvtypes | grep vnc** to get a list of all services offering vnc. The vnc installation targets should be available under a service named `YaST.installation.suse`.

2. Run **slptool findsrvs** *YaST.installation.suse* to get a list of installations available. Use the IP address and the port (usually `5901`) provided with your VNC viewer.

13.5.1.2   Connecting to the Installation Program

There are two ways to connect to a VNC server (the installation target in this case). You can either start an independent VNC viewer application on any operating system or connect using a Java-enabled Web browser.

Using VNC, you can control the installation of a Linux system from any other operating system, including other Linux flavors, Windows, or Mac OS.

On a Linux machine, make sure that the package `tightvnc` is installed. On a Windows machine, install the Windows port of this application, which can be obtained at the TightVNC home page (http://www.tightvnc.com/download.html).

To connect to the installation program running on the target machine, proceed as follows:

1. Start the VNC viewer.

2. Enter the IP address and display number of the installation target as provided by the SLP browser or the installation program itself:

```
ip_address:display_number
```

A window opens on your desktop displaying the YaST screens as in a normal local installation.

Using a Web browser to connect to the installation program makes you totally independent of any VNC software or the underlying operating system. As long as the browser application has Java support enabled, you can use any browser (Firefox, Internet Explorer, Chromium, Opera, etc.) to perform the installation of your Linux system.

To perform a VNC installation, proceed as follows:

1. Launch your preferred Web browser.

2. Enter the following at the address prompt:

```
http://ip_address_of_target:5801
```

3. Enter your VNC password when prompted to do so. The browser window now displays the YaST screens as in a normal local installation.

13.5.2 SSH Installation

Using SSH, you can remotely control the installation of your Linux machine using any SSH client software.

13.5.2.1 Preparing for SSH Installation

Apart from installing the appropriate software package (OpenSSH for Linux and PuTTY for Windows), you need to pass the appropriate boot options to enable SSH for installation. See *Section 13.4.2, "Using Custom Boot Options"* for details. OpenSSH is installed by default on any SUSE Linux–based operating system.

13.5.2.2 Connecting to the Installation Program

1. Retrieve the installation target's IP address. If you have physical access to the target machine, take the IP address the installation routine provides at the console after the initial boot. Otherwise take the IP address that has been assigned to this particular host in the DHCP server configuration.

2. At a command line, enter the following command:

```
ssh -X root@
ip_address_of_target
```

   Replace `ip_address_of_target` with the actual IP address of the installation target.

3. When prompted for a user name, enter `root`.

4. When prompted for the password, enter the password that has been set with the SSH boot option. After you have successfully authenticated, a command line prompt for the installation target appears.

5. Enter **yast** to launch the installation program. A window opens showing the normal YaST screens as described in *Chapter 6, Installation with YaST*.

14 Advanced Disk Setup

Sophisticated system configurations require specific disk setups. All common partitioning tasks can be done with YaST. To get persistent device naming with block devices, use the block devices below `/dev/disk/by-id` or `/dev/disk/by-uuid`. Logical Volume Management (LVM) is a disk partitioning scheme that is designed to be much more flexible than the physical partitioning used in standard setups. Its snapshot functionality enables easy creation of data backups. Redundant Array of Independent Disks (RAID) offers increased data integrity, performance, and fault tolerance. SUSE Linux Enterprise Server also supports multipath I/O (see *Book "Storage Administration Guide", Chapter 15 "Managing Multipath I/O for Devices"* for details), and there is also the option to use iSCSI as a networked disk (read more about iSCSI in *Book "Storage Administration Guide", Chapter 13 "Mass Storage over IP Networks: iSCSI"*).

14.1 Using the YaST Partitioner

With the expert partitioner, shown in *Figure 14.1, "The YaST Partitioner"*, manually modify the partitioning of one or several hard disks. You can add, delete, resize, and edit partitions, or access the soft RAID, and LVM configuration.

 Warning: Repartitioning the Running System

> Although it is possible to repartition your system while it is running, the risk of making a mistake that causes data loss is very high. Try to avoid repartitioning your installed system and always do a complete backup of your data before attempting to do so.

Device	Size	F	Enc	Type	FS Type	Label	Mount Point
/dev/sda	30.00 GiB			QEMU-HARDDISK			
/dev/sda1	2.01 GiB			Linux swap	Swap		swap
/dev/sda2	12.00 GiB			Linux native	BtrFS		/
/dev/sda3	15.99 GiB			Linux native	XFS		/home
tmpfs	946.71 MiB			TMPFS	TmpFS		/dev/shm
tmpfs	946.71 MiB			TMPFS	TmpFS		/run
tmpfs	946.71 MiB			TMPFS	TmpFS		/sys/fs/cgroup

FIGURE 14.1: THE YAST PARTITIONER

 Tip: IBM z Systems: Device Names

IBM z Systems recognizes only DASD and SCSI hard disks. IDE hard disks are not supported. This is why these devices appear in the partition table as `dasda` or `sda` for the first recognized device.

All existing or suggested partitions on all connected hard disks are displayed in the list of *Available Storage* in the YaST *Expert Partitioner* dialog. Entire hard disks are listed as devices without numbers, such as `/dev/sda` (or `/dev/dasda`). Partitions are listed as parts of these devices, such as `/dev/sda1` (or `/dev/dasda1`, respectively). The size, type, encryption status, file system, and mount point of the hard disks and their partitions are also displayed. The mount point describes where the partition appears in the Linux file system tree.

Several functional views are available on the left hand *System View*. Use these views to gather information about existing storage configurations, or to configure functions like `RAID`, `Volume Management`, `Crypt Files`, or view file systems with additional features, such as Btrfs, NFS, or `TMPFS`.

If you run the expert dialog during installation, any free hard disk space is also listed and automatically selected. To provide more disk space to SUSE® Linux Enterprise Server, free the needed space starting from the bottom toward the top of the list (starting from the last partition of a hard disk toward the first).

14.1.1   Partition Types

 Tip: IBM z Systems: Hard Disks

On IBM z Systems platforms, SUSE Linux Enterprise Server supports SCSI hard disks and DASDs (direct access storage devices). While SCSI disks can be partitioned as described below, DASDs can have no more than three partition entries in their partition tables.

Every hard disk has a partition table with space for four entries. Every entry in the partition table corresponds to a primary partition or an extended partition. Only one extended partition entry is allowed, however.

A primary partition simply consists of a continuous range of cylinders (physical disk areas) assigned to a particular operating system. With primary partitions you would be limited to four partitions per hard disk, because more do not fit in the partition table. This is why extended partitions are used. Extended partitions are also continuous ranges of disk cylinders, but an extended partition may be divided into *logical partitions* itself. Logical partitions do not require entries in the partition table. In other words, an extended partition is a container for logical partitions.

If you need more than four partitions, create an extended partition as the fourth partition (or earlier). This extended partition should occupy the entire remaining free cylinder range. Then create multiple logical partitions within the extended partition. The maximum number of logical partitions is 63, independent of the disk type. It does not matter which types of partitions are used for Linux. Primary and logical partitions both function normally.

Tip: GPT Partition Table

If you need to create more than 4 primary partitions on one hard disk, you need to use the GPT partition type. This type removes the primary partitions number restriction, and supports partitions bigger than 2 TB as well.

To use GPT, run the YaST Partitioner, click the relevant disk name in the *System View* and choose *Expert* › *Create New Partition Table* › *GPT*.

14.1.2   Creating a Partition

To create a partition from scratch select *Hard Disks* and then a hard disk with free space. The actual modification can be done in the *Partitions* tab:

1. Select *Add* and specify the partition type (primary or extended). Create up to four primary partitions or up to three primary partitions and one extended partition. Within the extended partition, create several logical partitions (see *Section 14.1.1, "Partition Types"*).

2. Specify the size of the new partition. You can either choose to occupy all the free unpartitioned space, or enter a custom size.

3. Select the file system to use and a mount point. YaST suggests a mount point for each partition created. To use a different mount method, like mount by label, select *Fstab Options*. For more information on supported file systems, see `root`.

4. Specify additional file system options if your setup requires them. This is necessary, for example, if you need persistent device names. For details on the available options, refer to *Section 14.1.3, "Editing a Partition"*.

5. Click *Finish* to apply your partitioning setup and leave the partitioning module.
   If you created the partition during installation, you are returned to the installation overview screen.

14.1.2.1 Btrfs Partitioning

The default file system for the root partition is Btrfs (see *Book "Administration Guide", Chapter 3 "System Recovery and Snapshot Management with Snapper"* and *Book "Storage Administration Guide", Chapter 1 "Overview of File Systems in Linux"* for more information on Btrfs). The root file system is the default subvolume and it is not listed in the list of created subvolumes. As a default Btrfs subvolume, it can be mounted as a normal file system.

 Important: Btrfs on an Encrypted Root Partition

The default partitioning setup suggests the root partition as Btrfs with /boot being a directory. If you need to have the root partition encrypted in this setup, make sure to use the GPT partition table type instead of the default MSDOS type. Otherwise the GRUB2 boot loader may not have enough space for the second stage loader.

It is possible to create snapshots of Btrfs subvolumes—either manually, or automatically based on system events. For example when making changes to the file system, **zypper** invokes the **snapper** command to create snapshots before and after the change. This is useful if you are not satisfied with the change **zypper** made and want to restore the previous state. As **snapper** invoked by **zypper** snapshots the *root* file system by default, it is reasonable to exclude specific directories from being snapshot, depending on the nature of data they hold. And that is why YaST suggests creating the following separate subvolumes.

SUGGESTED BTRFS SUBVOLUMES

/tmp /var/tmp /var/run

Directories with frequently changed content.

/var/spool

Contains user data, such as mails.

/var/lib

Holds dynamic data libraries and files plus state information pertaining to an application or the system.
By default, subvolumes with the option no copy on write are created for: /var/lib/ mariadb, /var/lib/pgsql, and /var/lib/libvirt/images.

/var/log

Contains system and applications' log files which should never be rolled back.

`/var/crash`

> Contains memory dumps of crashed kernels.

`/srv`

> Contains data files belonging to FTP and HTTP servers.

`/opt`

> Contains third party software.

 Tip: Size of Btrfs Partition

> Because saved snapshots require more disk space, it is recommended to reserve more space for Btrfs partition than for a partition not capable of snapshotting (such as Ext3). Recommended size for a root Btrfs partition with suggested subvolumes is 20GB.

14.1.2.1.1 Managing Btrfs Subvolumes using YaST

Subvolumes of a Btrfs partition can be now managed with the YaST *Expert partitioner* module. You can add new or remove existing subvolumes.

PROCEDURE 14.1: BTRFS SUBVOLUMES WITH YAST

1. Start the YaST *Expert Partitioner* with *System › Partitioner.*

2. Choose *Btrfs* in the left *System View* pane.

3. Select the Btrfs partition whose subvolumes you need to manage and click *Edit.*

4. Click *Subvolume Handling.* You can see a list off all existing subvolumes of the selected Btrfs partition. You can notice several `@/.snapshots/xyz/snapshot` entries—each of these subvolumes belongs to one existing snapshot.

5. Depending on whether you want to add or remove subvolumes, do the following:

   a. To remove a subvolume, select it from the list of *Exisitng Subvolumes* and click *Remove.*

   b. To add a new subvolume, enter its name to the *New Subvolume* text box and click *Add new.*

Creating a Partition

FIGURE 14.2: BTRFS SUBVOLUMES IN YAST PARTITIONER

6. Confirm with *OK* and *Finish*.

7. Leave the partitioner with *Finish*.

14.1.3   Editing a Partition

When you create a new partition or modify an existing partition, you can set various parameters. For new partitions, the default parameters set by YaST are usually sufficient and do not require any modification. To edit your partition setup manually, proceed as follows:

1. Select the partition.

2. Click *Edit* to edit the partition and set the parameters:

File System ID

Even if you do not want to format the partition at this stage, assign it a file system ID to ensure that the partition is registered correctly. Typical values are *Linux, Linux swap, Linux LVM*, and *Linux RAID*.

File System

To change the partition file system, click *Format Partition* and select file system type in the *File System* list.

SUSE Linux Enterprise Server supports several types of file systems. Btrfs is the Linux file system of choice for the root partition because of its advanced features. It supports copy-on-write functionality, creating snapshots, multi-device spanning, sub-volumes, and other useful techniques. XFS, Ext3 and JFS are journaling file systems. These file systems can restore the system very quickly after a system crash, using write processes logged during the operation. Ext2 is not a journaling file system, but it is adequate for smaller partitions because it does not require much disk space for management.

The default file system for the root partition is Btrfs. The default file system for additional partitions is XFS.

Swap is a special format that allows the partition to be used as a virtual memory. Create a swap partition of at least 256 MB. However, if you use up your swap space, consider adding more memory to your system instead of adding more swap space.

 Warning: Changing the File System

Changing the file system and reformatting partitions irreversibly deletes all data from the partition.

For details on the various file systems, refer to *Storage Administration Guide*.

Encrypt Device

If you activate the encryption, all data is written to the hard disk in encrypted form. This increases the security of sensitive data, but reduces the system speed, as the encryption takes some time to process. More information about the encryption of file systems is provided in *Book "Security Guide", Chapter 11 "Encrypting Partitions and Files"*.

Editing a Partition

Mount Point

> Specify the directory where the partition should be mounted in the file system tree. Select from YaST suggestions or enter any other name.

Fstab Options

> Specify various parameters contained in the global file system administration file (/ etc/fstab). The default settings should suffice for most setups. You can, for example, change the file system identification from the device name to a volume label. In the volume label, use all characters except / and space.
>
> To get persistent devices names, use the mount option *Device ID*, *UUID* or *LABEL*. In SUSE Linux Enterprise Server, persistent device names are enabled by default.

> ### Note: IBM z Systems: Mounting by Path
>
> > Since mounting by ID causes problems on IBM z Systems when using disk-to-disk copying for cloning purposes, devices are mounted by path in /etc/fstab on IBM z Systems by default.

> If you prefer to mount the partition by its label, you need to define one in the *Volume label* text entry. For example, you could use the partition label HOME for a partition intended to mount to /home.
>
> If you intend to use quotas on the file system, use the mount option *Enable Quota Support*. This must be done before you can define quotas for users in the YaST *User Management* module. For further information on how to configure user quota, refer to *Section 11.3.4, "Managing Quotas"*.

3. Select *Finish* to save the changes.

 ## Note: Resize File Systems

To resize an existing file system, select the partition and use *Resize*. Note, that it is not possible to resize partitions while mounted. To resize partitions, unmount the relevant partition before running the partitioner.

14.1.4 Expert Options

After you select a hard disk device (like *sda*) in the *System View* pane, you can access the *Expert* menu in the lower right part of the *Expert Partitioner* window. The menu contains the following commands:

Create New Partition Table

This option helps you create a new partition table on the selected device.

 Warning: Creating a New Partition Table

Creating a new partition table on a device irreversibly removes all the partitions and their data from that device.

Clone This Disk

This option helps you clone the device partition layout (but not the data) to other available disk devices.

14.1.5 Advanced Options

After you select the host name of the computer (the top-level of the tree in the *System View* pane), you can access the *Configure* menu in the lower right part of the *Expert Partitioner* window. The menu contains the following commands:

Configure iSCSI

To access SCSI over IP block devices, you first need to configure iSCSI. This results in additionally available devices in the main partition list.

Configure Multipath

Selecting this option helps you configure the multipath enhancement to the supported mass storage devices.

14.1.6 More Partitioning Tips

The following section includes a few hints and tips on partitioning that should help you make the right decisions when setting up your system.

Tip: Cylinder Numbers

Note, that different partitioning tools may start counting the cylinders of a partition with `0` or with `1`. When calculating the number of cylinders, you should always use the difference between the last and the first cylinder number and add one.

14.1.6.1 Using swap

Swap is used to extend the available physical memory. It is then possible to use more memory than physical RAM available. The memory management system of kernels before 2.4.10 needed swap as a safety measure. Then, if you did not have twice the size of your RAM in swap, the performance of the system suffered. These limitations no longer exist.

Linux uses a page called "Least Recently Used" (LRU) to select pages that might be moved from memory to disk. Therefore, running applications have more memory available and caching works more smoothly.

If an application tries to allocate the maximum allowed memory, problems with swap can arise. There are three major scenarios to look at:

System with no swap

The application gets the maximum allowed memory. All caches are freed, and thus all other running applications are slowed. After a few minutes, the kernel's out-of-memory kill mechanism activates and kills the process.

System with medium sized swap (128 MB–512 MB)

At first, the system slows like a system without swap. After all physical RAM has been allocated, swap space is used as well. At this point, the system becomes very slow and it becomes impossible to run commands from remote. Depending on the speed of the hard disks that run the swap space, the system stays in this condition for about 10 to 15 minutes until the out-of-memory kill mechanism resolves the issue. Note that you will need a certain amount of swap if the computer needs to perform a "suspend to disk". In that case, the swap size should be large enough to contain the necessary data from memory (512 MB–1GB).

System with lots of swap (several GB)

It is better to not have an application that is out of control and swapping excessively in this case. If you use such application, the system will need many hours to recover. In the process, it is likely that other processes get timeouts and faults, leaving the system in an undefined state, even after terminating the faulty process. In this case, do a hard machine reboot and try to get it running again. Lots of swap is only useful if you have an application that relies on this feature. Such applications (like databases or graphics manipulation programs) often have an option to directly use hard disk space for their needs. It is advisable to use this option instead of using lots of swap space.

If your system is not out of control, but needs more swap after some time, it is possible to extend the swap space online. If you prepared a partition for swap space, add this partition with YaST. If you do not have a partition available, you can also use a swap file to extend the swap. Swap files are generally slower than partitions, but compared to physical RAM, both are extremely slow so the actual difference is negligible.

PROCEDURE 14.2: ADDING A SWAP FILE MANUALLY

To add a swap file in the running system, proceed as follows:

1. Create an empty file in your system. For example, if you want to add a swap file with 128 MB swap at `/var/lib/swap/swapfile`, use the commands:

```
mkdir -p /var/lib/swap
dd if=/dev/zero of=/var/lib/swap/swapfile bs=1M count=128
```

2. Initialize this swap file with the command

```
mkswap /var/lib/swap/swapfile
```

 Note: Changed UUID for Swap Partitions when Formatting via mkswap

Do not reformat existing swap partitions with **mkswap** if possible. Reformatting with **mkswap** will change the UUID value of the swap partition. Either reformat via YaST (will update `/etc/fstab`) or adjust `/etc/fstab` manually.

3. Activate the swap with the command

```
swapon /var/lib/swap/swapfile
```

To disable this swap file, use the command

```
swapoff /var/lib/swap/swapfile
```

More Partitioning Tips

4. Check the current available swap spaces with the command

```
cat /proc/swaps
```

Note that at this point, it is only temporary swap space. After the next reboot, it is no longer used.

5. To enable this swap file permanently, add the following line to `/etc/fstab`:

```
/var/lib/swap/swapfile swap swap defaults 0 0
```

14.1.7   Partitioning and LVM

From the *Expert partitioner,* access the LVM configuration by clicking the *Volume Management* item in the *System View* pane. However, if a working LVM configuration already exists on your system, it is automatically activated upon entering the initial LVM configuration of a session. In this case, all disks containing a partition (belonging to an activated volume group) cannot be repartitioned. The Linux kernel cannot reread the modified partition table of a hard disk when any partition on this disk is in use. If you already have a working LVM configuration on your system, physical repartitioning should not be necessary. Instead, change the configuration of the logical volumes.

At the beginning of the physical volumes (PVs), information about the volume is written to the partition. To reuse such a partition for other non-LVM purposes, it is advisable to delete the beginning of this volume. For example, in the VG `system` and PV `/dev/sda2`, do this with the command **dd** `if=/dev/zero of=/dev/sda2 bs=512 count=1`.

 Warning: File System for Booting

The file system used for booting (the root file system or `/boot`) must not be stored on an LVM logical volume. Instead, store it on a normal physical partition.

In case you want to change your `/usr` or `swap`, refer to .

For more details about LVM, see *Book* "Storage Administration Guide".

14.2 LVM Configuration

This section briefly describes the principles behind the Logical Volume Manager (LVM) and its multipurpose features. In *Section 14.2.2, "LVM Configuration with YaST"*, learn how to set up LVM with YaST.

 Warning: Back up Your Data

Using LVM is sometimes associated with increased risk such as data loss. Risks also include application crashes, power failures, and faulty commands. Save your data before implementing LVM or reconfiguring volumes. Never work without a backup.

14.2.1 The Logical Volume Manager

The LVM enables flexible distribution of hard disk space over several file systems. It was developed because sometimes the need to change the segmenting of hard disk space arises just after the initial partitioning has been done. Because it is difficult to modify partitions on a running system, LVM provides a virtual pool (volume group, VG for short) of memory space from which logical volumes (LVs) can be created as needed. The operating system accesses these LVs instead of the physical partitions. Volume groups can occupy more than one disk, so that several disks or parts of them may constitute one single VG. This way, LVM provides a kind of abstraction from the physical disk space that allows its segmentation to be changed in a much easier and safer way than with physical repartitioning. Background information regarding physical partitioning can be found in *Section 14.1.1, "Partition Types"* and *Section 14.1, "Using the YaST Partitioner"*.

DISK		
PART	PART	PART
MP	MP	MP

DISK 1			DISK 2		
PART	PART	PART	PART	PART
VG 1			VG 2		
LV 1		LV 2	LV 3	LV4
MP		MP	MP	MP

FIGURE 14.3: PHYSICAL PARTITIONING VERSUS LVM

Figure 14.3, "Physical Partitioning versus LVM" compares physical partitioning (left) with LVM segmentation (right). On the left side, one single disk has been divided into three physical partitions (PART), each with a mount point (MP) assigned so that the operating system can gain access. On the right side, two disks have been divided into two and three physical partitions each. Two LVM volume groups (VG 1 and VG 2) have been defined. VG 1 contains two partitions from DISK 1 and one from DISK 2. VG 2 contains the remaining two partitions from DISK 2. In LVM, the physical disk partitions that are incorporated in a volume group are called physical volumes (PVs). Within the volume groups, four LVs (LV 1 through LV 4) have been defined. They can be used by the operating system via the associated mount points. The border between different LVs do not need to be aligned with any partition border. See the border between LV 1 and LV 2 in this example.

LVM features:

- Several hard disks or partitions can be combined in a large logical volume.

- Provided the configuration is suitable, an LV (such as /usr) can be enlarged if free space is exhausted.

- With LVM, it is possible to add hard disks or LVs in a running system. However, this requires hotpluggable hardware.

- It is possible to activate a "striping mode" that distributes the data stream of an LV over several PVs. If these PVs reside on different disks, the read and write performance is enhanced, as with RAID 0.

- The snapshot feature enables consistent backups (especially for servers) of the running system.

With these features, LVM is ready for heavily used home PCs or small servers. LVM is well-suited for the user with a growing data stock (as in the case of databases, music archives, or user directories). This would allow file systems that are larger than the physical hard disk. Another advantage of LVM is that up to 256 LVs can be added. However, working with LVM is different from working with conventional partitions. Instructions and further information about configuring LVM is available in the official LVM HOWTO at http://tldp.org/HOWTO/LVM-HOWTO/.

Starting from Kernel version 2.6, LVM version 2 is available, which is backward-compatible with the previous LVM and enables the continued management of old volume groups. When creating new volume groups, decide whether to use the new format or the backward-compatible version. LVM 2 does not require any kernel patches. It uses the device mapper integrated in kernel 2.6. This kernel only supports LVM version 2. Therefore, when talking about LVM, this section always refers to LVM version 2.

14.2.1.1   Thin Provisioning

Starting from Kernel version 3.4, LVM supports thin provisioning. A thin-provisioned volume has a virtual capacity and a real capacity. *Virtual* capacity is the volume storage capacity that is available to a host. *Real* capacity is the storage capacity that is allocated to a volume copy from a storage pool. In a fully allocated volume, the virtual capacity and real capacity are the same. In a thin-provisioned volume, however, the virtual capacity can be much larger than the real capacity. If a thin-provisioned volume does not have enough real capacity for a write operation, the volume is taken offline and an error is logged.

For more general information, see http://wikibon.org/wiki/v/Thin_provisioning.

14.2.2   LVM Configuration with YaST

The YaST LVM configuration can be reached from the YaST Expert Partitioner (see *Section 14.1, "Using the YaST Partitioner"*) within the *Volume Management* item in the *System View* pane. The Expert Partitioner allows you to edit and delete existing partitions and also create new ones that need to be used with LVM. The first task is to create PVs that provide space to a volume group:

1. Select a hard disk from *Hard Disks*.

2. Change to the *Partitions* tab.

3. Click *Add* and enter the desired size of the PV on this disk.

4. Use *Do not format partition* and change the *File System ID* to *0x8E Linux LVM*. Do not mount this partition.

5. Repeat this procedure until you have defined all the desired physical volumes on the available disks.

14.2.2.1   Creating Volume Groups

If no volume group exists on your system, you must add one (see *Figure 14.4, "Creating a Volume Group"*). It is possible to create additional groups by clicking *Volume Management* in the *System View* pane, and then on *Add Volume Group*. One single volume group is usually sufficient.

1. Enter a name for the VG, for example, `system`.

2. Select the desired *Physical Extend Size*. This value defines the size of a physical block in the volume group. All the disk space in a volume group is handled in blocks of this size.

3. Add the prepared PVs to the VG by selecting the device and clicking *Add*. Selecting several devices is possible by holding Ctrl while selecting the devices.

4. Select *Finish* to make the VG available to further configuration steps.

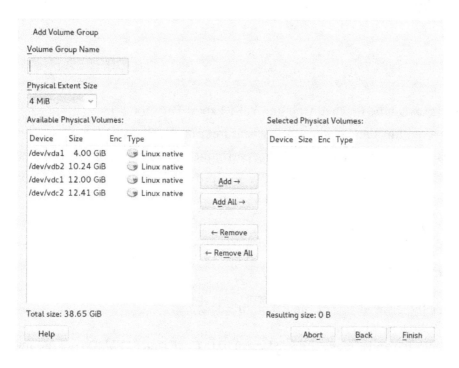

FIGURE 14.4: CREATING A VOLUME GROUP

If you have multiple volume groups defined and want to add or remove PVs, select the volume group in the *Volume Management* list and click *Resize*. In the following window, you can add or remove PVs to the selected volume group.

14.2.2.2 Configuring Logical Volumes

After the volume group has been filled with PVs, define the LVs which the operating system should use in the next dialog. Choose the current volume group and change to the *Logical Volumes* tab. *Add, Edit, Resize,* and *Delete* LVs as needed until all space in the volume group has been occupied. Assign at least one LV to each volume group.

FIGURE 14.5: LOGICAL VOLUME MANAGEMENT

Click *Add* and go through the wizard-like pop-up that opens:

1. Enter the name of the LV. For a partition that should be mounted to `/home`, a name like `HOME` could be used.

2. Select the type of the LV. It can be either *Normal Volume, Thin Pool,* or *Thin Volume*. Note that you need to create a thin pool first, which can store individual thin volumes. The big advantage of thin provisioning is that the total sum of all thin volumes stored in a thin pool can exceed the size of the pool itself.

3. Select the size and the number of stripes of the LV. If you have only one PV, selecting more than one stripe is not useful.

4. Choose the file system to use on the LV and the mount point.

By using stripes it is possible to distribute the data stream in the LV among several PVs (striping). However, striping a volume can only be done over different PVs, each providing at least the amount of space of the volume. The maximum number of stripes equals to the number of PVs, where Stripe "1" means "no striping". Striping only makes sense with PVs on different hard disks, otherwise performance will decrease.

 Warning: Striping

> YaST cannot, at this point, verify the correctness of your entries concerning striping. Any mistake made here is apparent only later when the LVM is implemented on disk.

If you have already configured LVM on your system, the existing logical volumes can also be used. Before continuing, assign appropriate mount points to these LVs. With *Finish*, return to the YaST Expert Partitioner and finish your work there.

14.3 Soft RAID Configuration

The purpose of RAID (redundant array of independent disks) is to combine several hard disk partitions into one large *virtual* hard disk to optimize performance and/or data security. Most RAID controllers use the SCSI protocol because it can address a larger number of hard disks in a more effective way than the IDE protocol. It is also more suitable for the parallel command processing. There are some RAID controllers that support IDE or SATA hard disks. Soft RAID provides the advantages of RAID systems without the additional cost of hardware RAID controllers. However, this requires some CPU time and has memory requirements that make it unsuitable for high performance computers.

With SUSE® Linux Enterprise Server , you can combine several hard disks into one soft RAID system. RAID implies several strategies for combining several hard disks in a RAID system, each with different goals, advantages, and characteristics. These variations are commonly known as *RAID levels*.

Common RAID levels are:

RAID 0

This level improves the performance of your data access by spreading out blocks of each file across multiple disk drives. Actually, this is not really a RAID, because it does not provide data backup, but the name *RAID 0* for this type of system is commonly used. With RAID 0, two or more hard disks are pooled together. Performance is enhanced, but the RAID system is destroyed and your data lost if even one hard disk fails.

RAID 1

This level provides adequate security for your data, because the data is copied to another hard disk 1:1. This is known as *hard disk mirroring*. If one disk is destroyed, a copy of its contents is available on the other one. All disks but one could be damaged without endangering your data. However, if the damage is not detected, the damaged data can be mirrored to the undamaged disk. This could result in the same loss of data. The writing performance suffers in the copying process compared to using single disk access (10 to 20 % slower), but read access is significantly faster in comparison to any one of the normal physical hard disks. The reason is that the duplicate data can be parallel-scanned. Generally it can be said that Level 1 provides nearly twice the read transfer rate of single disks and almost the same write transfer rate as single disks.

RAID 5

RAID 5 is an optimized compromise between Level 0 and Level 1, in terms of performance and redundancy. The hard disk space equals the number of disks used minus one. The data is distributed over the hard disks as with RAID 0. *Parity blocks*, created on one of the partitions, exist for security reasons. They are linked to each other with XOR, enabling the contents to be reconstructed by the corresponding parity block in case of system failure. With RAID 5, no more than one hard disk can fail at the same time. If one hard disk fails, it must be replaced as soon as possible to avoid the risk of losing data.

RAID 6

To further increase the reliability of the RAID system, it is possible to use RAID 6. In this level, even if two disks fail, the array still can be reconstructed. With RAID 6, at least 4 hard disks are needed to run the array. Note that when running as software raid, this configuration needs a considerable amount of CPU time and memory.

RAID 10 (RAID 1+0)

This RAID implementation combines features of RAID 0 and RAID 1: the data is first mirrored to separate disk arrays, which are inserted into a new RAID 0; type array. In each RAID 1 sub-array, one disk can fail without any damage to the data. A minimum of four disks and an even number of disks is needed to run a RAID 10. This type of RAID is used for database application where a huge load is expected.

Other RAID Levels

Several other RAID levels have been developed (RAID 2, RAID 3, RAID 4, RAIDn, RAID 10, RAID 0 + 1, RAID 30, RAID 50, etc.), some being proprietary implementations created by hardware vendors. These levels are not very common and therefore are not explained here.

14.3.1 Soft RAID Configuration with YaST

The YaST *RAID* configuration can be reached from the YaST Expert Partitioner, described in *Section 14.1, "Using the YaST Partitioner"*. This partitioning tool enables you to edit and delete existing partitions and create new ones to be used with soft RAID:

1. Select a hard disk from *Hard Disks*.

2. Change to the *Partitions* tab.

3. Click *Add* and enter the desired size of the raid partition on this disk.

4. Use *Do not Format the Partition* and change the *File System ID* to *0xFD Linux RAID*. Do not mount this partition.

5. Repeat this procedure until you have defined all the desired physical volumes on the available disks.

For RAID 0 and RAID 1, at least two partitions are needed—for RAID 1, usually exactly two and no more. If RAID 5 is used, at least three partitions are required, RAID 6 and RAID 10 require at least four partitions. It is recommended to use partitions of the same size only. The RAID partitions should be located on different hard disks to decrease the risk of losing data if one is defective (RAID 1 and 5) and to optimize the performance of RAID 0. After creating all the partitions to use with RAID, click *RAID › Add RAID* to start the RAID configuration.

In the next dialog, choose between RAID levels 0, 1, 5, 6 and 10. Then, select all partitions with either the "Linux RAID" or "Linux native" type that should be used by the RAID system. No swap or DOS partitions are shown.

Tip: Classify Disks

For RAID types where the order of added disks matters, you can mark individual disks with one of the letters A to E. Click the *Classify* button, select the disk and click of the *Class X* buttons, where X is the letter you want to assign to the disk. Assign all available RAID disks this way, and confirm with *OK*. You can easily sort the classified disks with the *Sorted* or *Interleaved* buttons, or add a sort pattern from a text file with *Pattern File*.

FIGURE 14.6: RAID PARTITIONS

To add a previously unassigned partition to the selected RAID volume, first click the partition then *Add*. Assign all partitions reserved for RAID. Otherwise, the space on the partition remains unused. After assigning all partitions, click *Next* to select the available *RAID Options*.

In this last step, set the file system to use, encryption and the mount point for the RAID volume. After completing the configuration with *Finish*, see the `/dev/md0` device and others indicated with *RAID* in the expert partitioner.

Soft RAID Configuration with YaST

14.3.2 Troubleshooting

Check the file `/proc/mdstat` to find out whether a RAID partition has been damaged. If th system fails, shut down your Linux system and replace the defective hard disk with a new one partitioned the same way. Then restart your system and enter the command **mdadm /dev/mdX --add /dev/sdX**. Replace 'X' with your particular device identifiers. This integrates the hard disk automatically into the RAID system and fully reconstructs it.

Note that although you can access all data during the rebuild, you may encounter some performance issues until the RAID has been fully rebuilt.

14.3.3 For More Information

Configuration instructions and more details for soft RAID can be found in the HOWTOs at:

- `/usr/share/doc/packages/mdadm/Software-RAID.HOWTO.html`

- http://raid.wiki.kernel.org

Linux RAID mailing lists are available, such as http://marc.info/?l=linux-raid.

III Updating and Upgrading SUSE Linux Enterprise

15 Life Cycle and Support

If you are not familiar with SUSE Linux Enterprise updates, upgrades and service packs in general, this chapter will give you some background information on terminology, SUSE product lifecycles and Service Pack releases, and recommended upgrade policies.

15.1 Terminology

This section uses several terms. To understand the information, read the definitions below:

Backporting

Backporting is the act of adapting specific changes from a newer version of software and applying it to an older version. The most commonly used case is fixing security holes in older software components. Usually it is also part of a maintenance model to supply enhancements or (less commonly) new features.

Delta RPM

A delta RPM consists only of the binary diff between two defined versions of a package, and therefore has the smallest download size. Before being installed, the full RPM package is rebuilt on the local machine.

Downstream

A metaphor of how software is developed in the open source world (compare it with *upstream*). The term *downstream* refers to people or organizations like SUSE who integrate the source code from upstream with other software to build a distribution which is then used by end users. Thus, the software flows downstream from its developers via the integrators to the end users.

Extensions,
Add-On Products

Extensions and third party add-on products provide additional functionality of product value to SUSE Linux Enterprise Server. They are provided by SUSE and by SUSE partners, and they are registered and installed on top of the base product SUSE Linux Enterprise Server.

Major Release,

General Availability (GA) Version

> The Major Release of SUSE Linux Enterprise (or any software product) is a new version which brings new features and tools, decommissions previously deprecated components and comes with backwards incompatible changes.

Migration

> Updating to a Service Pack (SP) by using the online update tools or an installation medium to install the respective patches. It updates all packages of the installed system to the latest state.

Migration Targets

> Set of compatible products to which a system can be migrated, containing the version of the products/extensions and the URL of the repository. Migration targets can change over time and depend on installed extensions.

Modules

> Modules are fully supported parts of SUSE Linux Enterprise Server with a different life cycle. They have a clearly defined scope and are delivered via online channel only. Registering at the SUSE Customer Center, SMT (Subscription Management Tool), or SUSE Manager is a prerequisite for being able to subscribe to these channels.

Package

> A package is a compressed file in `rpm` format that contains all files for a particular program, including optional components like configuration, examples, and documentation.

Patch

> A patch consists of one or more packages and may be applied by means of delta RPMs. It may also introduce dependencies to packages that are not installed yet.

Service Packs (SP)

> Combines several patches into a form that is easy to install or deploy. Service packs are numbered and usually contain security fixes, updates, upgrades, or enhancements of programs.

Upstream

A metaphor of how software is developed in the open source world (compare it with *downstream*). The term *upstream* refers to the original project, author or maintainer of a software that is distributed as source code. Feedback, patches, feature enhancements, or other improvements flow from end users or contributors to upstream developers. They decide if the request will be integrated or rejected.

If the project members decide to integrate the request, it will show up in newer versions of the software. An accepted request will benefit all parties involved.

If a request is not accepted, it may be for different reasons. Either it is in a state that is not compliant with the project's guidelines, it is invalid, it is already integrated, or it is not in the interest or roadmap of the project. An unaccepted request makes it harder for upstream developers as they need to synchronize their patches with the upstream code. This practice is generally avoided, but sometimes it is still needed.

Update

Installation of a newer *minor* version of a package, which usually contains security or bug fixes.

Upgrade

Installation of a newer *major* version of a package or distribution, which brings *new features*.

15.2 Product Life Cycle

SUSE has the following life cycle for products:

- SUSE Linux Enterprise Server has a 13-year life-cycle: 10 years of general support and 3 years of extended support.

- SUSE Linux Enterprise Desktop has a 10-year life-cycle: 7 years of general support and 3 years of extended support.

- Major releases are made every 4 years. Service packs are made every 12-14 months.

SUSE supports previous service packs for 6 months after the release of the new service pack. *Figure 15.1, "Major Releases and Service Packs"* depicts some mentioned aspects.

FIGURE 15.1: MAJOR RELEASES AND SERVICE PACKS

If you need additional time to design, validate and test your upgrade plans, Long Term Service Pack Support can extend the support you get by an additional 12 to 36 months in 12-month increments, giving you a total of between 2 and 5 years of support on any service pack (see *Figure 15.2, "Long Term Service Pack Support"*).

FIGURE 15.2: LONG TERM SERVICE PACK SUPPORT

15.3 Support Levels

The range for extended support levels starts from year 10 and ends in year 13. These contain continued L3 engineering level diagnosis and reactive critical bug fixes. These support levels proactively update trivial local root exploits in Kernel or other root exploits directly executable without user interaction. Furthermore they support existing workloads, software stacks, and hardware with limited package exclusion list. Find an overview in *Table 15.1, "Security Updates and Bug Fixes"*.

TABLE 15.1: SECURITY UPDATES AND BUG FIXES

	General Support for Most Recent Service Pack (SP)			General Support for Previous SP, with LTSS	Extended Support with LTSS
Feature	Year 1-5	Year 6-7	Year 8-10	Year 4-10	Year 10-13
Technical Services	Yes	Yes	Yes	Yes	Yes
Access to Patches and Fixes	Yes	Yes	Yes	Yes	Yes
Access to Documentation and Knowledge Base	Yes	Yes	Yes	Yes	Yes
Support for Existing Stacks and Workloads	Yes	Yes	Yes	Yes	Yes
Support for New Deployments	Yes	Yes	Limited (Based on partner and customer requests)	Limited (Based on partner and customer requests)	No
Enhancement Requests	Yes	Limited (Based on partner and customer requests)	Limited (Based on partner and customer requests)	No	No

Feature	General Support for Most Recent Service Pack (SP)			General Support for Previous SP, with LTSS	Extended Support with LTSS
	Year 1-5	Year 6-7	Year 8-10	Year 4-10	Year 10-13
Hardware Enablement and Optimization	Yes	Limited (Based on partner and customer requests)	Limited (Based on partner and customer requests)	No	No
Driver updates via SUSE Solid-Driver Program (formerly PLDP)	Yes	Yes	Limited (Based on partner and customer requests)	Limited (Based on partner and customer requests)	No
Backport of Fixes from recent SP	Yes	Yes	Limited (Based on partner and customer requests)	N/A	N/A
Critical Security Updates	Yes	Yes	Yes	Yes	Yes
Defect Resolution	Yes	Yes	Limited (Severity Level 1 and 2 defects only)	Limited (Severity Level 1 and 2 defects only)	Limited (Severity Level 1 and 2 defects only)

15.4 Repository Model

The repository layout corresponds to the product lifecycles. *Table 15.2, "Repository Layout for SUSE Linux Enterprise 11 SP3/SP4 and for SUSE Linux Enterprise 12 SP1"* contains a list of all relevant repositories.

TABLE 15.2: REPOSITORY LAYOUT FOR SUSE LINUX ENTERPRISE 11 SP3/SP4 AND FOR SUSE LINUX ENTERPRISE 12 SP1

Type	SLES	SLED
Required Repositories	11 SP3 SLES11-SP3-Pool SLES11-SP3-Updates 11 SP4 SLES11-SP4-Pool SLES11-SP4-Updates 12 SLES12-GA-Pool SLES12-GA-Updates 12 SP1 SLES12-SP1-Pool SLES12-SP1-Updates	11 SP3 SLED11-SP3-Pool SLED11-SP3-Updates 11 SP4 SLED11-SP4-Pool SLED11-SP4-Updates 12 SLED12-GA-Pool SLED12-GA-Updates 12 SP1 SLED12-SP1-Pool SLED12-SP1-Updates
Optional Repositories	11 SP3 SLES11-SP3-Debuginfo-Core SLES11-SP3-Debuginfo-Updates SLES11-SP3-Extension-Store SLES11-Extra 12 SLES12-GA-Debuginfo-Core SLES12-GA-Debuginfo-Updates 12 SP1	11 SP3 SLED11-SP3-Debuginfo-Core SLED11-SP3-Debuginfo-Updates SLED11-SP3-Extension-Store SLED11-Extra 12 SLED12-GA-Debuginfo-Core SLED12-GA-Debuginfo-Updates 12 SP1

Type	SLES	SLED
	SLES12-SP1-Debuginfo-Core	SLED12-SP1-Debuginfo-Core
	SLES12-SP1-Debuginfo-Updates	SLED12-SP1-Debuginfo-Updates
NEW: *Module* Specific Repositories	12/12 SP1 sle-module-web-scripting sle-module-adv-systems-manage-ment sle-module-public-cloud sle-module-legacy	12/12 SP1 Currently no modules for SLED

Updates

Maintenance updates to packages in the corresponding Core or Pool repository.

Pool

Containing all binary RPMs from the installation media, plus pattern information and support status metadata.

Debuginfo-Pool,
Debuginfo-Updates

These repositories contain static content. Of these two, only the Debuginfo-Updates repository receives updates. Enable these repositories if you need to install libraries with debug information in case of an issue.

15.4.1 Origin of Packages

SUSE Linux Enterprise 11 SP3/SP4. With the update to SP3 there are only two repositories available: SLES11-SP3-Pool and SLES11-SP3-Updates. Since SP4, any previous repositories are not visible anymore.

SUSE Linux Enterprise 12 and SP1. With the update to SUSE Linux Enterprise 12 there are only two repositories available: SLES12-GA-Pool and SLES12-GA-Updates. Any previous repositories from SUSE Linux Enterprise 11 are disabled.

15.4.2 Register and Unregister Repositories with SUSEConnect

On registration, the system receives repositories from the SUSE Customer Center (see https://scc.suse.com/) or a local registration proxy like SMT. The repository names map to specific URIs in the customer center. To list all available repositories on your system, use **zypper** as follows:

```
root # zypper repos -u
```

This gives you a list of all available repositories on your system. Each repository is listed by its alias, name and whether it is enabled and will be refreshed. The option -u gives you also the URI from where it originated.

To register your machine, run SUSEConnect, for example:

```
root # SUSEConnect -r REGCODE
```

If you want to unregister your machine, from SP1 and above you can use SUSEConnect too:

```
root # SUSEConnect --de-register
```

16 Backporting Source Code

SUSE extensively uses backports, for example for the migration of current software fixes and features into released SUSE Linux Enterprise packages. The information in this chapter helps you understand why it can be deceptive to compare version numbers to judge the capabilities and the security of SUSE Linux Enterprise software packages. You will understand how SUSE keeps the system software secure and current while maintaining compatibility for your application software on top of SUSE Linux Enterprise products. You will also learn how to check which public security issues actually are addressed in your SUSE Linux Enterprise system software, and how current your software really is.

16.1 Reasons for Backporting

Upstream developers are primarily concerned with advancing the software they develop. Often they combine fixing bugs with introducing new features which have not yet received extensive testing and which may introduce new bugs.

For distribution developers, it is important to distinguish between:

- bugfixes with a limited potential for disrupting functionality; and

- changes that may disrupt existing functionality.

Usually, distribution developers do not follow all upstream changes when a package has become part of a released distribution. Usually they stick instead with the upstream version that they initially released and create patches based on upstream changes to fix bugs. This practice is known as *backporting*.

Distribution developers generally will only introduce a newer version of software in two cases:

- when the changes between their packages and the upstream versions have become so large that backporting is no longer feasible, or

- for software that inherently ages badly, like anti-malware software.

SUSE uses backports extensively as we strike a good balance between several concerns for enterprise software. The most important of them are:

- Having stable interfaces (APIs) that software vendors can rely on when building products for use on SUSE's enterprise products.

- Ensuring that packages used in the release of SUSE's enterprise products are of the highest quality and have been thoroughly tested, both in themselves and as part of the whole enterprise product.

- Maintaining the various certifications of SUSE's enterprise products by other vendors, like certifications for Oracle or SAP products.

- Allowing SUSE's developers to focus on making the next version of the product as good as they can make it, rather than them having to spread their focus thinly across a wide range of releases.

- Keeping a clear view of what is in a particular enterprise release, so that our support can provide accurate and timely information about it.

16.2 Reasons against Backports

It is a general policy rule that no new upstream versions of a package are introduced into our enterprise products. This rule is not an absolute rule however. For a limited class of packages, in particular anti-virus software, security concerns weigh heavier than the conservative approach that is preferable from the perspective of quality assurance. For packages in that class, occasionally newer versions are introduced into a released version of an enterprise product line.

Sometimes also for other types of packages the choice is made to introduce a new version rather than a backport. This is done when producing a backport is not economically feasible or when there is a very relevant technical reason to introduce the newer version.

16.3   The Implications of Backports for Interpreting Version Numbers

Because of the practice of backporting, one cannot simply compare version numbers to determine whether a SUSE package contains a fix for a particular issue or has had a particular feature added to it. With backporting, the upstream part of a SUSE package's version number merely indicates what upstream version the SUSE package is based on. It may contain bug fixes and features that are not in the corresponding upstream release, but that have been backported into the SUSE package.

One particular area where this limited value of version numbers when backporting is involved can cause problems is with security scanning tools. Some security vulnerability scanning tools (or particular tests in such tools) operate solely on version information. These tools/tests are thus prone to generating "false positives" (claims that a vulnerable piece of software has been found which in fact is not vulnerable) when backports are involved. When evaluating reports from security scanning tools, one should always investigate whether an entry is based on a version number or on an actual test of whether an actual vulnerability exists.

16.4   How to Check Which Bugs are Fixed and Which Features are Backported and Available

There are several locations where information regarding backported bug fixes and features are stored:

- The package's changelog:

```
rpm -q --changelog name-of-installed-package
rpm -qp --changelog packagefile.rpm
```

  The output briefly documents the change history of the package.

- The package changelog may contain entries like bsc#1234 ("*Bugzilla Suse.Com*") that refer to bugs in SUSE's Bugzilla tracking system or links to other bugtracking systems. Because of confidentiality policies, not all such information may be accessible to you.

- A package may contain a /usr/share/doc/*packagename*/README.SUSE file which contains general, high-level information specific to the SUSE package.

- The RPM source package contains the patches that were applied during the building of the regular binary RPMs as separate files that can be interpreted if you are familiar with reading source code. See *Book "Administration Guide", Chapter 4 "Managing Software with Command Line Tools", Section 4.1.2.1 "Installing or Downloading Source Packages"* for installing sources of SUSE Linux Enterprise software, see *Book "Administration Guide", Chapter 4 "Managing Software with Command Line Tools", Section 4.2.5 "Installing and Compiling Source Packages"* for building packages on SUSE Linux Enterprise and see the Maximum RPM [http://www.rpm.org/max-rpm/] book for the inner workings of SUSE Linux Enterprise software package builds.

- For security bug fixes, consult the SUSE security announcements [http://www.suse.com/support/security/#1]. These often refer to bugs through standardized names like CAN-2005-2495 which are maintained by the Common Vulnerabilities and Exposures (CVE) [http://cve.mitre.org] project.

17 Upgrading SUSE Linux Enterprise

SUSE® Linux Enterprise (SLE) allows to update an existing system to the new version, for example, going from SLE 11 SP4 to SLE 12. No new installation is needed. Existing data, such as home and data directories and system configuration, is kept intact. You can update from a local CD or DVD drive or from a central network installation source.

This chapter explains how to manually upgrade your SUSE Linux Enterprise system, be it by DVD, network, an automated process, or SUSE Manager.

17.1   General Preparations

Before starting the update procedure, make sure your system is properly prepared. Among others, preparation involves backing up data and checking the release notes.

17.1.1   Partitioning and Disk Space

Before starting your update, make note of the root partition. The command **df** / lists the device name of the root partition. For example, in *Example 17.1, "List with* **df** *-h"*, the root partition to write down is /dev/sda3 (mounted as /).

EXAMPLE 17.1: LIST WITH df -h

```
Filesystem      Size  Used Avail Use% Mounted on
/dev/sda3        74G   22G   53G  29% /
tmpfs           506M     0  506M   0% /dev/shm
/dev/sda5       116G  5.8G  111G   5% /home
/dev/sda1        44G    4G   40G   9% /data
```

Software tends to "grow" from version to version. Therefore, take a look at the available partition space with **df** before updating. If you suspect you are running short of disk space, secure your data before updating and repartitioning your system. There is no general rule regarding how much space each partition should have. Space requirements depend on your particular partitioning profile and the software selected.

17.1.2   Check Space on Btrfs Root File Systems

If you use Btrfs as root file systems on your machine, make sure there is enough free space. Getting disk space can be done with these two commands:

```
root # btrfs filesystem df /
root # df /
```

The results of the two commands show similar numbers of how much disk space is used. However, the problem with Btrfs and free space is that you do not know what is referenced in a snapshot and what is not; you cannot calculate how much disk space a change would need.

In the worst case, an upgrade needs as much disk space as the current root file system (without /.snapshot). Besides any Btrfs file systems, check for free space on other file systems as well. The following recommendation has been proven:

- For all file systems including Btrfs you need enough free disk space to download and install big RPMs. The space of old RPMs are only freed after new RPMs are installed.

- For Btrfs with snapshots, you need at minimum as much free space as your current installation takes. It is recommended to have twice as much free space as the current installation. If you do not have enough free space, you can try to delete old snapshots with **snapper** like this:

```
root # snapper list
root # snapper delete NUMBER
```

However, this may not help in all cases. Before migration, most snapshots occupy only little space.

17.1.3   Check the Release Notes

In the release notes you can find additional information on what has changed since the previous release of SUSE Linux Enterprise. Verify there if your specific hardware or set up needs special considerations, which of your favorite specific software packages have changed significantly, and which precautions you should take in addition to the general recommendations of this section. The release notes also provide last-minute information and known issues that could not make it to the manual on time.

The current version of the release notes document containing the latest information on SUSE Linux Enterprise Server can be read online at http://www.suse.com/doc/.

17.1.4 Make a Backup

Before updating, copy existing configuration files to a separate medium (such as tape device, removable hard disk, etc.) to back up the data. This primarily applies to files stored in /etc and some directories and files in /var and /opt. You may also want to write the user data in /home (the HOME directories) to a backup medium. Back up this data as root. Only root has read permissions for all local files.

If you have selected *Update an Existing System* as the installation mode in YaST, you can choose to do a (system) backup at a later point in time. You can choose to include all modified files and files from the /etc/sysconfig directory. However, this is not a complete backup, as all the other important directories mentioned above are missing. Find the backup in the /var/adm/backup directory.

17.1.5 Migrate your MySQL Database

As of SUSE Linux Enterprise 12, SUSE switched from MySQL to MariaDB. Before you start any upgrade, it is highly recommended to back up your database.

To perform the database migration, do the following:

1. Log in to your SUSE Linux Enterprise 11 machine.

2. Create a dump file:

```
root # mysqldump -u root -p --all-databases > mysql_backup.sql
```

   By default, **mysqldump** does not dump the INFORMATION_SCHEMA or performance_schema database. For more details refer to https://dev.mysql.com/doc/refman/5.5/en/mysqldump.html.

3. Store your dump file, the configuration file /etc/my.cnf, and the directory /etc/mysql/ for later investigation (*NOT* installation!) in a safe place.

4. Perform your upgrade. After the upgrade, your former configuration file /etc/my.cnf is still intact. You can find the new configuration in the file /etc/my.cnf.rpmnew.

5. Configure your MariaDB database to your needs. Do *NOT* use the former configuration file and directory, but use it as a reminder and adapt it.

6. Make sure you start the MariaDB server:

```
root # systemctl start mysql
```

If you want to start the MariaDB server on every boot, enable the service:

```
root # systemctl enable mysql
```

7. Verify that MariaDB is running properly by connecting to the database:

```
root # mysql -u root -p
```

17.1.6 Migrate your PostgreSQL Database

SLE11 SP3 and SLE12 GA get a newer version of the PostgreSQL database as a maintenance update. Because of the required migration work of the database, there is no automatic upgrade process. As such, the switch from one version to another needs to be done manually.

The migration process is conducted by the **pg_upgrade** command which is an alternative method of the classic dump and reload. In comparison with the "dump & reload" method, **pg_upgrade** makes the migration less time-consuming.

Each PostgreSQL version stores its files in different, version-dependant directories. After the update the directories will change to:

SLE11 SP3/SP4

/usr/lib/postgresql91/ to /usr/lib/postgresql94/

SLE12 GA

/usr/lib/postgresql93/ to /usr/lib/postgresql94/

To perform the database migration, do the following:

1. Make sure the following preconditions are fulfilled:

- If not already done, upgrade any package of the old PostgreSQL version to the latest release through a maintenance update.

- Create a backup of your existing database.

- Install the packages of the new PostgreSQL major version. For SLE12 this means to install `postgresql94-server` and all the packages it depends on.

- Install the package `postgresql94-contrib` which contains the command **pg_upgrade**.

- Make sure you have enough free space in your PostgreSQL data area, which is `/var/lib/pgsql/data` by default. If space is tight, try to reduce size with the following SQL command on each database (can take very long!):

```
VACUUM FULL
```

2. Stop the PostgreSQL server:

```
root # /usr/sbin/rcpostgresql stop
```

3. Rename your old data directory:

```
root # mv /var/lib/pgsql/data /var/lib/pgsql/data.old
```

4. Create a new data directory:

```
root # mkdir -p /var/lib/pgsql/data
```

5. If you have changed your configuration files in the old version, copy the files `postgresql.conf` `pg_hba.conf` to your new `data` directory:

```
root # cp /var/lib/pgsql/data.old/*.conf \
    /var/lib/pgsql/data
```

6. Initialize your new database instance either manually with **initdb** or by starting and stopping PostgreSQL, which will do it automatically:

```
root # /usr/sbin/rcpostgresql start
root # /usr/sbin/rcpostgresql stop
```

7. Start the migration process and replace the *OLD* placeholder with the older version:

```
root # pg_upgrade \
  --old-datadir "/var/lib/pgsql/data.old" \
  --new-datadir "/var/lib/pgsql/data" \
  --old-bindir "/usr/lib/postgresqlOLD/bin/" \
  --new-bindir "/usr/lib/postgresql94/bin/"
```

8. Start your new database instance:

```
root # /usr/sbin/rcpostgresql start
```

9. Check if the migration was successful. There is no general tool to automate this step. It depends on your use case how much and what you want to test.

10. Remove any old PostgreSQL packages and your old data directory:

```
root # zypper search -s postgresqlOLD | xargs zypper rm -u
root # rm -rf /var/lib/pgsql/data.old
```

17.1.7   Shut Down Virtual Machine Guests

If your machine serves as a VM Host Server for KVM or Xen, make sure to properly shut down all running VM Guests prior to the update. Otherwise you may not be able to access the guests after the update.

17.2 Supported Upgrade Paths for SLE

> **❗ Important: Cross-architecture Upgrades Are Not Supported**
>
> Cross-architecture upgrades, such as upgrading from a 32-bit version of SUSE Linux Enterprise Server to the 64-bit version, or upgrading from big endian to little endian are *not* supported!
>
> Specifically, SLE 11 on POWER (big endian) to SLE 12 SP1 on POWER (new: little endian!), is *not* supported.
>
> Also, since SUSE Linux Enterprise 12 is 64-bit only, upgrades from any 32-bit SUSE Linux Enterprise 11 systems to SUSE Linux Enterprise 12 and later are *not* supported.

Before you perform any migration, read *Section 17.1, "General Preparations"*.

Upgrading from SUSE Linux Enterprise 10 (any Service Pack)

There is no supported direct migration path to SUSE Linux Enterprise 12. A fresh installation is recommended instead.

Upgrading from SUSE Linux Enterprise 11 GA, SP1 or SP2

There is no supported direct migration path to SUSE Linux Enterprise 12. You need at least SLE 11 SP3 before you can proceed to SLE 12.

If you cannot do a fresh install, you need to first update from SLE 11 GA to SP1, then from SLE 11 SP1 to SP2, and then from SLE 11 SP2 to SP3. These steps are described in the *SUSE Linux Enterprise 11 Deployment Guide* [https://www.suse.com/documentation/sles11/]. Then proceed with *Section 17.3, "Supported Methods for Upgrading SUSE Linux Enterprise"*.

Upgrading from SUSE Linux Enterprise 11 SP3 or SP4

Refer to *Section 17.3, "Supported Methods for Upgrading SUSE Linux Enterprise"* for details.

Upgrading from SUSE Linux Enterprise 12 to SP1

Refer to *Chapter 18, Service Pack Migration* for details.

17.3 Supported Methods for Upgrading SUSE Linux Enterprise

Upgrading from SUSE Linux Enterprise 11 SP3 to SUSE Linux Enterprise 12, SUSE Linux Enterprise 11 SP3 to SUSE Linux Enterprise 12 SP1, or SUSE Linux Enterprise 11 SP4 to SUSE Linux Enterprise 12 SP1 is supported using one of the following methods:

- Manual upgrade, booting from an installation medium (see *Section 17.4, "Upgrading Manually from SLE 11 SP3 to SLE 12 SP1, Using an Installation Source"*).

- Semi-automated migration, possible via SSH (see *Section 17.5, "Migrating Automatically from SLE 11 SP3 or SP4 to SLE 12 SP1"*) or with *Chapter 18, Service Pack Migration*.

17.4 Upgrading Manually from SLE 11 SP3 to SLE 12 SP1, Using an Installation Source

Before you upgrade your system, read *Section 17.1, "General Preparations"* first.

To upgrade your system this way, you need to boot from an installation source, like you would do for a fresh installation. However, when the boot screen appears, you need to select *Upgrade* (instead of *Installation*). The installation source to boot from can be one of the following:

- A local installation medium (like a DVD, or an ISO image on a USB mass storage device). For detailed instructions, see *Section 17.4.1, "Upgrading from an Installation Medium"*.

- A network installation source. You can either boot from the local medium and then select the respective network installation type, or boot via PXE. For detailed instructions, see *Section 17.4.2, "Upgrading from a Network Installation Source"*.

17.4.1 Upgrading from an Installation Medium

The procedure below describes booting from a DVD as an example, but you can also use another local installation medium like an ISO image on a USB mass storage device. The way to select the boot method and to start up the system from the medium depends on the system architecture and on whether the machine has a traditional BIOS or UEFI. For details, see the links below.

1. Insert DVD 1 of the SUSE Linux Enterprise 12 SP1 installation medium and boot your machine. A *Welcome* screen is displayed, followed by the boot screen.

2. Select the respective boot method to start the system from the medium (see *Section 6.1, "Choosing the Installation Method"*).

3. Start up the system from the medium (see *Section 6.2, "System Start-up for Installation"*).

4. Proceed with the upgrade process as described in *Section 17.6, "Starting the Upgrade Process After Booting"*.

17.4.2 Upgrading from a Network Installation Source

If you want to start an upgrade from a network installation source, make sure that the following requirements are met:

REQUIREMENTS FOR UPGRADING FROM A NETWORK INSTALLATION SOURCE

Network Installation Source

A network installation source is set up according to *Section 13.2, "Setting Up the Server Holding the Installation Sources"*.

Network Connection and Network Services

Both the installation server and the target machine have a functioning network connection. The network must provide the following services: a name service, DHCP (optional, but needed for booting via PXE), and OpenSLP (optional).

Installation Media

You have a SUSE Linux Enterprise DVD 1 (or a local ISO image) at hand to boot the target system *or* a target system that is set up for booting via PXE according to *Section 13.3.5, "Preparing the Target System for PXE Boot"*. **Refer to** *Chapter 13, Remote Installation* **for** in-depth information on starting the upgrade from a remote server.

When upgrading from network installation source, you can either boot from the local medium and then select the respective network installation type, or boot via PXE. Select the method of your choice and proceed as described in *Procedure 17.2* or *Procedure 17.3*.

This procedure describes booting from a DVD as an example, but you can also use another local installation medium like an ISO image on a USB mass storage device. The way to select the boot method and to start up the system from the medium depends on the system architecture and on whether the machine has a traditional BIOS or UEFI. For details, see the links below.

1. Insert DVD 1 of the SUSE Linux Enterprise 12 SP1 installation media and boot your machine. A *Welcome* screen is displayed, followed by the boot screen.

2. Select the type of network installation source you want to use (FTP, HTTP, NFS, SMB, or SLP). Usually you get this choice by pressing F4 , but in case your machine is equipped with UEFI instead of a traditional BIOS, you may need to manually adjust boot parameters. For details, see *Installing from a Network Server* in *Chapter 6, Installation with YaST*.

3. Proceed with the upgrade process as described in *Section 17.6, "Starting the Upgrade Process After Booting"*.

PROCEDURE 17.3: MANUALLY UPGRADING FROM SLE 11 SP3 OR SP4 TO SLE 12 SP1 VIA NETWORK
INSTALLATION SOURCE—BOOTING VIA PXE

To perform an upgrade from a network installation source using PXE Boot, proceed as follows:

1. Adjust the setup of your DHCP server to provide the address information needed for booting via PXE. For details, see *Section 13.3.5, "Preparing the Target System for PXE Boot"*.

2. Set up a TFTP server to hold the boot image needed for booting via PXE. Use DVD 1 of your SUSE Linux Enterprise 12 SP1 installation media for this or follow the instructions in *Section 13.3.2, "Setting Up a TFTP Server"*.

3. Prepare PXE Boot and Wake-on-LAN on the target machine.

4. Initiate the boot of the target system and use VNC to remotely connect to the installation routine running on this machine. For more information, see *Section 13.5.1, "VNC Installation"*.

5. Proceed with the upgrade process as described in *Section 17.6, "Starting the Upgrade Process After Booting"*.

17.5 Migrating Automatically from SLE 11 SP3 or SP4 to SLE 12 SP1

Before you upgrade your system, read *Section 17.1, "General Preparations"* first. To perform an automated migration, proceed as follows:

PROCEDURE 17.4: AUTOMATED MIGRATION FROM SUSE LINUX ENTERPRISE 11 SP3 TO SUSE LINUX ENTERPRISE 12 SP1

1. Copy the installation Kernel `linux` and the file `initrd` from `/boot/x86_64/loader/` from your first installation DVD to your system's `/boot` directory:

   ```
   cp -vi DVDROOT/boot/x86_64/loader/linux /boot/linux.upgrade
   cp -vi DVDROOT/boot/x86_64/loader/initrd /boot/initrd.upgrade
   ```

   `DVDROOT` denotes the path where your system mounts the DVD, usually `/run/media/$USER/$DVDNAME`.

2. Open the GRUB legacy configuration file `/boot/grub/menu.lst` and add another section. For other boot loaders, edit the respective configuration file(s). Adjust device names and the `root` parameter accordingly. For example:

   ```
   title Linux Upgrade Kernel
   kernel (hd0,0)/boot/linux.upgrade root=/dev/sda1 upgrade=1 OPTIONAL_PARAMETERS
   initrd (hd0,0)/boot/initrd.upgrade
   ```

   `OPTIONAL_PARAMETERS` denote additional boot parameters which you might need to boot your system and perform the upgrade. These may be kernel parameters needed for your system—check if you need to review and copy those from an existing GRUB entry. They also may be SUSE linuxrc parameters, documented online [http://en.opensuse.org/Linuxrc].

3. If the upgrade should be done automated (see *Section 26.2, "Running the Automated Upgrade"*), add the `autoupgrade=1` to the end of the `kernel` line in your GRUB configuration.

4. Reboot your machine and select the newly added section from the boot menu (here: *Linux Upgrade Kernel*). You can use **grubonce** to preselect the newly created GRUB entry for an unattended automatic reboot into the newly created entry. You can also use **reboot** to initiate the reboot from the command line.

5. Proceed with the usual upgrade process as described in *Section 17.6, "Starting the Upgrade Process After Booting"*.

6. After the upgrade process was finished successfully, remove the installation Kernel and initrd files (`/boot/linux.upgrade` and `/boot/initrd.upgrade`). They are not needed anymore.

17.6 Starting the Upgrade Process After Booting

1. After you have booted (either from an installation medium or the network), select the *Upgrade* entry on the boot screen.

 Warning: Wrong Choice May Lead to Data Loss

   If you select *Installation* instead of *Upgrade*, data may be lost later. You need to be extra careful to not destroy your data partitions by doing a fresh installation, e.g. by repartitioning the disks (which can destroy the existing partitions) or by reformatting the data partitions (which erases all data on them).

   Make sure to select *Upgrade* here.

   YaST starts the installation system.

2. On the *Welcome* screen choose *Language* and *Keyboard* and accept the license agreement. Proceed with *Next*.
   YaST checks your partitions for already installed SUSE Linux Enterprise systems.

3. On the *Select for Upgrade* screen, select the partition to upgrade and click *Next*.
   YaST mounts the selected partition and displays all repositories that have been found on the partition that you want to upgrade.

4. On the *Previously Used Repositories* screen, adjust the status of the repositories: enable those you want to include in the upgrade process and disable any repositories that are no longer needed. Proceed with *Next*.

5. On the *Registration* screen, select whether to register the upgraded system now (by entering your registration data and clicking *Next*) or if to *Skip Registration*. For details on registering your system, see *Section 17.8, "Registering Your System"*.

The following *Installation Settings* screen is the last step before the upgrade starts.

6. Review the *Installation Settings* for the upgrade, especially the *Update Options*. Choose between the following options:

   - *Only Update Installed Packages*, in which case you might miss new features shipped with the latest SUSE Linux Enterprise version.

   - *Update with Installation of New Software and Features*. Click *Select Patterns* if you want to enable or disable patterns and packages according to your wishes.

    Note: Choice of Desktop

   If you used KDE before upgrading to SUSE Linux Enterprise 12 (`DEFAULT_WM` in `/etc/sysconfig/windowmanager` was set to `kde*`), your desktop environment will automatically be replaced with GNOME after the upgrade. By default, the KDM display manager will be replaced with GDM.

   To change the choice of desktop environment or window manager, adjust the software selection by clicking *Select Patterns*.

7. If all settings are according to your wishes, start the installation and removal procedure by clicking *Update*.

8. After the upgrade process was finished successfully, check for any "orphaned packages". Orphaned packages are packages which belong to no active repository anymore. The following command gives you a list of these:

```
zypper packages --orphaned
```

With this list, you can decide if a package is still needed or can be deinstalled safely.

17.7 Updating via SUSE Manager

SUSE Manager is a server solution for providing updates, patches, and security fixes for SUSE Linux Enterprise clients. It comes with a set of tools and a Web-based user interface for management tasks.

The SUSE Manager documentation at https://www.suse.com/documentation/suse_manager/ book_susemanager_install/data/s1-maintenance-update.html gives an overview of its features and instructions on how to set up server and clients.

17.8 Registering Your System

If you skipped the registration step during the installation, you can register your system at any time using the *Product Registration* module in YaST.

Registering your systems has these advantages:

- Getting support

- Getting security updates and bug fixes

- Access to SUSE Customer Center

1. Start YaST and select *Software* › *Product Registration* to open the *Registration* dialog.

2. Provide the *E-mail* address associated with the SUSE account you or your organization uses to manage subscriptions. In case you do not have a SUSE account yet, go to the SUSE Customer Center home page (https://scc.suse.com/) to create one.

3. Enter the *Registration Code* you received with your copy of SUSE Linux Enterprise Server.

4. Proceed with *Next* to start the registration process. If one or more local registration servers are available on your network, you can choose one of them from a list. Alternatively, choose *Cancel* to ignore the local registration servers and register with the default SUSE registration server.
   During registration the online update channels will be added to your installation setup. After successful registration, YaST lists extensions, add-ons, and modules that are available for your system. To select and install them, proceed with *Section 9.1, "Installing Modules and Extensions from Online Channels".*

17.9 Retaining Kernel Packages

When installing a new kernel with YaST or Zypper, SUSE Linux Enterprise preserves the last two kernels and the running one. Usually this is sufficient.

However, there may be situations where you need to preserve more kernel versions, for example, for testing purposes. To enable this, SUSE Linux Enterprise supports the *multiversion kernel feature*. By enabling and configuring this feature the default behavior can be changed and configured to:

- delete an old kernel only after the system has been rebooted successfully with the new kernel

- keep a specified number of older kernels as fallback

- keep a specific kernel version

After the successful reboot, a script will compare the list of installed kernels with the settings in `/etc/zypp/zypp.conf` and delete those kernels that are no longer needed.

17.9.1   Enabling the Multiversion Kernel Feature

The default behavior is defined in the configuration file `/etc/zypp/zypp.conf`:

```
root # grep ^multiversion /etc/zypp/zypp.conf
multiversion = provides:multiversion(kernel)
multiversion.kernels = latest,latest-1,running
```

Remove any hash mark (#) before the line `multiversion` above to enable this feature (which should already be the case). The second line is used to configure *which* kernels need to be preserved. You need to enable both, otherwise the system will keep *all* kernels and it will fill up your hard disk.

The `multiversion.kernels` line can contain several keywords in different combinations and order:

`latest`

　　Keep kernel with the highest version number

`latest-N`

　　Keep kernel with the Nth highest version number; N is a number starting from 1

`running`

　　Keep the current running kernel

`oldest`

> Keep kernel with the lowest version number (the kernel on the released product)

`oldest-N`

> Keep kernel with the *N* th lowest version number

`3.12.28-4.6`

> Keep this exact kernel version

17.9.2 Use Case: Deleting an Old Kernel After Reboot Only

You want to make sure that an old kernel will only be deleted after the system has rebooted successfully of the new kernel.

Change the following line in `/etc/zypp/zypp.conf`:

```
multiversion.kernels = latest,running
```

The previous parameters tell the system to keep the latest kernel and the running one only if they differ.

17.9.3 Use Case: Keeping Older Kernels as Fallback

You want to keep one or more kernel versions to have one or more "spare" kernels.

This use case can be useful if you need kernels for testing reasons. In case something goes wrong, for example, your machine does not boot, you still can use one or more kernel versions which are known to be good.

Change the following line in `/etc/zypp/zypp.conf`:

```
multiversion.kernels = latest,latest-1,latest-2,running
```

When you reboot your system after the installation of a new kernel, the system will keep three kernels: the new and running kernel (configured as `latest,running`), the previous kernel version of the new kernel (configured as `latest-1`), and the predecessor of the previous kernel version (configured as `latest-2`).

17.9.4 Use Case: Keep a Specific Kernel Version

You make regular system updates and install new kernel versions. However, you are also compiling your own kernel version for various reasons and want to make sure that the system will keep it.

Change the following line in `/etc/zypp/zypp.conf`:

```
multiversion.kernels = latest,3.12.28-4.20,running
```

When you reboot your system after the installation of a new kernel, the system will keep two kernels: the new and running kernel (configured as `latest,running`) and your self-compiled kernel (configured as `3.12.28-4.20`).

18 Service Pack Migration

SUSE offers now new tools with some interesting features to system administrators for online service pack migration. These are simple command line tools, an intuitive graphical user interface, support for "rollback" of service packs, and some more. This chapter explains how to do a service pack migration step by step with the new tools.

18.1 Supported Scenarios and Versions

SUSE supports the following scenarios, be it offline or online:

Online

    SUSE Customer Center, Subscription Management Tool (SMT), SUSE Manager

Offline

    Boot DVD, flash disk, ISO image, AutoYaST, "plain RPM" and third-party tools

The following versions are supported:

Online

    SUSE Linux Enterprise 12

Offline

    SUSE Linux Enterprise 11 SP3/SP4, SUSE Linux Enterprise 12

Manually/Third-Party

    SUSE Linux Enterprise 12

18.2 Service Pack Migration Workflow

A service pack migration can be executed by either YaST, **zypper**, AutoYaST, RPM, or third-party tools. Only the first two are described in this chapter. Regardless of the method, a service pack migration consists of the following steps:

1. Find possible migration targets.

2. Select a migration target.

3. Request and enable new repositories.

4. Run the migration.

The list of migration targets depends on the products you have installed. If you have an extension installed for which the new SP is not yet available, it could be that no migration target is offered to you.

The list of migration targets available for your host will always be retrieved from the SUSE Customer Center and depend on installed products or extensions and may change over time—which means that, for example, migration from SLE12 GA to SP2 may be possible for one host, but not possible for another.

18.3   Migrating with YaST (Online Migration Tool)

To perform a service pack migration with YaST, use the *Online Migration* tool. By default, YaST does not install any packages from a third-party repository. If a package was installed from a third-party repository, YaST prevents packages from being replaced with the same package coming from SUSE.

Note that when performing the SP migration, YaST will install all recommended packages. Especially in the case of custom minimal installations, this may increase the installation size of the system significantly. To change this default behaviour, adjust /etc/zypp/zypp.conf and set the following variable:

```
solver.onlyRequires = true
```

This changes the behavior of all package operations, such as the installation of patches or new packages.

To start the service pack migration, do the following:

1. Install the latest updates to get the *Online Migration* module.

2. Install the package yast2-migration and its dependencies.

3. Restart YaST, otherwise the newly installed module will not be shown in the control center.

4. Start the *Online Migration* module from the *Software* section in YaST.

YaST will show possible migration targets and a summary.

5. Select a migration target and proceed with *Next*.

6. In case the Online Migration tool offers update repositories, decide if you want them. It is recommended to proceed with *Yes*.

7. If the Online Migration tool finds obsolete repositories coming from DVD or a local server, it is highly recommended to disable them. Old repositories from SUSE Customer Center or Subscription Management Tool are removed automatically.

8. Check the summary and proceed with the migration by clicking *Next*. Confirm with *Start Update*.

9. After the successful migration restart your system.

18.4 Migrating with Zypper

To perform a service pack migration with Zypper, use the command line tool **zypper** `migration`.

Note that when performing the SP migration, Zypper will install all recommended packages. Especially in the case of custom minimal installations, this may increase the installation size of the system significantly. To change this default behaviour, adjust `/etc/zypp/zypp.conf` and set the following variable:

```
solver.onlyRequires = true
installRecommends=false # or commented
```

This changes the behavior of all package operations, such as the installation of patches or new packages. To change the behavior of Zypper for a single invocation, add the parameter `--no-recommends` to your command line.

To start the service pack migration, do the following:

1. Log in to your SUSE Linux Enterprise 12 machine.

2. Install the latest updates.

3. Install the packages `zypper-migration-plugin` and their dependencies.

4. Run the **zypper** migration:

```
root # zypper migration
Executing 'zypper  patch-check'

Refreshing service 'SUSE_Linux_Enterprise_Server_12_x86_64'.
Loading repository data...
Reading installed packages...
0 patches needed (0 security patches)


Available migrations:

    1 | SUSE Linux Enterprise Server 12 SP1 x86_64
```

By default, Zypper uses the option `--no-allow-vendor-change` which is passed to **zypper** dup. If a package was installed from a third-party repository, this option prevents packages from being replaced with the same package coming from SUSE.

5. If Zypper finds obsolete repositories coming from DVD or a local server, it is highly recommended to disable them. Old SCC or SMT repositories are removed automatically.

6. Review all the changes, especially the packages that are going to be removed. Proceed by typing y (the exact number of packages to upgrade can vary on your system):

```
266 packages to upgrade, 54 to downgrade, 17 new, 8 to reinstall, 5 to remove,
 1 to change arch.
Overall download size: 285.1 MiB. Already cached: 0 B  After the operation,
 additional 139.8 MiB will be used.
Continue? [y/n/? shows all options] (y):
```

Use the [Shift]–[Page ↑] or [Shift]–[Page ↓] keys to scroll in your shell.

7. After successful migration restart your system.

IV Imaging and Creating Products

19 Creating Images with KIWI

KIWI is a system for creating operating system images. With KIWI you can create LiveCDs, LiveDVDs, flash disks to use for Linux-supported hardware platforms and virtual disks for virtualization and cloud systems (like Xen, KVM, VMware, EC2 and more). The images created by KIWI can also be used in a PXE environment to boot from network.

For comprehensive KIWI documentation, see https://github.com/openSUSE/kiwi or install the `kiwi-doc` package on your system.

With YaST Image Creator, SUSE Linux Enterprise Server also provides a graphical interface for KIWI. For details, refer to *Chapter 23, Creating Images with YaST Image Creator*.

20 Creating Images with SUSE Studio

SUSE Studio is an online image creation tool which allows you to build and test appliances in a Web browser. It supports creation of virtual appliances and live systems, based on either openSUSE or SUSE Linux Enterprise. Apart from the publicly hosted SUSE Studio release that is available at http://susestudio.com/, there is also SUSE Studio Onsite. It is a SUSE Studio release intended for installation on a server machine behind the firewall.

For the SUSE Studio Onsite documentation, see https://www.suse.com/documentation/suse_studio/. For the SUSE Studio documentation, refer to https://susestudio.com/help/.

21 Creating Add-on Products With Add-on Product Creator

An add-on is a special designed media, usually a CD or DVD, to extend SUSE Linux Enterprise Server with your product. The Add-on Product Creator was developed to support customers and partners and simplify third-party software distribution for all SUSE products.

To be able to use the Add-on Product Creator you need to install the package `yast2-add-on-creator` from the SUSE Software Development Kit. The SDK is a module for SUSE Linux Enterprise and is available via an online channel from the SUSE Customer Center. Alternatively, go to http://download.suse.com/, search for `SUSE Linux Enterprise Software Development Kit` and download it from there. Refer to *Chapter 9, Installing Modules, Extensions, and Third Party Add-On Products* for details.

21.1 Creating Images

To create an image of an add-on product, proceed as follows:

1. Start YaST and open the *Add-on Creator* module.

2. If you have not created an add-on before, click *Create an Add-on from the Beginning* to start. Alternatively, you may create the add-on based on an existing add-on product. Specify the path to the directory containing the data—this may also be a mounted ISO image or a CD/DVD.
   In case you have already created an add-on, the window lists all existing add-ons. You may *Edit* or *Delete* them. Choose *Add* to create a new one.
   This tutorial explains how to *Create an Add-on from the Beginning*.

3. Enter the name (*Add-on Product Label*) and the version of your add-on and provide additional information:

- Under *Required Product* choose the SUSE Linux product for which to create the add-on.

- Select the path to a directory containing the add-on product packages.

- Optionally, choose the path to a directory containing RPM packages from the *Required Product*. Typically, these packages originate in the required product (already chosen) and are not part of the add-on itself, but other packages from the add-on depend on them. These packages will not be added to the add-on product, but can be used to create patterns.

Proceed with *Next*.

4. Each installation media contains a content file and a product file defining the add-on product. Use this dialog to provide the data for both files. Select an entry and choose *Edit* to set or change a value. Alternatively, double-click an entry. See *Help* for more information and possible values.

To import values from an existing content or product file, choose the respective *Import* button.

You need to at least enter values for *Product architectures*, *Product name* and *Vendor name* of the content file. Proceed with *Next*.

5. Enter or change the package descriptions on the next screen. Use *Add Language* to insert a new language and add translated descriptions (this step is optional). You may also *Import* existing package descriptions.

Proceed with *Next*.

6. Optionally, add patterns in the next step. With patterns you can group your RPM packages. Use *New* to add a new pattern name and change the respective attributes in the list below. Check *Required Pattern* for patterns that will automatically be selected for installation when installing the add-on product.

Proceed with *Next*.

7. Provide a path to the output directory. If you rather want to create an ISO image, check *Create ISO Image* and provide a file name. Select *Create Changelog* to create a file containing the changelog entries of all packages included in your product. Additionally, you can modify the workflow and add files:

- Use *Configure Workflow* to enter files to customize your product workflow. This way you can, for example, insert additional dialogs with options into the add-on installation process that are needed for the correct product operation. See *Help* for more information.

- Use *Optional Files* to the following files to your add-on product:

    info.txt
    > A text file containing general information about the add-on product.

    License Files
    > Add files containing license information in various languages. The files are named `license.LANGUAGE`, for example `license.en_US`.

    README Files
    > Add README files with a name of your choice.

    Enter the content of the files in the respective text boxes. Alternatively, *Import* the content from an existing file.

    Proceed with *Next*.

8. Sign your add-on product with your GPG key to provide evidence of the origin of your product. If you do not have a key, create one first and enter the respective passphrase twice.

9. Check your settings in the configuration summary and proceed with *Finish*. Choose the *Back* buttons to change a setting.

21.2 Add-on Structure

An add-on product contains the following files and directories:

`ARCHIVES.gz`
> Contains information about all packages included (the output of `rpm -qil` for each package). This file is compressed with gzip.

`Changelog`
> Contains all the changes of the RPM files ordered by date of change.

`content`

> The content file created during the add-on setup.

`content.asc`

> The GPG signature file.

`content.key`, `gpg-pubkey-NUMBER.asc`

> The public GPG key.

`INDEX.gz`

> A list of all RPM files. This file is compressed with gzip.

`ls-lR.gz`

> A list of all files and directories of the add-on product medium. This file is compressed with gzip.

`media.N/`

> Contains files with basic information about the add-on media set. The directory is numbered, so `media.1/` is for the first add-on medium (for example DVD1). Additional media have a consecutive number.

`suse/`

> Contains sub directories with architecture-specific information. Exceptions are `noarch/` for architecture-independent packages, and `src/` for source packages. Proprietary software packages are stored under `nosrc/`.

22 Creating Images with YaST Product Creator

The YaST Product Creator is a graphical tool to provide creation of installable images. To be able to use it you need to install the package `yast2-product-creator` from the SUSE Software Development Kit. The SDK is a module for SUSE Linux Enterprise and is available via an online channel from the SUSE Customer Center. Alternatively download it from http://download.suse.com/. (Search for `SUSE Linux Enterprise Software Development Kit`). Refer to *Chapter 9, Installing Modules, Extensions, and Third Party Add-On Products* for details.

22.1 Creating Images

To create an image of a product, proceed as follows:

1. Start YaST and open the *Product Creator* module.

2. If you are starting the Product Creator for the first time, enter the configuration name and choose the method for adding packages to the ISO image.
   In case you have already created a product, the window shows a list of all existing products. You may *Edit* or *Delete* them. Choose *Add* to create a new one.

3. Select or deselect package sources to be used within the product by selecting an entry and choosing *Select* or *Remove*, respectively.
   Choose *Create New* to start the YaST Add-on Product Creator for setting up a new software source. Start the YaST *Installation Sources* module afterwards and add the source you created. Restart the Product Creator to make the source available for selection.
   Proceed with *Next*.

    Note: Unsupported Target Architectures
   Do not change the target architecture. As of SUSE Linux Enterprise Server 12, the Product Creator does not support building of different architectures.

   Proceed with *Next*.

4. Select the base source from the list of repositories chosen in the previous step. If the resulting ISO image should be bootable, it must contain a `/boot` directory containing files needed to boot the system.
   Proceed with *Next*.

5. Enter the path in which to create the skeleton directory in the *Product Creator Configuration* screen. Choose whether to generate an ISO file or a directory tree.
   Activating *Copy only needed files* saves space. Optionally enter credits by specifying the *CD Publisher* and the *CD Preparer*.
   Proceed with *Next*.

6. Edit the content of the `isolinux.cfg` file, if it is a part of the configuration. Usually you can leave it as it is. If the file is not part of the configuration, add it now with *Load File*.
   Proceed with *Next*.

7. Select the software packages to be included in the product. The default view lets you select patterns. Choose *Details* to be able to select individual packages. The solver tries to solve all package dependencies automatically whenever you select new packages. In case it fails, you need to manually resolve the conflict. If a conflict cannot be solved, a source providing a needed package may be missing.
   Proceed with *Next*.

8. Sign your product with *Digitally Sign the Product on the Medium*, if needed. Provide a key for your product configuration. Signing your product with your GPG key provides evidence of the origin of your product.
   Proceed with *Next*.

9. Check your settings in the configuration summary and proceed with *Finish*. Choose the *Back* buttons to change a setting.

Your product definition is now completed. The Product Creator allows you to choose from the following actions:

- *Create Product*. Creates an ISO image of the selected product. If there is something missing, the process will be aborted. Correct the error and repeat the configuration.

- *Create Image with KIWI*. Use the pull-down menu to choose from different target formats, such as Live media or Xen images.

Creating Images

23 Creating Images with YaST Image Creator

The YaST Image Creator is a graphical interface for the KIWI imaging tool (see http://doc.opensuse.org/projects/kiwi/doc/ for more information on KIWI). With Image Creator, you can create a new KIWI configuration, or import an existing one and modify it, then build the image after the configuration is complete. Advanced users can save the configuration to disk, then modify it and build the image manually.

To be able to use it you need to install the package `yast2-product-creator` from the SUSE Software Development Kit. The SDK is a module for SUSE Linux Enterprise and is available via an online channel from the SUSE Customer Center. Alternatively download it from http://download.suse.com/. (Search for `SUSE Linux Enterprise Software Development Kit`). Refer to *Chapter 9, Installing Modules, Extensions, and Third Party Add-On Products* for details.

23.1 Creating Images

To create an image of a product, proceed as follows:

1. Start YaST and open the *Image Creator* module.

2. The window lists all existing images configuration. You may *Edit* or *Delete* them. Choose *Add* to create a new one.

3. Enter the name for the new *Kiwi Configuration*, and choose whether you want to begin from scratch, or base on existing KIWI configuration. In the latter case, provide a path to the existing KIWI configuration so that Image Creator can import it.

4. Choose the image type you need to build. There are several options - *Live ISO Image, Xen Image*, or *Virtual Disk Image*.

5. Select the output directory where you want to store the KIWI configuration.

6. If you are running Image Creator on a 64-bit architecture, you can force KIWI to configure the image for 32-bit architecture, and, moreover, limit it to i586 only.

7. Add the list of package repositories you need to use for your KIWI configuration. Click *Add* to add a new repository, or *Add from System* to add repositories that are configured in the system where Image Creator is running. If you need to modify details of an existing repository, select it and click *Edit*. To remove an unneeded repository, select it and click *Delete*.

Proceed with *Next*.

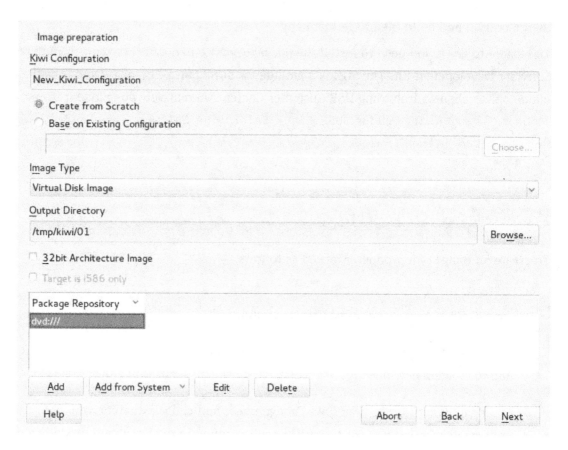

FIGURE 23.1: EDITING REPOSITORY IN IMAGE CREATOR

8. There are four tabs in the next screen. Here you can set more configuration options supported by KIWI to fine-tune the resulting image.

In the *Image Configuration* tab, you can set the image version and size, and then modify the software selection for the image in detail. You can specify patterns/packages for three package sections: packages included on the image, in the bootstrap, and packages intended to be deleted from the image.

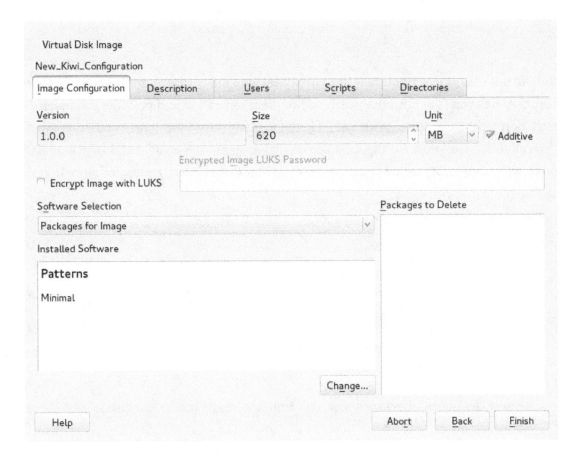

FIGURE 23.2: KIWI DETAILED CONFIGURATION IN IMAGE CREATOR

To change the list of packages and/or patterns intended for installation (or for ignoring), click *Change* and *YaST Package Selector* opens, where you can make your selection.

In the *Description* tab, fill in information about the author of the image, description, and the locale settings.

The *Users* tab lets you add new users who should be available on the target system.

Next, you can edit the configuration *Scripts* used to build your image.

Lastly, configure the directory with system configuration and scripts in the *Directories* tab.

9. After you finish configuring the image, click *Finish* to build it. YaST asks you to confirm your choice. If you decline, the configuration will be saved, and you are returned to the overview screen. If you confirm the build, KIWI is started, and you can see a progress window showing the KIWI log file.

If the image is successfully built, it is saved to the output directory specified earlier.

24 Deploying Customized Preinstallations

Rolling out customized preinstallations of SUSE Linux Enterprise Server to many identical machines spares you from installing each one of them separately and provides a standardized installation for the end users. With YaST Firstboot, create customized preinstallation images and determine the workflow for the final personalizing steps that involve end user interaction (as opposed to AutoYaST, which allows completely automated installations; for more information, see *Chapter 25, Automated Installation*).

Creating a custom installation, rolling it out to your hardware, and personalizing the final product involves the following steps:

1. Prepare the master machine whose disk needs to be cloned to the client machines. For more information, refer to *Section 24.1, "Preparing the Master Machine"*.

2. Customize the firstboot workflow. For more information, refer to *Section 24.2, "Customizing the Firstboot Installation"*.

3. Clone the master machine's disk and roll this image out to the clients' disks. For more information, refer to *Section 24.3, "Cloning the Master Installation"*.

4. Have the end user personalize the instance of SUSE Linux Enterprise Server. For more information, refer to *Section 24.4, "Personalizing the Installation"*.

24.1 Preparing the Master Machine

To prepare a master machine for a firstboot workflow, proceed as follows:

1. Insert the installation media into the master machine.

2. Boot the machine.

3. Perform a normal installation including all necessary configuration steps and wait for the installed machine to boot. Also install the `yast2-firstboot` package.

4. To define your own workflow of YaST configuration steps for the end user or to add your own YaST modules to this workflow, proceed to *Section 24.2, "Customizing the Firstboot Installation"*. Otherwise proceed directly to *Step 5*.

5. Enable firstboot as `root`:

Create an empty file `/var/lib/YaST2/reconfig_system` to trigger firstboot's execution. This file will be deleted after the firstboot configuration has been successfully accomplished. Create this file using the following command:

```
touch /var/lib/YaST2/reconfig_system
```

6. **Proceed to** *Section 24.3, "Cloning the Master Installation"*.

24.2 Customizing the Firstboot Installation

Customizing the firstboot installation workflow may involve several different components. Customizing them is optional. If you do not make any changes, firstboot performs the installation using the default settings. The following options are available:

- Customizing messages to the user, as described in *Section 24.2.1, "Customizing YaST Messages"*.

- Customizing licenses and license actions, as described in *Section 24.2.2, "Customizing the License Action"*.

- Customizing the release notes to display, as described in *Section 24.2.3, "Customizing the Release Notes"*.

- Customizing the order and number of components involved in the installation, as described in *Section 24.2.4, "Customizing the Workflow"*.

- Configuring additional optional scripts, as described in *Section 24.2.5, "Configuring Additional Scripts"*.

To customize any of these components, modify the following configuration files:

`/etc/sysconfig/firstboot`

Configure various aspects of firstboot (such as release notes, scripts, and license actions).

`/etc/YaST2/firstboot.xml`

Configure the installation workflow by enabling or disabling components or adding custom ones.

Provide translations for such a customized installation workflow, as described in *Section 24.2.6, "Providing Translations of the Installation Workflow"*.

Tip: Alternative Location of the Control File

`/etc/YaST2/firstboot.xml` is the default path for the control file, installed by the `yast2-firstboot` package. If you need to define a different location for the control file, edit `/etc/sysconfig/firstboot`, and change the `FIRSTBOOT_CONTROL_FILE` variable to your preferred location.

If you want to customize more than the workflow components, refer to the `control.xml` documentation at http://doc.opensuse.org/projects/YaST/SLES11/tdg/inst_in_general_chap.html#product_control.

24.2.1   Customizing YaST Messages

By default, an installation of SUSE Linux Enterprise Server contains several default messages that are localized and displayed at certain stages of the installation process. These include a welcome message, a license message, and a congratulatory message at the end of installation. You can replace any of these with your own versions and include localized versions of them in the installation. To include your own welcome message, proceed as follows:

1. Log in as `root`.

2. Open the `/etc/sysconfig/firstboot` configuration file and apply the following changes:

    a. Set `FIRSTBOOT_WELCOME_DIR` to the directory path where you want to store the files containing the welcome message and the localized versions, for example:

    ```
    FIRSTBOOT_WELCOME_DIR="/usr/share/firstboot/"
    ```

    b. If your welcome message has file names other than `welcome.txt` and `welcome_locale.txt` (where `locale` matches the ISO 639 language codes such as "cs" or "de"), specify the file name pattern in `FIRSTBOOT_WELCOME_PATTERNS`. For example:

    ```
    FIRSTBOOT_WELCOME_PATTERNS="mywelcome.txt"
    ```

    If unset, the default value of `welcome.txt` is assumed.

3. Create the welcome file and the localized versions and place them in the directory specified in the `/etc/sysconfig/firstboot` configuration file.

Proceed in a similar way to configure customized license and finish messages. These variables are `FIRSTBOOT_LICENSE_DIR` and `FIRSTBOOT_FINISH_FILE`.

Change the `SHOW_Y2CC_CHECKBOX` to "yes" if the user needs to be able to start YaST directly after performing the installation.

24.2.2   Customizing the License Action

You can customize the way the installation system reacts to a user's refusal to accept the license agreement. There are three different ways which the system could react to this scenario:

halt

The firstboot installation is aborted and the entire system shuts down. This is the default setting.

continue

The firstboot installation continues.

abort

The firstboot installation is aborted, but the system attempts to boot.

Make your choice and set `LICENSE_REFUSAL_ACTION` to the appropriate value.

24.2.3   Customizing the Release Notes

Depending on if you have changed the instance of SUSE Linux Enterprise Server you are deploying with firstboot, you probably need to educate the end users about important aspects of their new operating system. A standard installation uses release notes (displayed during one of the final stages of the installation) to provide important information to the users. To have your own modified release notes displayed as part of a firstboot installation, proceed as follows:

1. Create your own release notes file. Use the RTF format as in the example file in `/usr/share/doc/release-notes` and save the result as `RELEASE-NOTES.en.rtf` (for English).

2. Store optional localized versions next to the original version and replace the `en` part of the file name with the actual ISO 639 language code, such as `de` for German.

3. Open the firstboot configuration file from `/etc/sysconfig/firstboot` and set `FIRSTBOOT_RELEASE_NOTES_PATH` to the actual directory where the release notes files are stored.

24.2.4 Customizing the Workflow

By default, a standard firstboot workflow includes the following components:

- Language Selection

- Welcome

- License Agreement

- Host Name

- Network

- Time and Date

- Desktop

- root Password

- User Authentication Method

- User Management

- Hardware Configuration

- Finish Setup

This standard layout of a firstboot installation workflow is not mandatory. You can enable or disable certain components or integrate your own modules into the workflow. To modify the firstboot workflow, manually edit the firstboot configuration file `/etc/YaST2/firstboot.xml`. This XML file is a subset of the standard `control.xml` file that is used by YaST to control the installation workflow.

For an overview about proposals, see *Example 24.1, "Configuring the Proposal Screens"*. This provides you with enough background to modify the firstboot installation workflow. The basic syntax of the firstboot configuration file (plus how the key elements are configured) is explained with this example.

```
...
<proposals config:type="list">❶
    <proposal>❷
        <name>firstboot_hardware</name>❸
        <mode>installation</mode>❹
        <stage>firstboot</stage>❺
        <label>Hardware Configuration</label>❻
        <proposal_modules config:type="list">❼
            <proposal_module>printer</proposal_module>❽
        </proposal_modules>
    </proposal>
    <proposal>
    ...
    </proposal>
</proposals>
```

❶   The container for all proposals that should be part of the firstboot workflow.

❷   The container for an individual proposal.

❸   The internal name of the proposal.

❹   The mode of this proposal. Do not make any changes here. For a firstboot installation, this must be set to `installation`.

❺   The stage of the installation process at which this proposal is invoked. Do not make any changes here. For a firstboot installation, this must be set to `firstboot`.

❻   The label to be displayed on the proposal.

❼   The container for all modules that are part of the proposal screen.

❽   One or more modules that are part of the proposal screen.

The next section of the firstboot configuration file consists of the workflow definition. All modules that should be part of the firstboot installation workflow must be listed here.

EXAMPLE 24.2: CONFIGURING THE WORKFLOW SECTION

```
<workflows  config:type="list">
    <workflow>
        <defaults>
            <enable_back>yes</enable_back>
            <enable_next>yes</enable_next>
            <archs>all</archs>
        </defaults>
        <stage>firstboot</stage>
        <label>Configuration</label>
        <mode>installation</mode>
        … <!— list of modules  —>
        </modules>
    </workflow>
</workflows>
…
```

The overall structure of the `workflows` section is very similar to that of the `proposals` section. A container holds the workflow elements and the workflow elements all include stage, label and mode information (just as the proposals introduced in *Example 24.1, "Configuring the Proposal Screens"*). The most notable difference is the `defaults` section, which contains basic design information for the workflow components:

`enable_back`

  Include the *Back* button in all dialogs.

`enable_next`

  Include the *Next* button in all dialogs.

`archs`

  Specify the hardware architectures on which this workflow should be used.

EXAMPLE 24.3: CONFIGURING THE LIST OF WORKFLOW COMPONENTS

```
<modules  config:type="list">❶
    <module>❷
        <label>Language</label>❸
```

```
            <enabled config:type="boolean">false</enabled> ④
            <name>firstboot_language</name> ⑤
        </module>
    <modules>
```

① The container for all components of the workflow.

② The module definition.

③ The label displayed with the module.

④ The switch to enable or disable this component in the workflow.

⑤ The module name. The module itself must be located under `/usr/share/YaST2/clients` and have the `.ycp` file suffix.

To make changes to the number or order of proposal screens during the firstboot installation, proceed as follows:

1. Open the firstboot configuration file at `/etc/YaST2/firstboot.xml`.

2. Delete or add proposal screens or change the order of the existing ones:

   - To delete an entire proposal, remove the `proposal` element including all its sub-elements from the `proposals` section and remove the respective `module` element (with sub-elements) from the workflow.

   - To add a new proposal, create a new `proposal` element and fill in all the required sub-elements. Make sure that the proposal exists as a YaST module in `/usr/share/YaST2/clients`.

   - To change the order of proposals, move the respective `module` elements containing the proposal screens around in the workflow. Note that there may be dependencies to other installation steps that require a certain order of proposals and workflow components.

3. Apply your changes and close the configuration file.

You can always change the workflow of the configuration steps when the default does not meet your needs. Enable or disable certain modules in the workflow (or add your own custom ones). To toggle the status of a module in the firstboot workflow, proceed as follows:

Customizing the Workflow

1. Open the `/etc/YaST2/firstboot.xml` configuration file.

2. Change the value for the `enabled` element from `true` to `false` to disable the module or from `false` to `true` to enable it again.

```
<module>
    <label>Time and Date</label>
    <enabled config:type="boolean">true</enabled>
    <name>firstboot_timezone</name>
</module>
```

3. Apply your changes and close the configuration file.

To add a custom made module to the workflow, proceed as follows:

1. Create your own YaST module and store the module file *module_name*.ycp in `/usr/share/YaST2/clients`.

2. Open the `/etc/YaST2/firstboot.xml` configuration file.

3. Determine at which point in the workflow your new module should be run. In doing so, make sure that possible dependencies to other steps in the workflow are taken into account and resolved.

4. Create a new `module` element inside the `modules` container and add the appropriate sub-elements:

```
<modules config:type="list">
    …
    <module>
        <label>my_module</label>
        <enabled config:type="boolean">true</enabled>
        <name>filename_my_module</name>
    </module>
</modules>
```

a. Enter the label to be displayed on your module in the `label` element.

b. Make sure that `enabled` is set to `true` to have your module included in the workflow.

c. Enter the file name of your module in the `name` element. Omit the full path and the `.ycp` suffix.

5. Apply your settings and close the configuration file.

 Tip: Finding a Connected Network Interface For Auto-Configuration

If the target hardware may feature more than one network interface add the `network-autoconfig` package to the application image. `network-autoconfig` makes sure that during firstboot all available Ethernet interfaces are cycled until one is successfully configured with DHCP.

24.2.5 Configuring Additional Scripts

Firstboot can be configured to execute additional scripts after the firstboot workflow has been completed. To add additional scripts to the firstboot sequence, proceed as follows:

1. Open the `/etc/sysconfig/firstboot` configuration file and make sure that the path specified for `SCRIPT_DIR` is correct. The default value is `/usr/share/firstboot/scripts`.

2. Create your shell script, store it in the specified directory, and apply the appropriate file permissions.

24.2.6 Providing Translations of the Installation Workflow

Depending on the end user it could be desirable to offer translations of the customized workflow. Those translations could be necessary, if you customized the workflow by changing the `/etc/YaST2/firstboot.xml` file, as described in *Section 24.2.4, "Customizing the Workflow"*. This is different from the localization of customized YaST messages, which is already described in *Section 24.2.1, "Customizing YaST Messages"*.

If you have changed `/etc/YaST2/firstboot.xml` and introduced string changes, generate a new translation template file (`.pot` file) and use the `gettext` tool chain to translate and finally install the translated files in the YaST locale directories (`/usr/share/YaST2/locale`) as compiled `.mo` files. Proceed as follows:

1. Change the `textdomain` setting from:

   ```
   <textdomain>firstboot</textdomain>
   ```

   to, for example,

   ```
   <textdomain>firstboot-oem</textdomain>
   ```

2. Use **xgettext** to extract the translatable strings to the translation template file (`.pot` file), for example to `firstboot-oem.pot`:

   ```
   xgettext -L Glade -o firstboot-oem.pot /etc/YaST2/firstboot.xml
   ```

3. Start the translation process. Then package the translated files (`.LL_code.po` files) the same way as translations of the other projects and install the compiled `firstboot-oem.mo` files.

If you need translations for additional or changed YaST modules, provide translations within such a module itself. If you changed an existing module, make sure to change also its textdomain statement to avoid undesired side effects.

 Tip: For More Information

For more information about YaST development, refer to http://en.opensuse.org/openSUSE:YaST_development. Detailed information about YaST firstboot can be found at http://doc.opensuse.org/projects/YaST/SLES11/tdg/bk09ch01s02.html.

24.3   Cloning the Master Installation

Clone the master machine's disk using any of the imaging mechanisms available to you, and roll these images out to the target machines. For more information about imaging see http://doc.opensuse.org/projects/kiwi/doc/.

24.4 Personalizing the Installation

As soon as the cloned disk image is booted, firstboot starts and the installation proceeds exactly as laid out in *Section 24.2.4, "Customizing the Workflow"*. Only the components included in the firstboot workflow configuration are started. All other installation steps are skipped. The end user adjusts language, keyboard, network, and password settings to personalize the workstation. After this process is finished, a firstboot installed system behaves as any other instance of SUSE Linux Enterprise Server.

V Automated Installations

25 Automated Installation

AutoYaST allows you to install SUSE® Linux Enterprise on a large number of machines in parallel. The AutoYaST technology offers great flexibility to adjust deployments to heterogeneous hardware. This chapter tells you how to prepare a simple automated installation and lay out an advanced scenario involving different hardware types and installation purposes.

25.1   Simple Mass Installation

 Important: Identical Hardware

> This scenario assumes you are rolling out SUSE Linux Enterprise to a set of machines with identical hardware configuration.

To prepare for an AutoYaST mass installation, proceed as follows:

1. Create an AutoYaST profile that contains the installation details needed for your deployment as described in *Section 25.1.1, "Creating an AutoYaST Profile"*.

2. Determine the source of the AutoYaST profile and the parameter to pass to the installation routines as described in *Section 25.1.2, "Distributing the Profile and Determining the AutoYaST Parameter"*.

3. Determine the source of the SUSE Linux Enterprise installation data as described in *Section 25.1.3, "Providing the Installation Data"*.

4. Determine and set up the boot scenario for autoinstallation as described in *Section 25.1.4, "Setting Up the Boot Scenario"*.

5. Pass the command line to the installation routines by adding the parameters manually or by creating an `info` file as described in *Section 25.1.5, "Creating the info File"*.

6. Start the autoinstallation process as described in *Section 25.1.6, "Initiating and Monitoring the Autoinstallation"*.

25.1.1 Creating an AutoYaST Profile

An AutoYaST profile tells AutoYaST what to install and how to configure the installed system to get a completely ready-to-use system in the end. It can be created in several different ways:

- Clone a fresh installation from a reference machine to a set of identical machines

- Use the AutoYaST GUI to create and modify a profile to meet your requirements

- Use an XML editor and create a profile from scratch

To clone a fresh reference installation, proceed as follows:

1. Start a normal installation as described in *Chapter 6, Installation with YaST* and configure the system according to your needs. On the *Installation Settings* screen (*Section 6.13, "Installation Settings"*) choose *Clone System Configuration* and activate *Write AutoYaST profile to /root/autoinst.xml*.

2. A ready-to-use profile will be created at `/root/autoinst.xml`. It can be used to create clones of this particular installation.

To use the AutoYaST GUI to create a profile from an existing system configuration and modify it to your needs, proceed as follows:

1. As `root`, start YaST.

2. Select *Miscellaneous* › *Autoinstallation* to start the graphical AutoYaST front-end.

3. Select *Tools* › *Create Reference Profile* to prepare AutoYaST to mirror the current system configuration into an AutoYaST profile.

4. Apart from the default resources (like boot loader, partitioning, and software selection), you can add various other aspects of your system to the profile by checking the items in the list in *Create a Reference Control File*.

5. Click *Create* to have YaST gather all the system information and write it to a new profile.

6. To proceed, choose one of the following:

- If the profile is complete and matches your requirements, select *File* › *Save as* and enter a file name for the profile, such as `autoinst.xml`.

- Modify the reference profile by selecting the appropriate configuration aspects (such as "Hardware/Printer") from the tree view to the left and clicking *Configure*. The respective YaST module starts but your settings are written to the AutoYaST profile instead of applied to your system. When done, select *File* › *Save as* and enter a suitable name for the profile.

7. Leave the AutoYaST module with *File* › *Exit*.

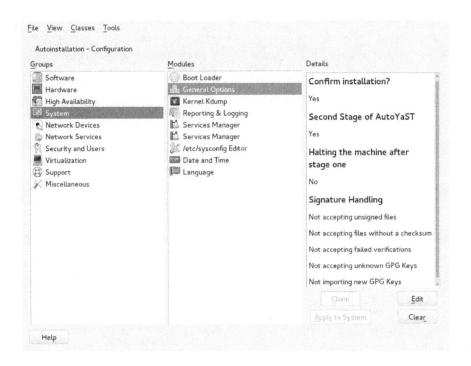

FIGURE 25.1: EDITING AN AUTOYAST PROFILE WITH THE AUTOYAST FRONT-END

25.1.2 Distributing the Profile and Determining the AutoYaST Parameter

The AutoYaST profile can be distributed in several different ways. Depending on the protocol used to distribute the profile data, different AutoYaST parameters are used to make the profile location known to the installation routines on the client. The location of the profile is passed to the installation routines by means of the boot prompt or an `info` file that is loaded upon boot. The following options are available:

Profile Location	Parameter	Description
File	`autoyast=file://path`	Makes the installation routines look for the control file in the specified path (relative to source root directory—`file:///autoinst.xml` if in the top directory of a CD-ROM).
Device	`autoyast=device://path`	Makes the installation routines look for the control file on a storage device. Only the device name is needed—`/dev/sda1` is wrong, use `sda1` instead.
NFS	`autoyast=nfs://server/path`	Has the installation routines retrieve the control file from an NFS server.
HTTP	`autoyast=http://server/path`	Has the installation routines retrieve the control file from an HTTP server.
HTTPS	`autoyast=https://server/path`	Has the installation routines retrieve the control file from an HTTPS server.

Profile Location	Parameter	Description
TFTP	`autoyast=tftp://server/path`	Has the installation routines retrieve the control file from a TFTP server.
FTP	`autoyast=ftp://server/path`	Has the installation routines retrieve the control file from an FTP server.

Replace the `server` and `path` placeholders with values matching your actual setup.

AutoYaST includes a feature that allows the binding of certain profiles to the client's MAC address. Without having to alter the `autoyast=` parameter, you can have the same setup install several different instances using different profiles.

To use this, proceed as follows:

1. Create separate profiles with the MAC address of the client as the file name and put them on the HTTP server that holds your AutoYaST profiles.

2. Omit the exact path including the file name when creating the `autoyast=` parameter, for example:

```
autoyast=tftp://192.168.1.115/
```

3. Start the autoinstallation.

YaST tries to determine the location of the profile in the following way:

1. YaST searches for the profile using its own IP address in uppercase hexadecimal, for example, `192.0.2.91` is `C000025B`.

2. If this file is not found, YaST removes one hex digit and tries again. This action is repeated eight times until the file with the correct name is found.

3. If that still fails, it tries locating a file with the MAC address of the clients as the file name. The MAC address of the example client is `0080C8F6484C`.

4. If the MAC address–named file cannot be found, YaST searches for a file named `default` (in lowercase). An example sequence of addresses where YaST searches for the AutoYaST profile looks as follows:

```
C000025B
C000025
C00002
C0000
C000
C00
C0
C
0080C8F6484C
default
```

25.1.3   Providing the Installation Data

The installation data can be provided by means of the product CDs or DVDs or using a network installation source. If the product CDs are used as the installation source, physical access to the client to be installed is needed, because the boot process needs to be initiated manually and the CDs need to be changed.

To provide the installation sources over the network, set up a network installation server (HTTP, NFS, FTP) as described in *Section 13.2.1, "Setting Up an Installation Server Using YaST"*. Use an `info` file to pass the server's location to the installation routines.

25.1.4   Setting Up the Boot Scenario

The client can be booted in several different ways:

Network Boot

As with a normal remote installation, autoinstallation can be initiated with Wake on LAN and PXE, the boot image and control file can be pulled in via TFTP, and the installation sources from any network installation server.

Bootable CD-ROM

You can use the original SUSE Linux Enterprise media to boot the system for autoinstallation and pull in the control file from a network location or a removable media. Alternatively, create your own custom CD-ROM holding both the installation sources and the AutoYaST profile.

The following sections provide a basic outline of the procedures for network boot or boot from CD-ROM.

25.1.4.1   Preparing for Network Boot

Network booting with Wake on LAN, PXE, and TFTP is discussed in *Section 13.1.3, "Remote Installation via VNC—PXE Boot and Wake on LAN"*. To make the setup introduced there work for autoinstallation, modify the featured PXE Linux configuration file (`/srv/tftp/pxelinux.cfg/` `default`) to contain the `autoyast` parameter pointing to the location of the AutoYaST profile. An example entry for a standard installation looks like this:

```
default linux

# default label linux
    kernel linux
    append initrd=initrd install=http://192.168.1.115/install/suse-enterprise/
```

The same example for autoinstallation looks like this:

```
default linux

# default label linux
    kernel linux
    append initrd=initrd install=http://192.168.1.115/install/suse-enterprise/ \
        autoyast=nfs://192.168.1.110/profiles/autoinst.xml
```

Replace the example IP addresses and paths with the data used in your setup.

25.1.4.2   Preparing to Boot from CD-ROM

There are several ways in which booting from CD-ROM can come into play in AutoYaST installations. Choose from the following scenarios:

Boot from SUSE Linux Enterprise Media, Get the Profile over the Network
Use this approach if a totally network-based scenario is not possible (for example, if your hardware does not support PXE) and you have physical access to system to install during most of the process.
You need:

- The SUSE Linux Enterprise media

- A network server providing the profile data (see *Section 25.1.2, "Distributing the Profile and Determining the AutoYaST Parameter"* for details)

- A removable media containing the `info` file that tells the installation routines where to find the profile
  or
  Access to the boot prompt of the system to install where you manually enter the `autoyast=` parameter

Boot and Install from SUSE Linux Enterprise Media, Get the Profile from a Removable Media
Use this approach if an entirely network-based installation scenario would not work. It requires physical access to the system to be installed for turning on the target machine, or, in the second case, to enter the profile's location at the boot prompt. In both cases, you may also need to change media depending on the scope of installation.
You need:

- The SUSE Linux Enterprise media

- A removable media holding both the profile and the `info` file
  or
  Access to the boot prompt of the target to enter the `autoyast=` parameter

If you need to install a limited number of software packages and the number of targets is relatively low, creating your own custom CD holding both the installation data and the profile itself might prove a good idea, especially if no network is available in your setup.

25.1.5   Creating the `info` File

The installation routines at the target need to be made aware of all the different components of the AutoYaST framework. This is done by creating a command line containing all the parameters needed to locate the AutoYaST components, installation sources, and the parameters needed to control the installation process.

Do this by manually passing these parameters at the boot prompt of the installation or by providing a file called `info` that is read by the installation routines (linuxrc). The former requires physical access to any client to install, which makes this approach unsuitable for large deployments. The latter enables you to provide the `info` file on some media that is prepared and inserted into the clients' drives prior to the autoinstallation. Alternatively, use PXE boot and include the linuxrc parameters in the `pxelinux.cfg/default` file as shown in *Section 25.1.4.1, "Preparing for Network Boot"*.

The following parameters are commonly used for linuxrc. For more information, refer to the AutoYaST package documentation under `/usr/share/doc/packages/autoyast`.

> ❗ **Important: Separating Parameters and Values**
>
> When passing parameters to linuxrc at the boot prompt, use `=` to separate parameter and value. When using an `info` file, separate parameter and value with `:`.

Keyword	Value
`netdevice`	The network device to use for network setup (for BOOTP/DHCP requests). Only needed if several network devices are available.
`hostip`	When empty, the client sends a BOOTP request. Otherwise the client is configured using the specified data.

Keyword	Value
netmask	Netmask for the selected network.
gateway	Default gateway.
nameserver	Name server.
autoyast	Location of the control file to use for the automatic installation, such as `autoyast=nfs//192.168.1.110/pro-files/`.
install	Location of the installation source, such as `install=nfs://192.168.1.110/CDs/`.
vnc	If set to `1`, enables VNC remote controlled installation.
VNCPassword	The password for VNC.
ssh	If set to `1`, enables SSH remote controlled installation.
netsetup	If set to `1`, sets up the network. Normally this is done automatically, but you need to set `netsetup=1` in case the installation repository is provided locally (for example, via DVD or local iso image) and the `info` file is loaded from the network.

If your autoinstallation scenario involves client configuration via DHCP and a network installation source, and you want to monitor the installation process using VNC, your `info` would look like this:

```
autoyast:profile_source install:install_source vnc:1 VNCPassword:some_password
```

If you prefer a static network setup at installation time, your info file would look like the following:

```
autoyast:profile_source \
install:install_source \
hostip:some_ip \
netmask:some_netmask \
gateway:some_gateway
```

The \ indicates that the line breaks have only been added for the sake of readability. All options must be entered as one continuous string.

The info data can be made available to linuxrc in various different ways:

- As a file on a removable media that is available on the client at installation time. Add the info parameter similar to info=cd:/info.

- As a file in the root directory of the initial RAM disk used for booting the system provided either from custom installation media or via PXE boot.

- As part of the AutoYaST profile. In this case, the AutoYaST file needs to be called info to enable linuxrc to parse it. An example for this approach is given below.

- By means of a URL that points to the location of the info file. The syntax for this looks like info=http://www.example.com/info.

linuxrc looks for a string (start_linuxrc_conf) in the profile that represents the beginning of the file. If it is found, it parses the content starting from that string and finishes when the string end_linuxrc_conf is found. The options are stored in the profile as follows:

```
....
  <install>
....
    <init>
      <info_file>
<![CDATA[
#
# Don't remove the following line:
# start_linuxrc_conf
```

```
#
install: nfs:server/path
vnc: 1
VNCPassword: test
autoyast: file:///info


# end_linuxrc_conf
# Do not remove the above comment
#
]]>


      </info_file>
    </init>
......
  </install>
....
```

linuxrc loads the profile containing the boot parameters instead of the traditional `info` file. The `install:` parameter points to the location of the installation sources. `vnc` and `VNCPassword` indicate the use of VNC for installation monitoring. The `autoyast` parameter tells linuxrc to treat `info` as an AutoYaST profile.

25.1.6 Initiating and Monitoring the Autoinstallation

After you have provided all the infrastructure mentioned above (profile, installation source, and `info` file), you can go ahead and start the autoinstallation. Depending on the scenario chosen for booting and monitoring the process, physical interaction with the client may be needed:

- If the client system boots from any kind of physical media, either product media or custom CDs, you need to insert these into the client's drives.

- If the client is not switched on via Wake on LAN, you need to at least switch on the client machine.

- If you have not opted for remote controlled autoinstallation, the graphical feedback from AutoYaST is sent to the client's attached monitor or, if you use a headless client, to a serial console.

To enable remote controlled autoinstallation, use the VNC or SSH parameters described in *Section 25.1.5, "Creating the* `info` *File"* and connect to the client from another machine as described in *Section 13.5, "Monitoring the Installation Process"*.

25.2 Rule-Based Autoinstallation

The following sections introduce the basic concept of rule-based installation using AutoYaST and provide an example scenario that enables you to create your own custom autoinstallation setup.

25.2.1 Understanding Rule-Based Autoinstallation

Rule-based AutoYaST installation allows you to cope with heterogeneous hardware environments:

- Does your site contain hardware of different vendors?

- Are the machines on your site of different hardware configuration (for example, using different devices or using different memory and disk sizes)?

- Do you intend to install across different domains and need to distinguish between them?

Rule-based autoinstallation starts with generating a custom profile to match a heterogeneous scenario by merging several profiles into one. Each rule describes one particular distinctive feature of your setup (such as disk size) and tells AutoYaST which profile to use when the rule matches. Several rules describing different features of your setup are combined in an AutoYaST `rules.xml` file. The rule stack is then processed and AutoYaST generates the final profile by merging the different profiles matching the AutoYaST rules into one. To illustrate this procedure, refer to *Section 25.2.2, "Example Scenario for Rule-Based Autoinstallation"*.

Rule-based AutoYaST offers you great flexibility in planning and executing your SUSE Linux Enterprise deployment. You can:

- Create rules for matching any of the predefined system attributes in AutoYaST

- Combine multiple system attributes (such as disk size and kernel architecture) into one rule by using logical operators

- Create custom rules by running shell scripts and passing their output to the AutoYaST framework. The number of custom rules is limited to five.

Note: For More Information

For more information about rule creation and usage with AutoYaST, refer to the package's documentation under `/usr/share/doc/packages/autoyast2/html/index.html`, Chapter *Rules and Classes*.

To prepare for a rule-based AutoYaST mass installation, proceed as follows:

1. Create several AutoYaST profiles that contain the installation details needed for your heterogeneous setup as described in *Section 25.1.1, "Creating an AutoYaST Profile"*.

2. Define rules to match the system attributes of your hardware setup as shown in *Section 25.2.2, "Example Scenario for Rule-Based Autoinstallation"*.

3. Determine the source of the AutoYaST profile and the parameter to pass to the installation routines as described in *Section 25.1.2, "Distributing the Profile and Determining the AutoYaST Parameter"*.

4. Determine the source of the SUSE Linux Enterprise installation data as described in *Section 25.1.3, "Providing the Installation Data"*.

5. Pass the command line to the installation routines by adding the parameters manually or by creating an `info` file as described in *Section 25.1.5, "Creating the `info` File"*.

6. Determine and set up the boot scenario for autoinstallation as described in *Section 25.1.4, "Setting Up the Boot Scenario"*.

7. Start the autoinstallation process as described in *Section 25.1.6, "Initiating and Monitoring the Autoinstallation"*.

25.2.2   Example Scenario for Rule-Based Autoinstallation

To get a basic understanding of how rules are created, think of the following example, depicted in *Figure 25.2, "AutoYaST Rules"*. One run of AutoYaST installs the following setup:

A Print Server

This machine only needs a minimal installation without a desktop environment and a limited set of software packages.

Workstations in the Engineering Department

These machines need a desktop environment and a broad set of development software.

Laptops in the Sales Department

These machines need a desktop environment and a limited set of specialized applications, such as office and calendaring software.

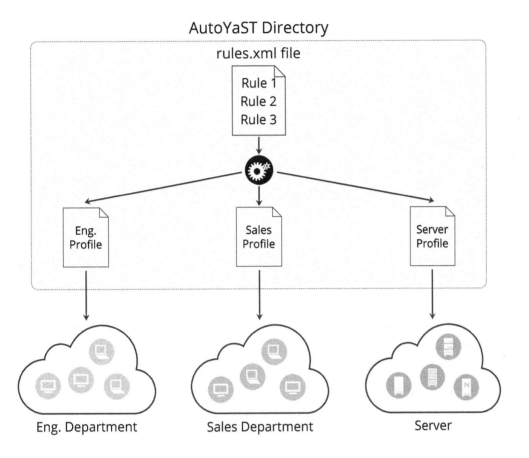

In a first step, use one of the methods outlined in *Section 25.1.1, "Creating an AutoYaST Profile"* to create profiles for each use case. In this example, you would create `print.xml`, `engineering.xml`, and `sales.xml`.

In the second step, create rules to distinguish the three hardware types from one another and to tell AutoYaST which profile to use. Use an algorithm similar to the following to set up the rules:

1. Does the machine have an IP of *192.168.2.253*? Then make it the print server.

2. Does the machine have PCMCIA hardware and feature an Intel chipset? Then consider it an Intel laptop and install the sales department software selection.

3. If none of the above is true, consider the machine a developer workstation and install accordingly.

Roughly sketched, this translates into a `rules.xml` file with the following content:

```
<?xml version="1.0"?>
<!DOCTYPE autoinstall SYSTEM "/usr/share/autoinstall/dtd/rules.dtd">
<autoinstall xmlns="http://www.suse.com/1.0/yast2ns" xmlns:config="http://
www.suse.com/1.0/configns">
  <rules config:type="list">
    <rule>
      <hostaddress>
     <match>192.168.2.253</match>
          <match_type>exact</match_type>
      </hostaddress>
      <result>
          <profile>print.xml</profile>
          <continue config:type="boolean">false</continue>
       </result>
    </rule>
    <rule>
      <haspcmcia>
          <match>1</match>
          <match_type>exact</match_type>
      </haspcmcia>
      <custom1>
          <script>
if grep -i intel /proc/cpuinfo > /dev/null; then
echo -n "intel"
```

Example Scenario for Rule-Based Autoinstallation

```
else
echo -n "non_intel"
fi;
            </script>
            <match>*</match>
            <match_type>exact</match_type>
        </custom1>
        <result>
            <profile>sales.xml</profile>
            <continue config:type="boolean">false</continue>
        </result>
        <operator>and</operator>
    </rule>
    <rule>
        <haspcmcia>
            <match>0</match>
            <match_type>exact</match_type>
        </haspcmcia>
    <result>
            <profile>engineering.xml</profile>
            <continue config:type="boolean">false</continue>
        </result>
    </rule>
</rules>
</autoinstall>
```

When distributing the rules file, make sure that the `rules` directory resides under the `profiles` directory, specified in the `autoyast=protocol:serverip/profiles/` URL. AutoYaST looks for a `rules` subdirectory containing a file named `rules.xml` first then loads and merges the profiles specified in the rules file.

The rest of the autoinstallation procedure is carried out as usual.

       Example Scenario for Rule-Based Autoinstallation

25.3 For More Information

For in-depth information about the AutoYaST technology, refer to *Book "AutoYaST"* or the documentation installed along with the software (`/usr/share/doc/packages/autoyast2`).

26 Automated Upgrade from SUSE Linux Enterprise 11 SP2 to 11 SP3

The following procedure is a way to do a mass upgrade unattended from SUSE Linux Enterprise 11 SP2 to SUSE Linux Enterprise 11 SP3. Several preparation steps are needed to create a suitable AutoYaST profile. AutoYaST finally will execute the upgrade process.

26.1 Preparing the AutoYaST Profile

The AutoYaST profile for the automated upgrade uses the same file format as the AutoYaST installation. For more information about AutoYaST, see *Chapter 25, Automated Installation* and *Book "AutoYaST"*.

However, there are some parts of the system (for example, partitioning) that do not make sense to be configured during the upgrade. On the other hand, it is useful to set upgrade-specific options by means of the AutoYaST profile.

26.1.1 Upgrade

The upgrade options define the behavior of the dependency solver during upgrade:

```
<upgrade>
  <only_installed_packages
    config:type="boolean">false</only_installed_packages>
  <stop_on_solver_conflict
    config:type="boolean">true</stop_on_solver_conflict>
</upgrade>
```

only_installed_packages

Set to `true` for package-based upgrades (recommended for upgrading to the next service pack of the same product) or `false` for pattern-based upgrades (recommended for an upgrade between versions of a product, for example, from SLES10 to SLES11).

```
stop_on_solver_conflict
```
Defines whether to show the proposal in case of failure to resolve package dependencies interactively (recommended to be set to `true`, but this could result in an interactive process, during which the user needs to resolve the conflicts manually).

26.1.2 Software Selection

The software selection options define, which components to select or deselect in addition to the results of the resolver:

```
<software>
  <packages config:type="list">
    <package>autoyast2-installation</package>
    <package>apparmor-profile-editor</package>
  </packages>
  <patterns config:type="list">
    <pattern>base</pattern>
  </patterns>
  <remove-packages config:type="list"/>
  <remove-patterns config:type="list"/>
</software>
```

It is especially important to set packages or patterns for being selected or deselected to resolve package conflicts and thus to avoid the need for interactive intervention. After the upgrade is done, the newly created `autoupg_updated.xml` file contains these packages and patterns plus those that were selected or deselected for any other reason.

26.1.3 Backup Before Upgrade

The backup before upgrade options match these features in the upgrade proposal.

```
<backup>
  <sysconfig config:type="boolean">true</sysconfig>
  <modified config:type="boolean">true</modified>
  <remove_old config:type="boolean">false</remove_old>
```

```
</backup>
```

`sysconfig`
> defines whether to back up sysconfig before upgrading.

`modified`
> defines whether to back up the modified configuration files before upgrading.

`remove_old`
> defines whether to remove old backups from previous upgrades.

26.2   Running the Automated Upgrade

To start the automated upgrade, boot the installation media and pass the AutoYaST profile to it. There are two ways to pass the profile to the system:

- Pass the profile to the kernel command line the same way as for the AutoYaST installation (use the `autoupgrade=1` `autoyast=http://host/path/profile.xml` parameter. For z Systems, this is the only possibility.

- Pass the `autoupgrade=1` parameter to the kernel command line. Before you start the upgrade, copy the profile to `/root/autoupg.xml`. Then there is no need for any additional kernel parameter.

The latter approach allows you to have a single installation kernel command line for even different machines—just copy the appropriate profile into its file system.

As long as you have only one SUSE Linux Enterprise system installed on your machine, there are no package conflicts and you did not set the profile to stop on the upgrade proposal, the complete process will be non-interactive. In case you enter the upgrade proposal, you can modify its settings for the upgrade.

After the upgrade finishes, YaST writes the `/root/autoupg-updated.xml` file, which contains the profile with applied software selection changes done in the proposal. This is especially useful in case of mass upgrades of machines with the same package selection. This way, conflict resolutions from one machine can easily be applied on other machines, which consequently will get these conflicts resolved automatically and the upgrade itself will be non-interactive.

If there are more SUSE Linux Enterprise systems installed on the machine, you will always be asked, which one to upgrade—there is no way to select it in advance.

26.3 GRUB 2 Menu Section for Booting into the Upgrade

An alternate way to boot the system is to create an additional section in the GRUB 2 menu (and similar for other boot loaders and other architectures), which starts the installation. The following example assumes that there is a separate /boot partition, which is referred in GRUB 2 as (hd0,0):

```
title Upgrade
    root (hd0,0)
    kernel /upgrade/linux
    install=inst_source_url autoupgrade=1
    autoyast=autoyast_profile_url vga=0x314
    initrd /upgrade/initrd
```

The above example assumes that the installation kernel and the installation initrd are located in the /boot/upgrade directory.

On z Systems, you must add the parameters to the PARM file—proceed the same way as you do when performing an AutoYaST-driven installation.

26.4 Second Stage of the Upgrade

The automated upgrade by default does not perform configuration changes during the second stage of the upgrade. The only exception is network configuration, which needs to be set to be preserved in the AutoYaST upgrade profile.

If configuration adjustment of some system areas is needed after the upgrade (for example, configuring a new service), add the relevant sections to the AutoYaST profile for the upgrade and the configuration of the selected system areas will be saved during the upgrade.

 Warning: AutoYaST Supplied Configuration Replaces Existing Configuration

Be warned that existing configuration of that system area will be replaced and thus destroyed by the AutoYaST configuration.

Normally, the only configuration adjustment, which should be done in the AutoYaST profile, is the registration of the system with Subscription Management Tool (SMT) or SUSE Customer Center (SCC). If this is missing, the system will not get the update repository and updates will not be possible—unless configured later again.

26.5 Limitations and Hints

26.5.1 NetworkManager and Registration

In case of using NetworkManager for managing network devices and network connections, network connection is not available during the second stage of the upgrade. This prevents the system from performing the registration.

26.5.2 Cleaning Up Upgrade Setting

If you do any changes in your system to trigger the upgrade process (for example, adding a new section to the boot loader menu), you probably want to remove it after the upgrade is done.

You can do it automatically with a post-installation script. Find an examples in *Book "AutoYaST", Chapter 4 "Configuration and Installation Options", Section 4.31 "Custom User Scripts"*. A sample script cleaning up GRUB 2's `menu.lst` is included in the sample `autoupg.xml` file. Make sure that the script matches your particular setup and that it does not remove more than you actually want!

26.5.3 For More Information

- **Linuxrc Documentation:** http://en.opensuse.org/SDB:Linuxrc

27 Automated Deployment of Preload Images

With KIWI you can create operating system images. This chapter describes the process of deploying a system image to an empty client machine. For this, you need to create a preload image which contains a bootable RAW image. This file contains two important parts: a partition table and the actual operating system. This RAW image will be written to the empty hard disk and the operating system extends to the remaining disk space at first boot.

To create such an image, see http://doc.opensuse.org/projects/kiwi/doc/. When you build the ISO image, you can find the RAW file in the destination directory. There are many ways to dump a raw image onto a disk.

- Plug the disk into a deployment server and copy the image to the raw device.

- Provide the raw image by means of an HTTP or FTP server and dump it on the disk of the client machine.

- Create a netboot image to get the image and dump it on the disk. This is a good method for mass deployment.

- Boot a rescue disk and do the dump manually from the rescue image.

For a quick start, it is good to use one of the methods described in *Section 27.1, "Deploying system manually from rescue image"*.

27.1 Deploying system manually from rescue image

Deploying with generated ISO file from KIWI:

1. Burn the ISO image you get from the KIWI building process on CD/DVD.

2. Boot from this medium onto the client machine.

3. Select the hard disk for installation.

4. Restart the client machine and boot from hard disk.

Deploying over rescue system:

1. Boot the client machine with a rescue system. Such systems are available on all SUSE installation CDs or DVDs.

2. Log in as `root`. Do not enter password.

3. Configure your network. If you have DHCP available in your network, this is merely the command **`ifup-dhcp eth0`**. If you must do this manually, use the command **`ip`** to configure your network. The output starting DHCP also tells you the IP address of the computer.

4. Listen on an unused port of your network like `1234` and dump the incoming data to disk with the following command:

```
netcat -l -p 1234 > /dev/sda
```

5. On the imaging server, send the raw image to the client machine with the command:

```
netcat <IP of client> 1234 < $HOME/preload_image/<image_name>
```

6. When the image is transferred, remove the rescue system from your CD or DVD drive and shut down the client machine. On reboot, the boot loader `GRUB` should be started on the client and the firstboot system will take over.

27.2   Automated Deployment with PXE Boot

When doing multiple installations of an operating system on similar hardware, it is useful to put some effort into preparing a mass deployment of the operating system and to minimize the time needed for the actual deployment. This chapter describes this process. The goal is to simply plug in a computer, connect it to a network, start a network boot, and wait until it powers down.

The following actions need to be performed to accomplish this task:

Set up a boot and install server

A dedicated machine is needed, that should be prepared to offer PXE boot and an FTP or Web server to provide a preload image. It is a good idea to give the machine enough memory to hold all necessary installation data in memory. For a default installation, you

Automated Deployment with PXE Boot

should have at least 4 GByte of memory. All the necessary tasks can be accomplished with SUSE Linux Enterprise Server. For more details, see *Section 27.2.1, "Set Up a Boot and Install Server"*.

Prepare a preload Image

The actual installation is done by the copying of a raw image of the operating system to the new hard disk. All features and settings must be prepared and tested carefully. To provide such an image, KIWI can be used (available in the SDK of the SUSE Linux Enterprise operating system). More information about image creation with KIWI is available at http://doc.opensuse.org/projects/kiwi/doc/. For more details about the requirements of the preload image, see *Section 27.2.2, "Creating a Preload Image"*.

KIWI is available from the SUSE Linux Enterprise SDK. The SDK is a module for SUSE Linux Enterprise and is available via an online channel from the SUSE Customer Center. Alternatively, go to http://download.suse.com/, search for `SUSE Linux Enterprise Software Development Kit` and download it from there. Refer to *Chapter 9, Installing Modules, Extensions, and Third Party Add-On Products* for details.

Create an initial system for deployment

This is a task that requires some Linux expertise. A description on how this can be achieved by means of an example installation is available at *Section 27.2.3, "Creating an Initial System to Deploy a Preload Image"*.

Configure the boot server for automatic deployment

PXE boot must be told to boot the installation system, that in turn will take the preload image from the server and copy it to the hard disk.

27.2.1   Set Up a Boot and Install Server

There are four steps to accomplish to perform this task after a SUSE Linux Enterprise Server installation:

1. Set up the installation source as described in *Section 13.2, "Setting Up the Server Holding the Installation Sources"*. Choose an HTTP, or FTP network server.

2. Set up a TFTP server to hold a boot image (this image will be created in a later step). This is described in *Section 13.3.2, "Setting Up a TFTP Server"*.

3. Set up a DHCP server to assign IP addresses to all machines and to reveal the location of the TFTP server to the target system. This is described in *Section 13.3.1, "Setting Up a DHCP Server"*.

4. Prepare the installation server PXE boot. This is described in further detail in *Section 13.3.3, "Using PXE Boot"*.

Note that the actual installation process will greatly benefit if you provide enough memory on this machine to hold the preload image. Also, using gigabit Ethernet will speed up the deployment process considerably (compared to slower networks).

27.2.2 Creating a Preload Image

The process of creating images with KIWI is described at http://doc.opensuse.org/projects/kiwi/doc/. However, to create a useful image for mass deployment, several considerations should be taken into account:

- A typical preload image will use the following type:

```
<type primary="true" filesystem="btrfs" boot="oemboot/suse-SLES12">vmx</type>
```

- During the setup of a preload image, the image creation process is run multiple times. The repositories needed to build the image should be available on the local computer.

- Depending on the desired usage of the preload, some effort should be invested in configuring firstboot. Find more details about firstboot in *Chapter 24, Deploying Customized Preinstallations*. With this method you can also require the user to do initial configurations at the first bootup of the system.

- Many additional features can be configured into the image, like adding update repositories or doing an update on initial bootup. However, it is impossible to describe all possibilities in this document, and (depending on the requirements) the creation of the preload image requires in-depth knowledge of the imaging system KIWI, and several other technologies used in SUSE Linux Enterprise Server.

The actual image to be deployed should be available from the FTP or HTTP server that you provided on the installation server.

27.2.3 Creating an Initial System to Deploy a Preload Image

To run an automatic deployment, it is necessary to start an initial Linux system on the target computer. During a typical installation, the kernel and initial RAM file system are read from some boot medium and started by the bios. The needed functionality can be implemented in the RAM file system , which together with the kernel will serve as the initial system.

The main features that must be provided by the initial system is the enabling of access to the hard disk and the making available of the network connection. Both of these functions are dependent on the hardware onto which you want to deploy. In theory it is possible to create an initial system from scratch, but to simplify this task it is also possible to modify the initial RAM file system used by the machine during boot.

The following procedure is only one example of how to create the needed initial RAM file system:

1. Do a standard installation of SUSE Linux Enterprise Server on the target system.

2. Install the package `busybox` on the system.

3. Create a new RAM file system with the following command:

   ```
   dracut -a busybox
   ```

   The parameter `-a busybox` adds the multi call binary `busybox` to the RAM file system. After doing this, many standard unix commands are available inside this system.

4. Copy the new RAM file system and the kernel to your boot server with the command:

   ```
   scp /boot/initrd /boot/vmlinuz pxe.example.com:
   ```

   Replace pxe.example.com with the name of your local boot server or IP address.

5. Log in to your boot server as user `root`, and create a directory where you can modify the RAM file system:

   ```
   mkdir ~/bootimage
   ```

6. Change your working directory to this directory with the command **cd ~/bootimage**.

7. Unpack the previously copied initial RAM file system with the command:

   ```
   zcat ../initrd | cpio -i
   ```

8. Edit the file run_all.sh.

9. Search for the following line, delete it and the rest of the file:

```
[ "$debug" ] && echo preping 21-nfs.sh
```

10. Add the following lines to the end of the files run_all.sh:

```
[ "$debug" ] && echo preping 92-install.sh
[ "$debug" ] && echo running 92-install.sh
source boot/92-install.sh
[ "$modules" ] && load_modules
```

11. Create a new script boot/92-install.sh with the following content:

```
#!/bin/bash
if [ "$(get_param rawimage)" ]; then
  rawimage=$(get_param rawimage)
  if  [ "$(get_param rawdevice)" ]; then
    rawdevice=$(get_param rawdevice)
    echo "wget -O ${rawdevice} ${rawimage}"
    wget -O ${rawdevice} ${rawimage}
    sync
    sleep 5
    echo "DONE"
  fi
fi
# /bin/bash
/bin/poweroff -f
```

12. If you want to have a debug shell before the computer switches off, remove the comment sign before /bin/bash.

13. Make this script executable with the command **chmod 755 boot/92-install.sh**.

14. Create a new initial RAM file system with the commands:

```
mkdir -p /srv/tftpboot
```

```
find . | cpio --quiet -H newc -o | gzip -9 -n > \
/srv/tftpboot/initrd.boot
```

15. Copy the kernel to this directory:

```
cp ../vmlinuz /srv/tftpboot/linux.boot
```

The initial RAM file system is now prepared to take two new kernel command line parameters. The parameter `rawimage=<URL>` is used to identify the location of the preload image. Any URL that is understood by wget can be used. The parameter `rawdevice=<device>` is used to identify the block device for the hard disk on the target machine.

27.2.4   Boot Server Configuration

The configuration of the boot server is covered in detail in several different chapters as listed in *Section 27.2.1, "Set Up a Boot and Install Server"*. This section should give a checklist that covers steps that are necessary to configure the system.

- Set up a DHCP server. The subnet where the machines are installed needs the additional lines:

```
filename "pxelinux.0";
next-server 192.168.1.115;
```

In this example, 192.168.1.115 is the ip address of the PXE server pxe.example.com.

- Configure a PXE server as described in *Section 13.3.3, "Using PXE Boot"*. When editing `/srv/tftpboot/pxelinux.cfg/default`, add the following entries:

```
default bootinstall
label bootinstall
  kernel linux.boot
  append initrd=initrd.boot \
  rawimage=ftp://192.168.1.115/preload/preloadimage.raw rawdevice=/dev/sda
```

- Set up an FTP server and copy your prepared preload image to `/srv/ftp/pre-load/preloadimage.raw`.

Test your setup by booting the target system with PXE network boot. This will automatically copy the prepared preload image to hard disk and switch off the machine when ready.

A Documentation Updates

This chapter lists content changes for this document.

This manual was updated on the following dates:

A.1 December 2015 (Initial Release of SUSE Linux Enterprise Server 12 SP1)

General

- *Book "Subscription Management Tool for SLES 12 SP1"* is now part of the documentation for SUSE Linux Enterprise Server.

- Add-ons provided by SUSE have been renamed to modules and extensions. The manuals have been updated to reflect this change.

- Numerous small fixes and additions to the documentation, based on technical feedback.

- The registration service has been changed from Novell Customer Center to SUSE Customer Center.

- In YaST, you will now reach *Network Settings* via the *System* group. *Network Devices* is gone (https://bugzilla.suse.com/show_bug.cgi?id=867809).

Chapter 2, Installation on AMD64 and Intel 64

- Removed pointers to the *Failsafe* boot option, which has been removed (Fate #317016).

Chapter 4, Installation on IBM z Systems

- Added installation instruction for KVM guests (FATE 319264).

- **Added** *Section 4.2.7, "The SUSE Linux Enterprise Server Boot Procedure on IBM z Systems".*

- Added *Section 6.2.3.4, "Using a Proxy During the Installation"* (Fate #318488).

- Added a warning on using unsigned drivers in secure boot mode to *Section 6.2.2.2, "The Boot Screen on Machines Equipped with UEFI"* (Fate #317593).

Chapter 8, Installing or Removing Software

- Added *Section 8.2.4.1, "Handling of Package Recommendations"* (Fate #318099).

Chapter 9, Installing Modules, Extensions, and Third Party Add-On Products

- Updated chapter to reflect the software changes to the former YaST *SUSE Customer Center Configuration* dialog (now called *Product Registration*) and the YaST *Add-On Products* module (Fate #318800).

Chapter 14, Advanced Disk Setup

- Mentioned that subvolumes for `/var/lib/mariadb`, `/var/lib/pgsql`, and `/var/lib/libvirt/images` are created with the option `no copy on write` by default to avoid extensive fragmenting with Btrfs.

Subscription Management

- The chapter about registering clients at a Subscription Management Tool server has been replaced by *Book "Subscription Management Tool for SLES 12 SP1", Chapter 8 "Configuring Clients to Use SMT"*.

Part III, "Updating and Upgrading SUSE Linux Enterprise"

- Split former update chapter into several independent chapters and combined them under this new part.

- Removed YaST Wagon chapter, as YaST Wagon is unsupported for SUSE Linux Enterprise Server 12 SP1.

- Added new chapter: *Chapter 18, Service Pack Migration*.

- Added *Section 17.1.5, "Migrate your MySQL Database"* and *Section 17.1.6, "Migrate your PostgreSQL Database"*.

- Integrated various new features: Fate #315161, Fate #318636, Fate #319128, Fate #319129, Fate #319138, Fate #319140.

- Listed both KIWI and SUSE Studio as imaging tools (Doc Comments #28481 and #28482).

Bugfixes

- Fixed path to `zpxe.exec` (https://bugzilla.suse.com/show_bug.cgi?id=937511).

- Added the `https` protocol to *Section 4.3.3, "Specifying the Installation Source and YaST Interface"* (https://bugzilla.suse.com/show_bug.cgi?id=951421).

- Consistent use of `yast`, `yast2.ssh`, `yast.ssh` for SSH based installation (https://bugzilla.suse.com/show_bug.cgi?id=956060).

- Consistent spelling of boot parameters (https://bugzilla.suse.com/show_bug.cgi?id=956054).

- PowerKVM: virt-install does not know about SLES12 (https://bugzilla.suse.com/show_bug.cgi?id=880918).

- Added documentation on the boot process for IBM z Systems (https://bugzilla.suse.com/show_bug.cgi?id=942772).

- Description of encrypted `/` and `/boot` on Btrfs was missing. Added an important note in *Section 6.9, "Suggested Partitioning"* **and** *Section 14.1.2.1, "Btrfs Partitioning"* (https://bugzilla.suse.com/show_bug.cgi?id=926951).

- Zypper multiversion kernels should be mentioned for SP2 Update (https://bugzilla.suse.com/show_bug.cgi?id=753809).

- SLES 12 Deployment Guide errors for zPXE installations (https://bugzilla.suse.com/show_bug.cgi?id=944384).

- AutoYaST hangs at "Configuring Bootloader ... 50%" with 512RAM (https://bugzilla.suse.com/show_bug.cgi?id=927237).

- Netsetup Parameters Wrong (https://bugzilla.suse.com/show_bug.cgi?id=928792).

- Documentation on not creating /usr as separate partition is missing (https://bugzilla.suse.com/show_bug.cgi?id=930267).

- Document how to enable SELinux during install (https://bugzilla.suse.com/show_bug.cgi?id=928158).

- YaST boot loader: supported scenarios needs updating clarification (https://bugzilla.suse.com/show_bug.cgi?id=939197).

A.2 February 2015 (Documentation Maintenance Update)

Section 6.10, "Clock and Time Zone"
> With NTP disabled it is recommended to avoid writing system time to the hardware clock. Thus set `SYSTOHC=no`.

Bugfixes

- Adjustments for SMT because of the switch from SUSE Customer Center to SUSE Customer Center (https://bugzilla.suse.com/show_bug.cgi?id=857639).

- *Section 11.3.2, "Enforcing Password Policies"*: Password Settings, Expiration Date is expiring user accounts in YAST Users module (https://bugzilla.suse.com/show_bug.cgi?id=743874).

- Various bugfixes for *Chapter 17, Upgrading SUSE Linux Enterprise*:

  - The named upgrade path does not work there is no working upgrade path from SLES 11 SP3 to SLES 12 on Linux for System z (https://bugzilla.suse.com/show_bug.cgi?id=907648).

  - [doc] 7.5 The Atomic Update (https://bugzilla.suse.com/show_bug.cgi?id=905330).

  - [doc] 7.5 Upgrading to SLE 12 (https://bugzilla.suse.com/show_bug.cgi?id=904188).

  - [doc] 7.4 Intermediate step: Updating SLE 11 SP2 to SLE 11 SP3 (https://bugzilla.suse.com/show_bug.cgi?id=904186).

- [doc] 7.2 Supported Upgrade Paths to SLE (https://bugzilla.suse.com/show_bug.cgi?id=904182).

- [doc] Potentially misleading info around the 6-months overlap in support (https://bugzilla.suse.com/show_bug.cgi?id=902463).

A.3 October 2014 (Initial Release of SUSE Linux Enterprise Server 12)

General

- Removed all KDE documentation and references because KDE is no longer shipped.

- Removed all references to SuSEconfig, which is no longer supported (Fate #100011).

- Move from System V init to systemd (Fate #310421). Updated affected parts of the documentation.

- YaST Runlevel Editor has changed to Services Manager (Fate #312568). Updated affected parts of the documentation.

- Removed all references to ISDN support, as ISDN support has been removed (Fate #314594).

- Removed all references to the YaST DSL module as it is no longer shipped (Fate #316264).

- Removed all references to the YaST Modem module as it is no longer shipped (Fate #316264).

- Btrfs has become the default file system for the root partition (Fate #315901). Updated affected parts of the documentation.

- The **dmesg** now provides human-readable time stamps in `ctime()` -like format (Fate #316056). Updated affected parts of the documentation.

- syslog and syslog-ng have been replaced by rsyslog (Fate #316175). Updated affected parts of the documentation.

- MariaDB is now shipped as the relational database instead of MySQL (Fate #313595). Updated affected parts of the documentation.

- SUSE-related products are no longer available from http://download.novell.com but from http://download.suse.com. Adjusted links accordingly.

- Novell Customer Center has been replaced with SUSE Customer Center. Updated affected parts of the documentation.

- /var/run is mounted as tmpfs (Fate #303793). Updated affected parts of the documentation.

- The following architectures are no longer supported: Itanium and x86. Updated affected parts of the documentation.

- The traditional method for setting up the network with `ifconfig` has been replaced by `wicked`. Updated affected parts of the documentation.

- A lot of networking commands are deprecated and have been replaced by newer commands (usually **ip**). Updated affected parts of the documentation.

```
arp: ip neighbor
ifconfig: ip addr, ip link
iptunnel: ip tunnel
iwconfig: iw
nameif: ip link, ifrename
netstat: ss, ip route, ip -s link, ip maddr
route: ip route
```

- Numerous small fixes and additions to the documentation, based on technical feedback.

Chapter 2, Installation on AMD64 and Intel 64

- Updated system requirements.

Chapter 3, Installation on IBM POWER

- Added POWER8 to the list of supported hardware (Fate #315272).

- SUSE Linux Enterprise Server 12 for POWER has moved to Little Endian. Updated affected parts of the documentation.

- Updated the list of supported platforms: Removed IBM Series z9 and z10 machines and added IBM zEnterprise BC12.

- Updated the memory and disk space requirements.

- Removed instructions on how to IPL from tape—this is no longer supported.

- Rewrote large parts of *Section 4.2.5, "Network Configuration"* to remove redundant information and make it more concise.

- Removed references to Token Ring, which is no longer supported (Fate #313154).

- Completely rewrote the chapter because of the new installation workflow.

- The installation routine now supports setting up multiple network devices during the installation (Fate #315680): *Section 6.6, "Network Settings"*

- The installation proposal contains a separate /home partition formatted with XFS (Fate #316637 and Fate #316624): *Section 6.9, "Suggested Partitioning"*

- Removed occurrences of the YaST Repair module which has been dropped (Fate #308670).

- Update repositories are added after having registered with SUSE Customer Center and can be used during installation (Fate #312012): *Section 6.8, "Extension Selection".*

- Extensions and modules can be added to the system during the installation (Fate #316548): *Section 6.7, "SUSE Customer Center Registration".*

- SUSE Linux Enterprise Desktop can be installed as an add-on on top of SUSE Linux Enterprise Server (Fate #316436): *Section 6.8, "Extension Selection".*

- The HW crypto stack for IBM z Systems can be selected for installation via a pattern (Fate #316143): *Section 6.13.1, "Software"*

- Automatically importing SSH keys from a previous installation can be disabled (Fate #314982): *Section 6.2.3.5, "Disabling the Import of SSH Host Keys and Users from a Previous Installation "*

Chapter 17, Upgrading SUSE Linux Enterprise

- Added new section: *Section 17.3, "Supported Methods for Upgrading SUSE Linux Enterprise".*

Chapter 7, Setting Up Hardware Components with YaST

- Removed the following sections as the respective YaST modules are no longer included: *Hardware Information, Setting Up Graphics Card and Monitor, Mouse Model,* and *Setting Up a Scanner.*

- Removed content about mouse setup and adjusted *Section 7.1, "Setting Up Your System Keyboard Layout".*

Chapter 8, Installing or Removing Software

- Completely rewrote *Section 8.4, "Keeping the System Up-to-date"* because of changes in the GNOME software updater.

Chapter 9, Installing Modules, Extensions, and Third Party Add-On Products

- Installing add-on products or software extensions is now also possible without access to physical media. Added the following new sections: *Section 17.8, "Registering Your System"* and *Section 9.1, "Installing Modules and Extensions from Online Channels".* Modified *Section 9.2, "Installing Extensions and Third Party Add-On Products from Media"* accordingly.

Subscription Management

- For registering clients against an SMT server, `suse_register` has been replaced with `SUSEConnect` (Fate #316585).

Bugfixes

- Updated chapter *Chapter 21, Creating Add-on Products With Add-on Product Creator* according to http://bugzilla.suse.com/show_bug.cgi?id=861855.

- Updated chapter *Chapter 22, Creating Images with YaST Product Creator* and added chapter *Chapter 23, Creating Images with YaST Image Creator* according to http://bugzilla.suse.com/show_bug.cgi?id=864033.

- Updated section *Section 8.4, "Keeping the System Up-to-date"* according to http://bugzilla.suse.com/show_bug.cgi?id=839692.

- Removed section *Using Fingerprint Authentication.* Further minor corrections and additions (http://bugzilla.suse.com/show_bug.cgi?id=857680).

- Removed obsolete parameter `OsaMedium` from parmfile and Cobbler examples (http://bugzilla.suse.com/show_bug.cgi?id=860404).

- Additions in section *Section 24.2, "Customizing the Firstboot Installation"* (http://bugzilla.suse.com/show_bug.cgi?id=861866).

- Added instructions on how to add secondary languages during installation (http://bugzilla.suse.com/show_bug.cgi?id=870482).

- Multiversion feature (more than one kernel installed) is enabled by default (http://bugzilla.suse.com/show_bug.cgi?id=891805).

- Warn about incompatible Kernel Module Packages (KPMs) (http://bugzilla.suse.com/show_bug.cgi?id=891805).

B GNU Licenses

This appendix contains the GNU Free Documentation License version 1.2.

GNU Free Documentation License

Copyright (C) 2000, 2001, 2002 Free Software Foundation, Inc. 51 Franklin St, Fifth Floor, Boston, MA 02110-1301 USA. Everyone is permitted to copy and distribute verbatim copies of this license document, but changing it is not allowed.

0. PREAMBLE

The purpose of this License is to make a manual, textbook, or other functional and useful document "free" in the sense of freedom: to assure everyone the effective freedom to copy and redistribute it, with or without modifying it, either commercially or non-commercially. Secondarily, this License preserves for the author and publisher a way to get credit for their work, while not being considered responsible for modifications made by others.

This License is a kind of "copyleft", which means that derivative works of the document must themselves be free in the same sense. It complements the GNU General Public License, which is a copyleft license designed for free software.

We have designed this License to use it for manuals for free software, because free software needs free documentation: a free program should come with manuals providing the same freedoms that the software does. But this License is not limited to software manuals; it can be used for any textual work, regardless of subject matter or whether it is published as a printed book. We recommend this License principally for works whose purpose is instruction or reference.

1. APPLICABILITY AND DEFINITIONS

This License applies to any manual or other work, in any medium, that contains a notice placed by the copyright holder saying it can be distributed under the terms of this License. Such a notice grants a world-wide, royalty-free license, unlimited in duration, to use that work under the conditions stated herein. The "Document", below, refers to any such manual or work. Any member of the public is a licensee, and is addressed as "you". You accept the license if you copy, modify or distribute the work in a way requiring permission under copyright law.

A "Modified Version" of the Document means any work containing the Document or a portion of it, either copied verbatim, or with modifications and/or translated into another language.

A "Secondary Section" is a named appendix or a front-matter section of the Document that deals exclusively with the relationship of the publishers or authors of the Document to the Document's overall subject (or to related matters) and contains nothing that could fall directly within that overall subject. (Thus, if the Document is in part a textbook of mathematics, a Secondary Section may not explain any mathematics.) The relationship could be a matter of historical connection with the subject or with related matters, or of legal, commercial, philosophical, ethical or political position regarding them.

The "Invariant Sections" are certain Secondary Sections whose titles are designated, as being those of Invariant Sections, in the notice that says that the Document is released under this License. If a section does not fit the above definition of Secondary then it is not allowed to be designated as Invariant. The Document may contain zero Invariant Sections. If the Document does not identify any Invariant Sections then there are none.

The "Cover Texts" are certain short passages of text that are listed, as Front-Cover Texts or Back-Cover Texts, in the notice that says that the Document is released under this License. A Front-Cover Text may be at most 5 words, and a Back-Cover Text may be at most 25 words.

A "Transparent" copy of the Document means a machine-readable copy, represented in a format whose specification is available to the general public, that is suitable for revising the document straightforwardly with generic text editors or (for images composed of pixels) generic paint programs or (for drawings) some widely available draw-ing editor, and that is suitable for input to text formatters or for automatic translation to a variety of formats suitable for input to text formatters. A copy made in an otherwise Transparent file format whose markup, or absence of markup, has been arranged to thwart or discourage subsequent modification by readers is not Transparent. An image format is not Transparent if used for any substantial amount of text. A copy that is not "Transparent" is called "Opaque".

Examples of suitable formats for Transparent copies include plain ASCII without markup, Texinfo input format, LaTeX input format, SGML or XML using a publicly available DTD, and standard-conforming simple HTML, PostScript or PDF designed for human modification. Examples of transparent image formats include PNG, XCF and JPG. Opaque formats include proprietary formats that can be read and edited only by proprietary word processors, SGML or XML for which the DTD and/or processing tools are not generally available, and the machine-generated HTML, PostScript or PDF produced by some word processors for output purposes only.

The "Title Page" means, for a printed book, the title page itself, plus such following pages as are needed to hold, legibly, the material this License requires to appear in the title page. For works in formats which do not have any title page as such, "Title Page" means the text near the most prominent appearance of the work's title, preceding the beginning of the body of the text.

A section "Entitled XYZ" means a named subunit of the Document whose title either is precisely XYZ or contains XYZ in parentheses following text that translates XYZ in another language. (Here XYZ stands for a specific section name mentioned below, such as "Acknowledgements", "Dedications", "Endorsements", or "History".) To "Preserve the Title" of such a section when you modify the Document means that it remains a section "Entitled XYZ" according to this definition.

The Document may include Warranty Disclaimers next to the notice which states that this License applies to the Document. These Warranty Disclaimers are considered to be included by reference in this License, but only as regards disclaiming warranties: any other implication that these Warranty Disclaimers may have is void and has no effect on the meaning of this License.

2. VERBATIM COPYING

You may copy and distribute the Document in any medium, either commercially or noncommercially, provided that this License, the copyright notices, and the license notice saying this License applies to the Document are reproduced in all copies, and that you add no other conditions whatsoever to those of this License. You may not use technical measures to obstruct or control the reading or further copying of the copies you make or distribute. However, you may accept compensation in exchange for copies. If you distribute a large enough number of copies you must also follow the conditions in section 3.

You may also lend copies, under the same conditions stated above, and you may publicly display copies.

3. COPYING IN QUANTITY

If you publish printed copies (or copies in media that commonly have printed covers) of the Document, numbering more than 100, and the Document's license notice requires Cover Texts, you must enclose the copies in covers that carry, clearly and legibly, all these Cover Texts: Front-Cover Texts on the front cover, and Back-Cover Texts on the back cover. Both covers must also clearly and legibly identify you as the publisher of these copies. The front cover must present the full title with all words of the title equally prominent and visible. You may add other material on the covers in addition. Copying with changes limited to the covers, as long as they preserve the title of the Document and satisfy these conditions, can be treated as verbatim copying in other respects.

If the required texts for either cover are too voluminous to fit legibly, you should put the first ones listed (as many as fit reasonably) on the actual cover, and continue the rest onto adjacent pages.

If you publish or distribute Opaque copies of the Document numbering more than 100, you must either include a machine-readable Transparent copy along with each Opaque copy, or state in or with each Opaque copy a computer-network location from which the general network-using public has access to download using public-standard network protocols a complete Transparent copy of the Document, free of added material. If you use the latter option, you must take reasonably prudent steps, when you begin distribution of Opaque copies in quantity, to ensure that this Transparent copy will remain thus accessible at the stated location until at least one year after the last time you distribute an Opaque copy (directly or through your agents or retailers) of that edition to the public.

It is requested, but not required, that you contact the authors of the Document well before redistributing any large number of copies, to give them a chance to provide you with an updated version of the Document.

4. MODIFICATIONS

You may copy and distribute a Modified Version of the Document under the conditions of sections 2 and 3 above, provided that you release the Modified Version under precisely this License, with the Modified Version filling the role of the Document, thus licensing distribution and modification of the Modified Version to whoever possesses a copy of it. In addition, you must do these things in the Modified Version:

A. Use in the Title Page (and on the covers, if any) a title distinct from that of the Document, and from those of previous versions (which should, if there were any, be listed in the History section of the Document). You may use the same title as a previous version if the original publisher of that version gives permission.

B. List on the Title Page, as authors, one or more persons or entities responsible for authorship of the modifications in the Modified Version, together with at least five of the principal authors of the Document (all of its principal authors, if it has fewer than five), unless they release you from this requirement.

C. State on the Title page the name of the publisher of the Modified Version, as the publisher.

D. Preserve all the copyright notices of the Document.

E. Add an appropriate copyright notice for your modifications adjacent to the other copyright notices.

F. Include, immediately after the copyright notices, a license notice giving the public permission to use the Modified Version under the terms of this License, in the form shown in the Addendum below.

G. Preserve in that license notice the full lists of Invariant Sections and required Cover Texts given in the Document's license notice.

H. Include an unaltered copy of this License.

I. Preserve the section Entitled "History", Preserve its Title, and add to it an item stating at least the title, year, new authors, and publisher of the Modified Version as given on the Title Page. If there is no section Entitled "History" in the Document, create one stating the title, year, authors, and publisher of the Document as given on its Title Page, then add an item describing the Modified Version as stated in the previous sentence.

J. Preserve the network location, if any, given in the Document for public access to a Transparent copy of the Document, and likewise the network locations given in the Document for previous versions it was based on. These may be placed in the "History" section. You may omit a network location for a work that was published at least four years before the Document itself, or if the original publisher of the version it refers to gives permission.

K. For any section Entitled "Acknowledgements" or "Dedications", Preserve the Title of the section, and preserve in the section all the substance and tone of each of the contributor acknowledgements and/or dedications given therein.

L. Preserve all the Invariant Sections of the Document, unaltered in their text and in their titles. Section numbers or the equivalent are not considered part of the section titles.

M. Delete any section Entitled "Endorsements". Such a section may not be included in the Modified Version.

N. Do not retitle any existing section to be Entitled "Endorsements" or to conflict in title with any Invariant Section.

O. Preserve any Warranty Disclaimers.

If the Modified Version includes new front-matter sections or appendices that qualify as Secondary Sections and contain no material copied from the Document, you may at your option designate some or all of these sections as invariant. To do this, add their titles to the list of Invariant Sections in the Modified Version's license notice. These titles must be distinct from any other section titles.

You may add a section Entitled "Endorsements", provided it contains nothing but endorsements of your Modified Version by various parties--for example, statements of peer review or that the text has been approved by an organization as the authoritative definition of a standard.

You may add a passage of up to five words as a Front-Cover Text, and a passage of up to 25 words as a Back-Cover Text, to the end of the list of Cover Texts in the Modified Version. Only one passage of Front-Cover Text and one of Back-Cover Text may be added by (or through arrangements made by) any one entity. If the Document already includes a cover text for the same cover, previously added by you or by arrangement made by the same entity you are acting on behalf of, you may not add another; but you may replace the old one, on explicit permission from the previous publisher that added the old one.

The author(s) and publisher(s) of the Document do not by this License give permission to use their names for publicity for or to assert or imply endorsement of any Modified Version.

5. COMBINING DOCUMENTS

You may combine the Document with other documents released under this License, under the terms defined in section 4 above for modified versions, provided that you include in the combination all of the Invariant Sections of all of the original documents, unmodified, and list them all as Invariant Sections of your combined work in its license notice, and that you preserve all their Warranty Disclaimers.

The combined work need only contain one copy of this License, and multiple identical Invariant Sections may be replaced with a single copy. If there are multiple Invariant Sections with the same name but different contents, make the title of each such section unique by adding at the end of it, in parentheses, the name of the original author or publisher of that section if known, or else a unique number. Make the same adjustment to the section titles in the list of Invariant Sections in the license notice of the combined work.

In the combination, you must combine any sections Entitled "History" in the various original documents, forming one section Entitled "History"; likewise combine any sections Entitled "Acknowledgements", and any sections Entitled "Dedications". You must delete all sections Entitled "Endorsements".

6. COLLECTIONS OF DOCUMENTS

You may make a collection consisting of the Document and other documents released under this License, and replace the individual copies of this License in the various documents with a single copy that is included in the collection, provided that you follow the rules of this License for verbatim copying of each of the documents in all other respects.

You may extract a single document from such a collection, and distribute it individually under this License, provided you insert a copy of this License into the extracted document, and follow this License in all other respects regarding verbatim copying of that document.

7. AGGREGATION WITH INDEPENDENT WORKS

A compilation of the Document or its derivatives with other separate and independent documents or works, in or on a volume of a storage or distribution medium, is called an "aggregate" if the copyright resulting from the compilation is not used to limit the legal rights of the compilation's users beyond what the individual works permit. When the Document is included in an aggregate, this License does not apply to the other works in the aggregate which are not themselves derivative works of the Document.

If the Cover Text requirement of section 3 is applicable to these copies of the Document, then if the Document is less than one half of the entire aggregate, the Document's Cover Texts may be placed on covers that bracket the Document within the aggregate, or the electronic equivalent of covers if the Document is in electronic form. Otherwise they must appear on printed covers that bracket the whole aggregate.

8. TRANSLATION

Translation is considered a kind of modification, so you may distribute translations of the Document under the terms of section 4. Replacing Invariant Sections with translations requires special permission from their copyright holders, but you may include translations of some or all Invariant Sections in addition to the original versions of these Invariant Sections. You may include a translation of this License, and all the license notices in the Document, and any Warranty Disclaimers, provided that you also include the original English version of this License and the original versions of those notices and disclaimers. In case of a disagreement between the translation and the original version of this License or a notice or disclaimer, the original version will prevail.

If a section in the Document is Entitled "Acknowledgements", "Dedications", or "History", the requirement (section 4) to Preserve its Title (section 1) will typically require changing the actual title.

9. TERMINATION

You may not copy, modify, sublicense, or distribute the Document except as expressly provided for under this License. Any other attempt to copy, modify, sublicense or distribute the Document is void, and will automatically terminate your rights under this License. However, parties who have received copies, or rights, from you under this License will not have their licenses terminated so long as such parties remain in full compliance.

10. FUTURE REVISIONS OF THIS LICENSE

The Free Software Foundation may publish new, revised versions of the GNU Free Documentation License from time to time. Such new versions will be similar in spirit to the present version, but may differ in detail to address new problems or concerns. See http://www.gnu.org/copyleft/.

Each version of the License is given a distinguishing version number. If the Document specifies that a particular numbered version of this License "or any later version" applies to it, you have the option of following the terms and conditions either of that specified version or of any later version that has been published (not as a draft) by the Free Software Foundation. If the Document does not specify a version number of this License, you may choose any version ever published (not as a draft) by the Free Software Foundation.

ADDENDUM: How to use this License for your documents

```
Copyright (c) YEAR YOUR NAME.

Permission is granted to copy, distribute and/or modify this document

under the terms of the GNU Free Documentation License, Version 1.2

or any later version published by the Free Software Foundation;

with no Invariant Sections, no Front-Cover Texts, and no Back-Cover

 Texts.

A copy of the license is included in the section entitled "GNU

Free Documentation License".
```

If you have Invariant Sections, Front-Cover Texts and Back-Cover Texts, replace the "with...Texts." line with this:

```
with the Invariant Sections being LIST THEIR TITLES, with the

Front-Cover Texts being LIST, and with the Back-Cover Texts being LIST.
```

If you have Invariant Sections without Cover Texts, or some other combination of the three, merge those two alternatives to suit the situation.

If your document contains nontrivial examples of program code, we recommend releasing these examples in parallel under your choice of free software license, such as the GNU General Public License, to permit their use in free software.

www.ingramcontent.com/pod-product-compliance
Lightning Source LLC
LaVergne TN
LVHW060135070326
832902LV00018B/2802